AN ANTHOLOGY OF
NATURE POETRY

An Anthology
of
Nature Poetry

made by

Viola Meynell

Jonathan Cape
Thirty Bedford Square
London

FIRST PUBLISHED AS *THE POET'S WALK*
1936

RE-ISSUED UNDER THE PRESENT TITLE 1941
REPRINTED 1942

JONATHAN CAPE LTD. 30 BEDFORD SQUARE, LONDON
AND 91 WELLINGTON STREET WEST, TORONTO

PRINTED IN GREAT BRITAIN IN THE CITY OF OXFORD
AT THE ALDEN PRESS
BOUND BY A. W. BAIN & CO. LTD., LONDON

CONTENTS

MORNING

SUMMER

AUTUMN

EVENING

WINTER

NIGHT

NATURE AND MAN (2)

ACKNOWLEDGMENTS

For permission to print copyright poems acknowledgments are due to:
The Oxford University Press for the poems by Gerard Manley Hopkins; Mrs.
Thomas and Faber and Faber for poems by Edward Thomas; Macmillan & Co.
Ltd. and the author's executors for 'Margaritae Sorori' from W. E. Henley's
Poems; Mr. Stanley Snaith for 'The Scarecrow'; William Blackwood & Sons Ltd.
for 'The Crow' and 'Daydreams', by William Canton; Mr. Gordon Bottomley
and Messrs. Constable for 'Eager Spring'; Macmillan & Co. Ltd. and the author's
executors for T. E. Brown's 'Go Back!' from *The Collected Poems of T. E. Brown*;
George Bell & Sons Ltd. for Coventry Patmore's 'Winter' and 'St. Valentine's
Day'; Mrs. Reginald McKenna for Michael McKenna's 'Mountains'; Mr. Martin
Armstrong for 'The Buzzards'; Mr. de la Mare for 'The Scribe' and 'Alone';
Mr. Sturge Moore for 'The Dying Swan' from *Collected Poems*, published by
Macmillan & Co. Ltd.; the Hon. V. Sackville-West for an excerpt from *The
Land*; Macmillan & Co. Ltd. and the author's executors for two poems from
The Collected Poems of Thomas Hardy; Messrs. Chatto & Windus for two poems
by R. L. Stevenson; the executors of A. E. Housman for two poems from *A
Shropshire Lad*; Mr. John Drinkwater and Sidgwick & Jackson Ltd. for 'Olton
Pools' from *Collected Poems*; R. Cobden-Sanderson Ltd. and the author's executors
for a poem by Harold Monro; Sir Henry Newbolt for 'High Wind' from *Poems
by M. E. Coleridge*, published by Elkin Mathews & Marrot; Messrs. Constable
and the author's executors for three poems by George Meredith; the Clarendon
Press for two poems from *The Shorter Poems of Robert Bridges*; Mrs. John Freeman
and Macmillan & Co. Ltd. for John Freeman's 'Stone Trees'; Mr. Padraic
Colum for 'The Plougher'; Lord Dunsany for 'The Wife of Llew' by Francis
Ledwidge; and John Lane, The Bodley Head Ltd. for John Davidson's poem
from *Ballads and Songs*.

INTRODUCTORY NOTE

THE test for inclusion in this Anthology was True Poetry, by English poets, where it dealt with Nature, through the vicissitudes of the centuries.

Nature had to worm her way patiently into the full consciousness of the poets. The sixteenth and seventeenth centuries' use for her was mostly Love's use – a *Night-piece* being improbably, then, a night-piece pure and simple, but addressed *to Julia*:

> Her Eyes the Glow-worme lend thee,
> The Shooting Starres attend thee . . .

and a *Sunne Rising* being a harangue to the

> Busie old foole, unruly Sunne

for his interference with love's seclusion. Nature, also in those centuries, with her flowers, stars, rainbows and waterfalls, fitted out the more Heavenly-minded poems with some of their symbolism: the sun *then* being that sun that

> Saw a greater Sun appear
> Than his bright Throne, or burning Axletree could bear.

The next century merited, of course, in its first half, the denunciation of Thomas Warton, in *The Enthusiast or The Lover of Nature*, on account of its preoccupation with 'gardens decked with art's vain pomp' rather than with the 'thrush-haunted copse': it was only unfortunate that the degree of wildness Warton himself achieved in his own latter half was still not without spires emerging 'from the grove's bosom', and 'ruin'd tops of Gothic battlements'. It was thus weighted that Nature arrived at the nineteenth century, when she was stripped of Love and battlements and every adornment, and stood alone.

Our own most up-to-date writers have become less Natureminded, at a time when people in general are increasingly so. It is for to-day's great new race of Nature-lovers that this poetry has been collected from poets typical of their times – or the great exceptions to their times.

The True-Poetry standard has lowered itself occasionally to admit something that seemed irresistible on other grounds. The 'curious' quality that much eighteenth-century verse has for our ears, makes us, while we read it, not desire anything better than, for instance, a description of sheep-dipping in which the sheep are 'the soft fearful People'.

> The clamour much of Men, and Boys, and Dogs,
> Ere the soft fearful People to the Flood
> Commit their woolly Sides,

– or the climax of ecstatic approval which asks, in regard to the sunset-sky:

> Can the pencil's mimic skill
> Copy the refulgent dye?

or the assurance to the Cuckoo in spring:

> Now Heaven repairs thy rural seat,
> And woods thy welcome sing.

And some poems have come in on their 'plot' – that is, for dealing with some facet of Nature otherwise ignored.

The earlier poets' contemporary spelling has been preferred. To read

> The Flowers like brave imbroydered Gerles

is to meet familiar words – and their meanings – afresh. On the other hand, a prejudice against Early English, or Scottish, or dialect, for casual reading, has been indulged, to the exclusion of some poems otherwise eligible.

V. M.

Nature
and Man
(1)

RETIREMENT

Fresh *fields* and *woods*! the earth's fair *face*,
God's *foot-stool* and man's *dwelling-place*.
I ask not why the first *Believer*
Did love to be a Country liver?
Who to secure pious content
Did pitch by *groves* and *wells* his tent;
Where he might view the boundless *skie*,
And all those glorious *lights* on high:
With flying *meteors*, *mists*, and *show'rs*,
Subjected *hills*, *trees*, *meads*, and *Flow'rs*:
And ev'ry minute bless the King
And wise Creatour of each thing.

I ask not why he did remove
To happy *Mamre's* holy grove,
Leaving the *Cities* of the plain
To *Lot* and his successless train?
All various Lusts in *Cities* still
Are found; they are the *Thrones* of Ill.
The dismal *Sinks*, where blood is spill'd,
Cages with much uncleanness fill'd.
But *rural shades* are the sweet sense
Of piety and innocence;
They are the *Meek's* calm region, where
Angels descend and rule the sphere:
Where heav'n lies *Leiguer*, and the *Dove*
Duely as *Dew* comes from above.
If *Eden* be on Earth at all
'Tis that which we the *Country* call.

HENRY VAUGHAN

HYMN: TO LIGHT

First born of *Chaos*, who so fair didst come
    From the old *Negro's* darksome womb!
    Which when it saw the lovely Child,
The melancholly Mass put on kind looks and smil'd.

Thou Tide of Glory which no Rest dost know,
    But ever Ebb, and ever Flow!
    Thou Golden shower of a true Jove!
Who does in thee descend, and Heav'n to Earth make Love!

Hail active Natures watchful Life and Health!
    Her Joy, her Ornament, and Wealth!
    Hail to thy Husband Heat, and Thee!
Thou the worlds beauteous Bride, and lusty Bridegroom He!

Say from what Golden Quivers of the Sky,
    Do all thy winged Arrows fly?
    Swiftness and Power by Birth are thine:
From thy Great Sire they came, thy Sire the word Divine.

'Tis, I believe, this Archery to show,
    That so much cost in Colours thou,
    And skill in Painting dost bestow,
Upon thy ancient Arms, the Gawdy Heav'nly Bow.

Swift as light Thoughts their empty Carriere run,
    Thy Race is finisht, when begun,
    Let a Post-Angel start with Thee,
And Thou the Goal of Earth shalt reach as soon as He:

Thou in the Moon's bright Chariot proud and gay,
    Dost thy bright wood of Stars survey;
    And all the year dost with thee bring
Of thousand flowry Lights thine own Nocturnal Spring.

Thou *Scythian*-like dost round thy Lands above
    The Suns gilt Tent for ever move,
    And still as thou in pomp dost go
The shining Pageants of the World attend thy show.

Nor amidst all these Triumphs dost thou scorn
    The humble Glow-worms to adorn,
    And with those living spangles gild,
(O Greatness without Pride!) the Bushes of the Field.

Night, and her ugly Subjects thou dost fright,
    And sleep, the lazy Owl of Night;
    Asham'd and fearful to appear
They screen their horrid shapes with the black Hemisphere.

With 'em there hastes, and wildly takes the Alarm,
    Of painted Dreams, a busie swarm,
    At the first opening of thine eye,
The various Clusters break, the antick Atomes fly.

The guilty Serpents, and obscener Beasts
    Creep conscious to their secret rests:
    Nature to thee does reverence pay;
Ill Omens, and ill Sights removes out of thy way.

At thy appearance, Grief itself is said,
    To shake his Wings, and rowse his Head.
    And cloudy care has often took
A gentle beamy Smile reflected from thy Look.

At thy appearance, Fear it self grows bold;
    Thy Sun-shine melts away his Cold.
    Encourag'd at the sight of Thee,
To the cheek Colour comes, and firmness to the knee.

Even Lust the Master of a hardn'd Face,
    Blushes if thou beest in the place,
    To darkness' Curtains he retires,
In Sympathizing Night he rolls his smoaky Fires.

When, Goddess, thou liftst up thy wakened Head,
    Out of the Mornings purple bed,
    Thy Quire of Birds about thee play,
And all the joyful world salutes the rising day.

The Ghosts, and Monster Spirits, that did presume
    A Bodies Priv'lege to assume,
    Vanish again invisibly,
And Bodies gain agen their visibility.

All the Worlds bravery that delights our Eyes
    Is but thy sev'ral Liveries,
    Thou the Rich Dye on them bestowest,
Thy nimble Pencil Paints this Landskape as thou go'st.

A Crimson Garment in the Rose thou wear'st;
    A Crown of studded Gold thou bear'st,
    The Virgin Lillies in their White,
Are clad but with the Lawn of almost Naked Light.

The Violet, springs little Infant, stands,
    Girt in thy purple Swadling-bands:
    On the fair Tulip thou dost dote:
Thou cloath'st it in a gay and party-colour'd Coat.

With Flame condenst thou dost the Jewels fix,
    And solid Colours in it mix:
    Flora her self envyes to see
Flowers fairer than her own, and durable as she.

Ah, Goddess! would thou could'st thy hand withhold,
    And be less Liberall to Gold;
    Didst thou less value to it give,
Of how much care (alas) might'st thou poor Man relieve!

To me the Sun is more delightful far,
    And all fair Dayes much fairer are.
    But few, ah wondrous few there be,
Who do not Gold prefer, O Goddess, ev'n to Thee.

Through the soft wayes of Heaven, and Air, and Sea,
    Which open all their Pores to Thee;
    Like a cleer River thou dost glide,
And with thy Living Stream through the close Channels slide

But where firm Bodies thy free course oppose,
    Gently thy source the Land o'erflowes;
    Takes there possession, and does make,
Of Colours mingled, Light, a thick and standing Lake.

But the vast Ocean of unbounded Day
    In th' Empyraean Heaven does stay.
    Thy Rivers, Lakes, and Springs below
From thence took first their Rise, thither at last must Flow.

ABRAHAM COWLEY

SONNET

The world is too much with us; late and soon,
Getting and spending, we lay waste our powers:
Little we see in Nature that is ours;
We have given our hearts away, a sordid boon!
This Sea that bares her bosom to the moon;
The winds that will be howling at all hours,
And are up-gathered now like sleeping flowers;
For this, for everything, we are out of tune;
It moves us not. – Great God! I'd rather be
A Pagan suckled in a creed outworn;
So might I, standing on this pleasant lea,
Have glimpses that would make me less forlorn;
Have sight of Proteus rising from the sea;
Or hear old Triton blow his wreathèd horn.

WILLIAM WORDSWORTH

GOD'S GRANDEUR

The world is charged with the grandeur of God.
   It will flame out, like shining from shook foil;
   It gathers to a greatness, like the ooze of oil
Crushed. Why do men then now not reck his rod?
Generations have trod, have trod, have trod;
   And all is seared with trade; bleared, smeared with toil;
   And wears man's smudge and shares man's smell: the soil
Is bare now, nor can foot feel, being shod.

And for all this, nature is never spent;
   There lives the dearest freshness deep down things;
And though the last lights off the black West went,
   Oh, morning, at the brown brink eastward, springs —
Because the Holy Ghost over the bent
   World broods with warm breast and with ah! bright wings.

GERARD MANLEY HOPKINS

THE SCRIBE

What lovely things
Thy hand hath made:
The smooth-plumed bird
In its emerald shade,
The seed of the grass,
The speck of stone
Which the wayfaring ant
Stirs – and hastes on!

Though I should sit
By some tarn in thy hills,
Using its ink
As the spirit wills
To write of Earth's wonders,
Its live, willed things,
Flit would the ages
On soundless wings
Ere unto Z

My pen drew nigh;
Leviathan told,
And the honey-fly:
And still would remain
My wit to try –
My worn reeds broken,
The dark tarn dry,
All words forgotten –
Thou, Lord, and I.

WALTER DE LA MARE

THE LATTICE AT SUNRISE

As on my bed at dawn I mused and pray'd,
   I saw my lattice pranckt upon the wall,
   The flitting birds and flaunting leaves withal –
A sunny phantom interlaced with shade.
'Thanks be to heaven!' in happy mood I said;
   'What sweeter aid my matins could befall
Than this fair glory from the East hath made?
   What holy sleights hath God, the Lord of all,
To bid us feel and see! We are not free
   To say we see not, for the glory comes
Nightly and daily like a flowing sea;
   His lustre pierceth thro' the midnight glooms,
And, at prime hour, behold! – He follows me
   With golden shadows to my secret rooms!

CHARLES TENNYSON TURNER

THE WISH

Well then; I now do plainly see,
This busie world and I shall ne'er agree;
The very *Honey* of all earthly joy
    Does of all meats the soonest *cloy*,
    And they (methinks) deserve my pity,
Who for it can endure the stings,
The *Crowd*, and *Buz*, and *Murmurings*
    Of this great *Hive, the City*.

    Ah, yet, e'er I descend to th' Grave
May I a *small House*, and *large Garden* have!
And a *few Friends*, and *many Books*, both true,
    Both wise, and both delightful too!
    And since *Love* ne'er will from me flee,
A *Mistress* moderately fair,
And good as *Guardian-Angels* are,
    Only belov'd and loving me!

    Oh, *Fountains*, when in you shall I
My self, eas'd of unpeaceful thoughts, espy?
Oh *Fields*! Oh *Woods*! when, when shall I be made
    The happy Tenant of your shade?
    Here's the Spring-head of *Pleasures* flood;
Where all the *Riches* lie, that she
    Has coyn'd and stampt for good.

    Pride and *Ambition* here,
Only in *far fetcht Metaphors* appear;
Here nought but *winds* can hurtful *Murmurs* scatter,
    And nought but *Eccho flatter*.
    The *Gods*, when they descended, hither
From Heav'n did always chuse their way;
And therefore we may boldly say,
    That 'tis the *way* too *thither*.

How happy here should I,
And one dear *She* live, and embracing dy!
She who is all the world, and can exclude
  In *desarts Solitude.*
    I should have then this only fear,
Lest men, when they my pleasures see,
Should hither throng to live like me,
    And so make a *City* here.

ABRAHAM COWLEY

OF SOLITUDE

Hail, old *Patrician* Trees, so great and good!
    Hail ye *Plebeian* under wood!
    Where the Poetique Birds rejoyce,
And for their quiet Nests and plenteous Food,
    Pay with their grateful voice.

Hail, the poor Muses richest Manor Seat!
    Ye Country Houses and Retreat,
    Which all the happy Gods so Love,
That for you oft they quit their Bright and Great
    Metropolis above.

Here Nature does a House for me erect,
    Nature the wisest Architect,
    Who those fond Artists does despise
That can the fair and living Trees neglect;
    Yet the Dead Timber prize.

Here let me careless and unthoughtful lying,
    Hear the soft winds above me flying,
    With all their wanton Boughs dispute,
And the more tuneful Birds to both replying
    Nor be my self too Mute.

A Silver stream shall roll his waters neer,
    Gilt with the Sun-beams here and there
    On whose enamel'd Bank I'll walk,
And see how prettily they Smile, and hear
    How prettily they Talk.

Ah wretched, and too Solitary Hee
    Who loves not his own Company!
    He'll feel the weight of 't many a day
Unless he call in Sin or Vanity
    To help to bear 't away.

Oh Solitude, first state of Human-kind!
　　Which blest remain'd till man did find
　　Even his own helpers Company.
As soon as two (alas!) together joyn'd,
　　The Serpent made up Three.

Though God himself, through countless Ages Thee
　　His sole Companion chose to bee,
　　Thee, Sacred Solitude alone,
Before the Branchy head of Numbers Tree
　　Sprang from the Trunk of One.

Thou (though men think thine an unactive part)
　　Dost break and tame th' unruly heart,
　　Which else would know no settled pace,
Making it move, well manag'd by thy Art,
　　With Swiftness and with Grace.

Thou the faint beams of Reasons scatter'd Light,
　　Dost like a Burning-glass unite,
　　Dost multiply the feeble Heat,
And fortifie the strength, till thou dost bright
　　And noble Fires beget.

Whilst this hard Truth I teach, methinks, I see
　　The Monster *London* laugh at me,
　　I should at thee too, foolish City,
If it were fit to laugh at Misery,
　　But thy Estate I pity.

Let but thy wicked men from out thee go,
　　And all the Fools that crowd thee so,
　　Even thou who dost thy Millions boast,
A Village less than *Islington* wilt grow,
　　A Solitude almost.

ABRAHAM COWLEY

28

From AN ODE UPON OCCASION OF HIS MAJESTIES PROCLAMATION IN THE YEARE 1630. COMMANDING THE GENTRY TO RESIDE UPON THEIR ESTATES IN THE COUNTRY

Onley the Island which wee sowe,
(A world without the world) so farre
From present wounds, it cannot showe
    An Ancient skarre.

White Peace (the beautiful'st of things)
Seemes here her everlasting rest
To fix, and spreads her downy wings
    Over the nest.

As when great *Jove* usurping Reigne
From the plagu'd world did her exile
And ty'd her with a golden chaine
    To one blest Isle:

Which in a sea of plenty swamme
And Turtles sang on ev'ry bowgh,
A safe retreat to all that came,
    As ours is now.

Yet wee, as if some foe were here,
Leave the despised Fields to clownes,
And come to save our selves as twere
    In walled Townes.

Hither we bring Wives, Babes, rich clothes
And Gemms; Till now my Soveraigne
The growing evill doth oppose:
    Counting in vaine

His care preserves us from annoy
Of enemyes his Realmes t' invade,
Unless hee force us to enjoy
    The peace hee made.

29

To rowle themselves in envy'd leasure
He therefore sends the landed Heyres,
Whilst hee proclaimes not his owne pleasure
                    So much as theirs.

The sapp and bloud o' th' land, which feed
Into the roote, and choackt the heart,
Are bid their quickning pow'r to spread
                    Through ev'ry part.

O, 'twas an act, not for my muse
To celebrate, nor the dull Age
Untill the country aire infuse
                    A purer rage!

And if the Fields as thankfull prove
For benefits receiv'd, as seed,
They will, to quite so great a love,
                    A *Virgill* breed.

A *Tytirus*, that shall not cease
Th' *Augustus* of our world to praise
In equall verse, author of peace
                    And *Halcyon* dayes.

Nor let the Gentry grudge to goe
Into those places whence they grew
But think them blest they may doe so
                    Who would pursue ...

Beleeve me Ladies you will finde
In that sweete life more solid joyes
More true contentment to the minde,
                    Than all Town toyes.

Nor *Cupid* there lesse bloud doth spill,
But heads his shafts with chaster love,
Not feathered with a Sparrowes quill,
                    But of a Dove.

30

There shall you heare the Nightingale
(The harmlesse Syren of the wood)
How prettily she tells a tale
                    Of rape and blood.

The lyrricke Larke, with all beside
Of nature's feathered quire: and all
The Common-wealth of Flowres int's pride
                    Behold you shall.

The Lillie (Queene) the (Royall) Rose,
The Gillyflowre (Prince of the bloud)
The (Courtyer) Tulip (gay in clothes),
                    The (Regall) Budd.

The Vilet (purple Senatour)
How they doe mock the pompe of State,
And all that at the surly doore
                    Of great ones waite.

Plant Trees you may, and see them shoote
Up with your children, to be serv'd
To your cleane boards and fair'st Fruite
                    To be preserv'd:

And learne to use their severall gummes,
'Tis innocence in the sweet blood
Of cherrye, Apricocks, and Plummes
                    To be imbru'd.

SIR RICHARD FANSHAWE

THE PASSIONATE SHEPHEARD TO HIS LOVE

Come live with mee, and be my love,
And we will all the pleasures prove,
That Vallies, groves, hills and fieldes,
Woods, or steepie mountaine yeelds.

And wee will sit upon the Rocks,
Seeing the Sheepheards feede theyr flocks,
By shallow Rivers, to whose falls,
Melodious byrds sing Madrigalls.

And I will make thee beds of Roses,
And a thousand fragrant poesies,
A cap of flowers, and a kirtle,
Imbroydred all with leaves of Mirtle.

A gowne made of the finest wooll,
Which from our pretty Lambes we pull,
Fayre lined slippers for the cold:
With buckles of the purest gold.

A belt of straw and Yvye buds,
With Corall Clasps and Amber studs,
And if these pleasures may thee move,
Then live with me, and be my Love.

The Shepheard Swaines shall dance and sing
For thy delight each May-morning:
If these delights thy minde may move,
Then live with mee, and be my love.

CHRISTOPHER MARLOWE

Sweet Country life, to such unknown,
Whose lives are others, not their own!
But serving Courts, and Cities, be
Less happy, less enjoying thee.
Thou never Plow'st the Oceans foame
To seek, and bring rough Pepper home:
Nor to the Eastern Ind dost rove
To bring from thence the scorched Clove.
Nor, with the losse of thy lov'd rest,
Bring'st home the Ingot from the West.
No, thy Ambition's Master-piece
Flies no thought higher then a fleece:
Or how to pay thy Hinds, and cleere
All scores; and so to end the yeere:
But walk'st about thine own dear bounds,
Not envying others larger grounds:
For well thou know'st, *'tis not th' extent*
Of Land makes life, but sweet content.
When now the Cock (the Plow-man's Horne)
Calls forth the lilly-wristed Morne;
Then to thy corn-fields thou dost goe,
Which though well soyl'd, yet thou dost know,
That the best compost for the Lands
Is the wise Master's Feet, and Hands.
There at the Plough thou find'st thy Teame,
With a Hind whistling there to them:
And cheer'st them up by singing how
The Kingdoms portion *is the Plow.*
This done, then to th' enameld Meads
Thou go'st; and as thy foot there treads,
Thou seest a present God-like Power
Imprinted in each Herb and Flower:
And smell'st the breath of great-ey'd Kine,
Sweet as the blossomes of the Vine.

Here thou behold'st thy large sleek Neat
Unto the Dew-laps up in meat:
And, as thou look'st, the wanton Steere,
The Heifer, Cow, and Oxe draw neere
To make a pleasing pastime there.
These seen, thou go'st to view thy flocks
Of sheep, (safe from the Wolfe and Fox)
And find'st their bellies there as full
Of short sweet grasse, as backs with wool.
And leav'st them (as they feed and fill)
A Shepherd piping on a hill.

ROBERT HERRICK

THRISE HAPPIE HEE...

Thrise happie hee, who by some shadie Grove
Farre from the clamarous World, doth live his owne,
Though solitare, yet who is not alone,
But doth converse with that Eternall Love.
O how more sweet is Birds harmonious Mone,
Or the hoarse Sobbings of the widow'd Dove?
Than those smoothe Whisperings neare a Princes Throne,
Which Good make doubtfull, doe the Evill approve.
O how more sweet is Zephyres wholesome Breath,
And Sighs perfum'd, which doe Flowres unfold,
Than that Applause vaine Honour doth bequeath?
How sweete are Streames to poyson drunke in Gold?
    The World is full of Horrours, Falshoods, Slights,
    Woods silent Shades have only true Delights.

WILLIAM DRUMMOND OF HAWTHORNDEN

From A COUNTRY LIFE: TO HIS BROTHER

The Damaskt medowes, and the peebly streames
  Sweeten and make soft your dreames:
The Purling springs, groves, birds, and well-weav'd Bowrs,
  With fields enameled with flowers,
Present their shapes, while fantasie discloses
  Millions of *Lillies* mixt with *Roses*.
Then dream ye heare the Lamb with many a bleat
  Woo'd to come suck the milkie Teat;
While *Faunus* in the Vision comes to keep
  From rav'ning wolves the fleecie sheep.
With thousand such enchanting dreams, which meet
  To make sleep not so sound as sweet:
Nor can these figures so thy rest endeare
  As not to up when Chanticlere
Warnes the last Watch; but with the Dawne dost rise
  To work, but first to sacrifice:
Making thy peace with Heav'n for some late fault,
  With Holy-meale and crackling salt.

ROBERT HERRICK

TO LYDIA BEING RETIRED
PRIVATELY INTO THE COUNTRY

Now to the secret groves is Lydia gone,
Stolen from us all, meaning to live alone
Among the silent woods, where she may be
From busy servants' entertainments free;
And hear the pleasant songsters of the groves
With whistling lays resound their growing loves;
With uncontrolling freedom view the trammels
Of Flora, which the fragrant meads enamels;
With pleasure walk and see the crystal brooks,
Catching the sportive fish with silver hooks;
Conversing with the flowery Napææ;
Making diversity of flowers agree
Bound up together; 'mong the shady trees
Dance in a circle with the Dryades;
Feeding on cleanly, though but homely food;
Esteemed the only goddess of the wood.
Oh how I fear those rural pleasures may
Entice her there to make a tedious stay:
But I with vows will frosty Hyems move
To haste the ruins of the leavy grove:
Pray cold-mouth Boreas kiss her tender cheek
To make her shelter in the town to seek,
Where conversation and warm fires do bring,
Though frost without doors lies, within a spring.

SAMUEL PORDAGE

From TO HIS MISTRESSE, WHEN SHE WAS GOING INTO THE COUNTRY

Goe and be happy, goe, and when you see
The trusty Ivy claspe its much lov'd tree,
And with its amorous intwinings cover
The welcome waiste of its imbracèd lover,
Thinke it our Embleme then, and prov'd to be
The happy shadow of my love and mee.
Goe, and be happy, and when some sweet brookes
(Calme as thy thoughts, and smooth as are thy lookes)
Show thee thy face, then let thy thoughts supply
And though I be not, thinke that I am by;
For if the heart be taken for whole man,
I must be by thee, be thou where thou can.
Goe, and when pretty birds on some small spray,
Neere to thy window welcome in the day:
Awake, and thinke, when their sweete notes you heare,
I was before-hand, and had sung them there.
Goe, and whate're thou chance to heare or see,
Be it bird, or brooke, or shade or tree;
If it delights thee, may my soule in it
Move thy true joys under that counterfeit.
So, aske not how I doe when you are there,
For at your mercy well or ill I fare.
For now me thinkes my heart so high doth swell,
It must inforce a breath, farewell, farewell.

THOMAS BEEDOME

THE GARDEN

This Garden does not take my eyes,
Though here you shew how art of men
Can purchase Nature at a price
Would stock old Paradise agen.

These glories while you dote upon,
I envie not your Spring nor pride,
Nay boast the Summer all your own,
My thoughts with lesse are satisfied.

Give me a little plot of ground,
Where might I with the Sun agree,
Though every day he walk the Round,
My Garden he should seldom see.

Those tulips that such wealth display,
To court my eye, shall lose their name,
Though now they listen, as if they
Expected I should praise their flame.

But I would see my self appear
Within the Violet's drooping head,
On which a melancholy tear
The discontented Morne hath shed.

Within their budds let Roses sleep,
And virgin Lillies on their stemme,
Till sighes from Lovers glide, and creep
Into their leaves to open them.

Ith' Center of my ground compose
Of Bays and Ewe my Summer room,
Which may so oft as I repose,
Present my Arbour, and my Tombe.

No woman here shall find me out,
Or if a chance do bring one hither,
I'le be secure, for round about
I'le moat it with my eyes foul weather.

No Bird shall live within my pale,
To charme me with their shames of Art,
Unlesse some wandring Nightingale
Come here to sing and break her heart.

Upon whose death I'le try to write
An Epitaph in some funeral stone,
So sad, and true, it may invite
Myself to die, and prove mine owne.

JAMES SHIRLEY

From THE SPLEEN

. . . Forced by soft violence of prayer,
The blithesome goddess soothes my care,
I feel the deity inspire,
And thus she models my desire.
Two hundred pounds half-yearly paid,
Annuity securely made,
A farm some twenty miles from town,
Small, tight, salubrious, and my own:
Two maids, that never saw the town,
A serving-man not quite a clown,
A boy to help to tread the mow,
And drive, while t'other holds the plough;
A chief, of temper formed to please,
Fit to converse, and keep the keys;
And better to preserve the peace,
Commission'd by the name of niece;
With understandings of a size
To think their master very wise.
May heaven (it's all I wish for) send
One genial room to treat a friend,
Where decent cupboard, little plate,
Display benevolence, not state.
And may my humble dwelling stand
Upon some chosen spot of land:
A pond before full to the brim,
Where cows may cool, and geese may swim;
Behind a green like velvet neat,
Soft to the eye, and to the feet;
Where odorous plants in evening fair
Breathe all around ambrosial air;
From Eurus, foe to kitchen ground,
Fenced by a slope with bushes crowned,
Fit dwelling for the feathered throng,
Who pay their quit-rents with a song;

With opening views of hill and dale,
Which sense and fancy too regale,
Where the half-cirque, which vision bounds,
Like amphitheatre surrounds:
And woods impervious to the breeze,
Thick phalanx of embodied trees,
From hills through plains in dusk array
Extended far, repel the day.
Here stillness, height, and solemn shade
Invite, and contemplation aid:
Here nymphs from hollow oaks relate
The dark decrees and will of fate,
And dreams beneath the spreading beech
Inspire, and docile fancy teach;
While soft as breezy breath of wind,
Impulses rustle through the mind:
Here Dryad's scorning Phoebus' ray,
While Pan melodious pipes away,
In measured motions frisk about,
'Till old Silenus puts them out.
There see the clover, pea, and bean,
Vie in variety of green;
Fresh pastures speckled o'er with sheep,
Brown fields their fallow sabbaths keep,
Plump Ceres golden tresses wear,
And poppy top-knots deck her hair,
And silver streams through meadows stray,
And Naiads on the margin play,
And lesser nymphs on side of hills
From plaything urns pour down the rills. . . .

MATTHEW GREEN

42

ODE ON SOLITUDE

Happy the man whose wish and care
   A few paternal acres bound,
Content to breath his native air
  'In his own ground.

Whose herds with milk, whose fields with bread,
   Whose flocks supply him with attire,
Whose trees in summer yield him shade,
   In winter fire.

Blest, who can unconcern'dly find
   Hours, days and years slide soft away,
In health of body, peace of mind,
    Quiet by day.

Sound sleep by night; study and ease,
   Together mixt; sweet recreation;
And innocence, which most does please,
    With meditation.

Thus let me live, unseen, unknown;
   Thus unlamented let me die,
Steal from the world, and not a stone
    Tell where I lie.

ALEXANDER POPE

ENGLAND

We have no grass locked up in ice so fast
That cattle cut their faces and at last,
When it is reached, must lie them down and starve,
With bleeding mouths that freeze too hard to move.
We have not that delirious state of cold
That makes men warm and sing when in Death's hold.
We have no roaring floods whose angry shocks
Can kill the fishes dashed against their rocks.
We have no winds that cut down street by street,
As easy as our scythes can cut down wheat.
No mountains here to spew their burning hearts
Into the valleys, on our human parts.
No earthquakes here, that ring church bells afar,
A hundred miles from where those earthquakes are.
We have no cause to set our dreaming eyes,
Like Arabs, on fresh streams in Paradise.
We have no wilds to harbour men that tell
More murders than they can remember well.
No woman here shall wake from her night's rest,
To find a snake is sucking at her breast.
Though I have travelled many and many a mile,
And had a man to clean my boots and smile
With teeth that had less bone in them than gold –
Give me this England now for all my world.

W. H. DAVIES

IN THE HIGHLANDS

In the highlands, in the country places,
Where the old plain men have rosy faces,
  And the young fair maidens
    Quiet eyes;
Where essential silence cheer and blesses,
And for ever in the hill-recesses
  Her more lovely music
    Broods and dies –

O to mount again where erst I haunted;
Where the old red hills are bird-enchanted,
  And the low green meadows
    Bright with sward;
And when even dies, the million-tinted,
And the night has come, and planets glinted,
  Lo, the valley, hollow
    Lamp-bestarr'd!

O to dream, O to awake and wander
There, and with delight to take and render,
  Through the trance of silence,
    Quiet breath!
Lo! for there, among the flowers and grasses,
Only the mightier movement sounds and passes;
  Only winds and rivers,
    Life and death.

ROBERT LOUIS STEVENSON

Silent Nymph, with curious eye!
Who the purple ev'ning lie
On the mountain's lonely van,
Beyond the noise of busy man,
Painting fair the form of things,
While the yellow linnet sings;
Or the tuneful nightingale
Charms the forest with her tale;
Come with all thy various hues,
Come, and aid thy sister Muse;
Now while Phoebus riding high
Gives lustre to the land and sky!
Grongar Hill invites my song,
Draw the landskip bright and strong;
Grongar, in whose mossy cells
Sweetly musing Quiet dwells:
Grongar, in whose silent shade
For the modest Muses made,
So oft I have, the even still,
At the fountain of a rill,
Sate upon a flow'ry bed,
With my hand beneath my head;
And stray'd my eyes o'er Towy's flood,
Over mead and over wood,
From house to house, from hill to hill,
Till Contemplation had her fill.
   About his chequer'd sides I wind,
And leave his brooks and meads behind,
And groves and grottoes where I lay,
And vistas shooting beams of day:
Wider and wider spreads the vale,
As circles on a smooth canal:
The mountains round, unhappy fate,
Sooner or later, of all height!

Withdraw their summits from the skies,
And lessen as the others rise:
Still the prospect wider spreads,
Adds a thousand woods and meads,
Still it widens, widens still,
And sinks the newly risen hill.

Now I gain the mountain's brow,
What a landskip lies below!
No clouds, no vapours intervene,
But the gay, the open scene
Does the face of Nature show,
In all the hues of Heaven's bow!
And swelling to embrace the light,
Spreads around beyond the sight.

Old castles on the cliffs arise,
Proudly tow'ring in the skies!
Rushing from the woods, the spires
Seem from hence ascending fires!
Half his beams Apollo sheds
On the yellow mountain heads!
Gilds the fleeces of the flocks;
And glitters on the broken rocks!

Below me trees unnumber'd rise,
Beautiful in various dyes:
The gloomy pine, the poplar blue,
The yellow beech, the sable yew,
The slender fir that taper grows,
The sturdy oak, with broad-spread boughs.
And beyond the purple grove,
Haunt of Phyllis, queen of love!
Gaudy as the op'ning dawn,
Lies a long and level lawn,
On which a dark hill, steep and high,
Holds and charms the wand'ring eye!
Deep are his feet in Towy's flood,
His sides are clothed with waving wood,

And ancient towers crown his brow,
That cast an awful look below;
Whose ragged walls the ivy creeps,
And with her arms from falling keeps.
So both a safety from the wind
On mutual dependence find.

'Tis now the raven's bleak abode;
'Tis now th'apartment of the toad;
And there the fox securely feeds,
And there the pois'nous adder breeds,
Conceal'd in ruins, moss and weeds:
While ever and anon there falls
Huge heaps of hoary, moulder'd walls.
Yet time has seen, that lifts the low,
And level lays the lofty brow,
Has seen this broken pile complete,
Big with the vanity of state:
But transient is the smile of Fate!
A little rule, a little sway,
A sunbeam in a winter's day,
Is all the proud and mighty have
Between the cradle and the grave.

And see the rivers how they run,
Thro' woods and meads, in shade and sun.
Sometimes swift and sometimes slow,
Wave succeeding wave they go
A various journey to the deep
Like human life to endless sleep!
Thus is nature's vesture wrought
To instruct our wand'ring thought;
Thus she dresses green and gay
To disperse our cares away.

Ever changing, ever new,
When will the landskip tire the view!
The fountain's fall, the river's flow,
The woody valleys, warm and low;

The windy summit, wild and high,
Roughly rushing on the sky!
The pleasant seat, the ruin'd tow'r,
The naked rock, the shady bow'r;
The town and village, dome and farm,
Each give each a double charm,
As pearls upon an Ethiop's arm.

See on the mountain's southern side,
Where the prospect opens wide,
Where the evening gilds the tide,
How close and small the hedges lie!
What streaks of meadows cross the eye!
A step, methinks, may pass the stream,
So little distant dangers seem;
So we mistake the future's face,
Ey'd through hope's deluding glass;
As yon summits soft and fair,
Clad in colours of the air,
Which, to those who journey near,
Barren, brown, and rough appear.
Still we tread, tir'd, the same coarse way,
The present's still a cloudy day.

O, may I with myself agree.
And never covet what I see:
Content me with an humble shade,
My passions tam'd, my wishes laid;
For while our wishes wildly roll,
We banish quiet from the soul:
'Tis thus the busy beat the air;
'And misers gather wealth and care.

Now, ev'n now my joy runs high,
As on the mountain turf I lie;
While the wanton zephyr sings
And in the vale perfumes his wings;
While the waters murmur deep,
While the shepherd charms his sheep;

While the birds unbounded fly,
And with music fill the sky.
Now, ev'n now my joy runs high.
   . Be full, ye courts, be great who will;
Search for Peace with all your skill:
Open wide the lofty door,
Seek her on the marble floor,
In vain ye search, she is not there,
In vain ye search the domes of care!
Grass and flowers Quiet treads,
On the meads and mountain heads,
Along with Pleasure close ally'd,
Ever by each other's side:
And often, by the murm'ring rill,
Hears the thrush while all is still,
Within the groves of Grongar Hill.

JOHN DYER

TO PENSHURST

Thou art not, Penshurst, built to envious show
Or touch or marble; nor canst boast a row
Of polish'd pillars, or a roofe of gold:
Thou hast no lantherne, whereof tales are told;
Or stayre, or courts; but stand'st an ancient pile,
And these grudg'd at, art reverenc'd the while.
Thou joy'st in better marks, of soile, of ayre,
Of wood, of water: therein thou art faie.
Thou hast thy walkes for health, as well as sport:
Thy *Mount*, to which thy *Dryads* do resort,
Where Pan and Bacchus their high feasts have made,
Beneath the broad beech, and the chestnut shade;
That taller tree, which of a nut was set,
At his great birth, where all the *Muses* met.
There, in the writhed barke, are cut the names
Of many a Sylvane, taken with his flames;
And thence the ruddy *Satyres* oft provoke
The lighter *Faunes*, to reach thy *Ladies* oke.
Thy copp's, too, nam'd of Gamage, thou hast there,
That never failes to serve thee season'd deere,
When thou wouldst feast, or exercise thy friends.
The lower land, that to the river bends,
Thy sheep, thy bullocks, kine, and calves do feed:
The middle ground thy Mares, and Horses breed.
Each banck doth yeeld thee Coneyes; and the topps
Fertile of wood, Ashore, and Sydney's copp's,
To crown thy open table, doth provide
The purpled Phesant, with the speckled side:
The painted Partrich lyes in every field,
And, for thy messe, is willing to be kill'd.
And if the high-swolne *Medway* faile thy dish,
Thou hast thy ponds, that pay thee tribute fish,
Fat, aged Carps that run into thy net.
And Pikes, now weary their own kinde to eat,

As loth, the second draught, or cast to stay,
Officiously, at first, themselves betray.
Bright Eels, that emulate them, and leap on land,
Before the fisher, or into his hand.
Then hath thy Orchard fruit, thy garden flowers,
Fresh as the ayre, and new as are the houres.
The early Cherry, with the later Plum,
Fig, Grape, and Quince, each in his time doth come:
The blushing Apricot, and woolly peach
Hang on thy wals, that every child may reach.
And though thy wals be of the country stone,
They'are rear'd with no man's ruine, no man's grone;
There's none, that dwell about them, wish them downe;
But all come in, the farmer and the clowne:
And no one empty-handed, to salute
Thy Lord, and Lady, though they have no sute.
Some bring a Capon, some a rurall Cake,
Some Nuts, some Apples; some that think they make
The better Cheeses, bring them; or else send
By their ripe daughters, whom they would commend
This way to husbands; and whose baskets beare
An Embleme of themselves, in plum, or peare.
But what can this (more than expresse their love)
Adde to thy free provisions, farre above
The need of such? whose liberall boord doth flow,
With all, that hospitality doth know!
Where comes no guest, but is allow'd to eat,
Without his feare, and of thy Lord's own meat:
Where the same beere, and bread, and selfe-same wine,
That is his Lordship's, shall be also mine.
And I not fain to sit (as some, this day,
At great mens tables) and yet dine away.
Here no man tels my cups; nor, standing by,
A waiter, doth my gluttony envy:
But gives me what I call, and lets me eate,
He knowes, below, he shall finde plentie of meate;

Thy tables hoord not up for the next day,
Nor, when I take my lodging, need I pray
For fire, or lights, or livorie: all is there;
As if thou, then, wert mine, or I raign'd here:
There's nothing I can wish, for which I stay.
That found King James, when hunting late, this way,
With his brave sonne, the Prince, they saw thy fires
Shine bright on every harth as the desires
Of thy *Penates* had beene set on flame,
To entertayne them; or the countrey came,
With all their zeale, to warme their welcome here.
What (great, I will not say, but) sodaine cheare
Didst thou, then, make 'hem! and what praise was heap'd
On thy good Lady, then! who therein reap'd
The just reward of her high huswifery;
To have her linen, plate, and all things nigh,
When she was farre; and not a roome, but drest,
As if it had expected such a guest!
These, Penshurst, are thy praise, and yet not all.
Thy Lady's noble, fruitfull, chaste withall.
His children thy great Lord may call his owne:
A fortune, in this age, but rarely knowne.
They are and have beene taught religion: Thence
Their gentler spirits have suck'd innocence.
Each morne, and even, they are taught, to pray
With the whole household, and may, every day,
Reade, in their virtuous parents' noble parts,
The mysteries of manners, armes, and arts.
Now, Penshurst, they that will proportion thee
With other edifices, when they see
Those proud, ambitious heaps, and nothing else,
May say, their lords have built, but thy Lord dwells.

BEN JONSON

THE HOUSE BEAUTIFUL

A naked house, a naked moor,
A shivering pool before the door,
A garden bare of flowers and fruit,
And poplars at the garden foot:
Such is the place that I live in,
Bleak without and bare within.

Yet shall your barren moor receive
The incomparable pomp of eve,
And the cold glories of the dawn
Behind your shivering trees be drawn;
And when the wind from place to place
Doth the unmoored cloud-galleons chase,
Your garden gloom and gleam again
With leaping sun, with glancing rain.
Here shall the wizard moon ascend
The heavens, in the crimson end
Of day's declining splendour; here
The army of the stars appear.
The neighbour hollows dry or wet
Spring shall with tender flowers beset;
And oft the morning muser see
Larks rising from the broomy lea,
And every fairy wheel and thread
Of cobweb dew-bediamonded.
When daisies go shall winter-time
Silver the simple grass with rime;
Autumnal frosts enchant the pool
And make the cart-ruts beautiful;
And when snow-bright the moor expands,
How shall your children clap their hands!
To make this earth, our hermitage,
A cheerful and a changeful page,
God's bright and intricate device
Of days and seasons doth suffice.

ROBERT LOUIS STEVENSON

TINTERN ABBEY

Five years have past; five summers, with the length
Of five long winters! and again I hear
These waters, rolling from their mountain-springs
With a sweet inland murmur. – Once again
Do I behold these steep and lofty cliffs,
That on a wild secluded scene impress
Thoughts of more deep seclusion: and connect
The landscape with the quiet of the sky.
The day is come when I again repose
Here, under this dark sycamore, and view
These plots of cottage-ground, these orchard-tufts,
Which at this season, with their unripe fruits,
Are clad in one green hue, and lose themselves
Among the woods and copses, nor disturb
The wild green landscape. Once again I see
These hedgerows, hardly hedgerows, little lines
Of sportive wood run wild: these pastoral farms,
Green to the very door; and wreaths or smoke
Sent up, in silence, from among the trees!
With some uncertain notice, as might seem
Of vagrant dwellers in the houseless woods,
Or of some Hermit's cave, where by his fire
The Hermit sits alone.
                              These beauteous Forms,
Through a long absence, have not been to me
As is a landscape to a blind man's eye:
But oft, in lonely rooms, and 'mid the din
Of towns and cities, I have owed to them,
In hours of weariness, sensations sweet,
Felt in the blood, and felt along the heart;
And passing even into my purer mind,
With tranquil restoration: – feelings too
Of unremembered pleasure: such, perhaps,
As have no slight or trivial influence
On that best portion of a good man's life,

His little, nameless, unremembered acts
Of kindness and of love. Nor less, I trust,
To them I may have owed another gift,
Of aspect more sublime; that blessed mood,
In which the burthen of the mystery,
In which the heavy and the weary weight
Of all this unintelligible world,
Is lightened: – that serene and blessed mood,
In which the affections gently lead us on, –
Until, the breath of this corporeal frame
And even the motion of our human blood
Almost suspended, we are laid asleep
In body, and become a living soul:
While with an eye made quiet by the power
Of harmony, and the deep power of joy,
We see into the life of things.

                                               If this

Be but a vain belief, yet, oh! how oft,
In darkness, and amid the many shapes
Of joyless daylight; when the fretful stir
Unprofitable, and the fever of the world,
Have hung upon the beatings of my heart,
How oft, in spirit, have I turned to thee,
O sylvan Wye! Thou wanderer thro' the woods,
How often has my spirit turned to thee!

   And now, with gleams of half-extinguished thought,
With many recognitions dim and faint,
And somewhat of a sad perplexity,
The picture of the mind revives again:
While here I stand, not only with the sense
Of present pleasure, but with pleasing thoughts
That in this moment there is life and food
For future years. And so I dare to hope,
Though changed, no doubt, from what I was when first
I came among these hills; when like a roe
I bounded o'er the mountains, by the sides
Of the deep rivers, and the lonely streams,

Wherever nature led: more like a man.
Flying from something that he dreads, than one
Who sought the thing he loved. For nature then
(The coarser pleasures of my boyish days,
And their glad animal movements all gone by)
To me was all in all. – I cannot paint
What then I was. The sounding cataract
Haunted me like a passion: the tall rock,
The mountain, and the deep and gloomy wood,
Their colours and their forms, were then to me
An appetite; a feeling and a love,
That had no need of a remoter charm,
By thought supplied, or any interest
Unborrowed from the eye. – That time is past,
And all its aching joys are now no more,
And all its dizzy raptures. Not for this
Faint I, nor mourn nor murmur; other gifts
Have followed, for such loss, I would believe,
Abundant recompence. For I have learned
To look on nature, not as in the hour
Of thoughtless youth: but hearing oftentimes
The still, sad music of humanity,
Nor harsh nor grating, though of ample power
To chasten and subdue. And I have felt
A presence that disturbs me with the joy
Of elevated thoughts: a sense sublime
Of something far more deeply interfused,
Whose dwelling is the light of setting suns,
And the round ocean and the living air,
And the blue sky, and in the mind of man:
A motion and a spirit, that impels
All thinking things, all objects of all thought,
And rolls through all things. Therefore am I still
A lover of the meadows and the woods,
And mountains; and of all that we behold
From this green earth; of all the mighty world
Of eye and ear, both what they half create,

And what perceive; well pleased to recognize
In nature and the language of the sense,
The anchor of my purest thoughts, the nurse,
The guide, the guardian of my heart, and soul
Of all my moral being.
                                    Nor perchance,
If I were not thus taught, should I the more
Suffer my genial spirits to decay:
For thou art with me, here, upon the banks
Of this fair river; thou, my dearest Friend,
My dear, dear Friend, and in thy voice I catch
The language of my former heart, and read
My former pleasures in the shooting lights
Of thy wild eyes. Oh! yet a little while
May I behold in thee what I was once,
My dear, dear Sister! and this prayer I make,
Knowing that Nature never did betray
The heart that loved her; 'tis her privilege,
Through all the years of this our life, to lead
From joy to joy: for she can so inform
The mind that is within us, so impress
With quietness and beauty, and so feed
With lofty thoughts, that neither evil tongues,
Rash judgments, nor the sneers of selfish men,
Nor greetings where no kindness is, nor all
The dreary intercourse of daily life,
Shall e'er prevail against us, or disturb
Our cheerful faith, that all which we behold
Is full of blessings. Therefore let the moon
Shine on thee in thy solitary walk;
And let the misty mountain winds be free
To blow against thee: and in after years,
When these wild ecstasies shall be matured
Into a sober pleasure, when thy mind
Shall be a mansion for all lovely forms,
Thy memory be as a dwelling-place
For all sweet sounds and harmonies; oh! then,

If solitude, or fear, or pain, or grief,
Should be thy portion, with what healing thoughts
Of tender joy wilt thou remember me,
And these my exhortations! Nor, perchance
If I should be where I no more can hear
Thy voice, nor catch from thy wild eyes these gleams
Of past existence, wilt thou then forget
That on the banks of this delightful stream
We stood together; and that I, so long
A worshipper of Nature, hither came
Unwearied in that service: rather say
With warmer love, oh! with far deeper zeal
Of holier love. Nor wilt thou then forget,
That after many wanderings, many years
Of absence, these steep woods and lofty cliffs,
And this green pastoral landscape, were to me
More dear, both for themselves and for thy sake!

WILLIAM WORDSWORTH

Wandering by the river's edge,
I love to rustle through the sedge
And through the woods of reed to tear
Almost as high as bushes are.
Yet, turning quick with shudder chill,
As danger ever does from ill,
Fear's moment ague quakes the blood,
While plop the snake coils in the flood
And, hissing with a forked tongue,
Across the river winds along.
In coat of orange, green, and blue
Now on a willow branch I view,
Grey waving to the sunny gleam,
Kingfishers watch the ripple stream
For little fish that nimble bye
And in the gravel shallows lie.

Eddies run before the boats,
Gurgling where the fisher floats,
Who takes advantage of the gale
And hoists his handkerchief for sail
On osier twigs that form a mast –
While idly lies, nor wanted more,
The spirit that pushed him on before.

There's not a hill in all the view,
Save that a forked cloud or two
Upon the verge of distance lies
And into mountains cheats the eyes.
And as to trees the willows wear
Lopped heads as high as bushes are;
Some taller things the distance shrouds
That may be trees or stacks or clouds
Or may be nothing; still they wear
A semblance where there's nought to spare.

Among the tawny tasselled reed
The ducks and ducklings float and feed.
With head oft dabbing in the flood
They fish all day the weedy mud,
And tumbler-like are bobbing there,
Heels topsy-turvy in the air.

The geese in troops come droving up,
Nibble the weeds, and take a sup;
And, closely puzzled to agree,
Chatter like gossips over tea.
The gander with his scarlet nose
When strife's at height will interpose,
And, stretching neck to that and this,
With now a mutter, now a hiss,
A nibble at the feathers too,
A sort of 'pray be quiet do',
And turning as the matter mends,
He stills them into mutual friends;
Then in a sort of triumph sings
And throws the water o'er his wings.

Ah, could I see a spinney nigh,
A puddock riding in the sky
Above the oaks with easy sail
On stilly wings and forked tail,
Or meet a heath of furze in flower,
I might enjoy a quiet hour,
Sit down at rest, and walk at ease,
And find a many things to please.
But here my fancy's moods admire
The naked levels till they tire,
Nor e'en a molehill cushion meet
To rest on when I want a seat.

Here's little save the river scene
And grounds of oats in rustling green
And crowded growth of wheat and beans,
That with the hope of plenty leans
And cheers the farmer's gazing brow,
Who lives and triumphs in the plough –
One sometimes meets a pleasant sward
Of swarthy grass; and quickly marred
The plough soon turns it into brown,
And, when again one rambles down
The path, small hillocks burning lie
And smoke beneath a burning sky.
Green paddocks have but little charms
With gain the merchandise of farms;
And, muse and marvel where we may,
Gain mars the landscape every day –
The meadow grass turned up and copt,
The trees to stumpy dotterels lopt,
The hearth with fuel to supply
For rest to smoke and chatter bye;
Giving the joy of home delights,
The warmest mirth on coldest nights.
And so for gain, that joy's repay,
Change cheats the landscape every day,
Nor trees nor bush about it grows
That from the hatchet can repose,
And the horizon stooping smiles
O'er treeless fens of many miles.
Spring comes and goes and comes again
And all is nakedness and fen.

JOHN CLARE

. . . Turn to the watery world! – but who to thee
(A wonder yet unview'd) shall paint – the Sea?
Various and vast, sublime in all its forms,
When lull'd by zephyrs, or when roused by storms,
Its colours changing, when from clouds and sun
Shades after shades upon the surface run;
Embrown'd and horrid now, and now serene,
In limpid blue, and evanescent green;
And oft the foggy banks on ocean lie,
Lift the fair sail, and cheat th'experienced eye.

   Be it the summer-noon: a sandy space
The ebbing tide has left upon its place;
Then just the hot and stony beach above,
Light twinkling streams in bright confusion move;
(For heated thus, the warmer air ascends,
And with the cooler in its fall contends) –
Then the broad bosom of the ocean keeps
An equal motion; swelling as it sleeps,
Then slowly sinking; curling to the strand,
Faint, lazy waves o'ercreep the rigid sand,
Or tap the tarry boat with gentle blow,
And back return in silence, smooth and slow.
Ships in the calm seem anchor'd; for they glide
On the still sea, urged solely by the tide:
Art thou not present, this calm scene before,
Where all beside is pebbly length of shore,
And far as eye can reach, it can discern no more?

   Yet sometimes comes a ruffling cloud to make
The quiet surface of the ocean shake;
As an awaken'd giant with a frown
Might show his wrath, and then to sleep sink down.

   View now the Winter-storm! above, one cloud,
Black and unbroken, all the skies o'ershroud:
Th'unwieldy porpoise through the day before
Had roll'd in view of boding men on shore;

And sometimes hid and sometimes show'd his form,
Dark as the cloud, and furious as the storm.
    All where the eye delights, yet dreads to roam,
The breaking billows cast the flying foam
Upon the billows rising – all the deep
Is restless change; the waves so swell'd and steep,
Breaking and sinking, and the sunken swells,
Nor one, one moment, in its station dwells:
But nearer land you may the billows trace,
As if contending in their watery chase;
May watch the mightiest till the shoal they reach,
Then break and hurry to their utmost stretch;
Curl'd as they come, they strike with furious force,
And then re-flowing, take their grating course,
Raking the rounded flints, which ages past,
Roll'd by their rage, and shall to ages last.
    Far off the Petrel in the troubled way
Swims with her brood, or flutters in the spray;
She rises often, often drops again,
And sports at ease on the tempestuous main.
    High o'er the restless deep, above the reach
Of gunner's hope, vast flights of Wild-ducks stretch;
Far as the eye can glance on either side,
In a broad space and level line they glide;
All in their wedge-like figures from the north,
Day after day, flight after flight, go forth.
    In-shore their passage tribes of Sea-gulls urge,
And drop for prey within the sweeping surge;
Oft in the rough opposing blast they fly
Far back, then turn, and all their force apply
While to the storm they give their weak complaining cry;
Or clap the sleek white pinion to the breast,
And in the restless ocean dip for rest. . . .

GEORGE CRABBE

SONNET: ON THE SEA

It keeps eternal whisperings around
  Desolate shores, and with its mighty swell
  Gluts twice ten thousand Caverns, till the spell
Of Hecate leaves them their old shadowy sound.
Often 'tis in such gentle temper found,
  That scarcely will the very smallest shell
  Be mov'd for days from where it sometime fell,
When last the winds of Heaven were unbound.
Oh ye! who have your eye-balls vex'd and tir'd,
  Feast them upon the wideness of the Sea;
    Oh ye! whose ears are dinn'd with uproar rude,
Or fed too much with cloying melody —
    Sit ye near some old Cavern's Mouth, and brood
Until ye start, as if the sea-nymphs quir'd!

JOHN KEATS

THE THAMES FROM COOPER'S HILL

My eye descending from the Hill surveys
Where *Thames* amongst the wanton vallies strays.
Thames, the most lov'd of all the Oceans sons,
By his old Sire to his embraces runs,
Hasting to pay his tribute to the Sea
Like mortal life to meet Eternity.
Though with those streams he no resemblance hold,
Whose foam is Amber, and their Gravel Gold;
His genuine, and less guilty wealth t'explore,
Search not his bottom, but survey his shore;
O'er which he kindly spreads his spacious wing,
And hatches plenty for th' ensuing Spring.
Nor then destroys it with too fond a stay,
Like Mothers which their Infants overlay.
Nor with a sudden and impetuous wave,
Like profuse Kings, resumes the wealth he gave.
No unexpected inundations spoil
The mowers hopes, nor mock the plowmans toil:
But God-like his unwearied Bounty flows;
First loves to do, then loves the Good he does.
Nor are his Blessings to his banks confin'd,
But free, and common, as the Sea or Wind;
When he to boast, or to disperse his stores,
Full of the tributes of his grateful shores,
Visits the world, and in his flying towers
Brings home to us, and makes both Indies ours;
Finds wealth where 'tis, bestows it where it wants,
Cities in deserts, woods in Cities plants.
So that to us no thing, no place is strange,
While his fair bosom is the world's exchange.
O could I flow like thee, and make thy stream
My great example, as it is my theme!
Though deep, yet clear, though gentle, yet not dull,
Strong without rage, without o'er-flowing full.

SIR JOHN DENHAM

THE ANGLER'S WISH

I in these flow'ry Meades wo'd be:
These Christal streams should solace me;
To whose harmonious bubling noise,
I with my Angle wo'd rejoice,
  Sit here, and see the Turtle-dove,
  Court his chaste Mate to acts of love,

Or on that bank feel the West wind
Breathe health and plenty, please my mind
To see sweet dew-drops kisse these flowers,
And then washt off by April-showers:
  Here hear my Clora sing a song,
  There see a Blackbird feed her young.

Or a laverock build her nest;
Here give my weary spirits rest,
And raise my low pitcht thoughts above
Earth, or what poor mortals love:
  Thus free from lawsuits, and the noise
  Of Princes' Courts, I wo'd rejoyce.

Or with my Bryan, and a book,
Loyter long dayes near Shawford-brook;
There sit by him, and eat my meat,
There see the Sun both rise and set:
There bid good morning to next day,
There meditate my time away:
  And angle on, and beg to have
  A quiet passage to a welcome grave.

ISAAK WALTON

HUMBLE FOLK

Above our lane two rows of larches lean,
And lissom, rosy pines with wild black hair –
One slim, bright-fingered chestnut in between.
In blossom-time and berry-time and snow
Are muffled sounds of feet that come and go
Forever, from the cones and falling spines
And the sad, homeless rhythm of the pines.
These are our friends; we feel the griefs they bear;
We know the larches' thin young April song;
The heavy, dark endeavour of the cone
That goes alone
Among the thick, obliterating dust –
Impelled by something faint and strong
Within her, by the lust
Of death, towards the red and living tree.
Our fingers and the chestnut's touch and hold
The blue light and the gold,
And in a little drop them listlessly.
We know so few things more than these –
The larch that moans in rain
And every March puts roses on again;
The wise, mute chestnut listening to the bees;
The pine
That drinks the icy wind like wine.
We ask no better birth than their brown roots;
We dare not dream of immortality
Unshared by their brown fruits.
And when the wild bee's voice
Grows faint for us, we only ask to lie
Like two straight trees cut down together,
Not fearing any weather,
Too soundly sleeping even to rejoice.

MARY WEBB

From THE FARMER'S BOY

(MILKING AND CHEESE-MAKING)

... His simple errand done, he homeward hies;
Another instantly its place supplies.
The clattering dairy-maid immersed in steam
Singing and scrubbing midst her milk and cream,
Bawls out, 'Go fetch the cows': he hears no more,
For pigs, and ducks, and turkeys, throng the door,
And sitting hens, for constant war prepared;
A concert strange to that which late he heard.
Straight to the meadow then he whistling goes;
With well-known hallo calls his lazy cows:
Down the rich pasture heedlessly they graze,
Or hear the summons with an idle gaze;
For well they know the cow-yard yields no more
Its tempting fragrance, nor its wintry store.
Reluctance marks their steps, sedate and slow;
The right of conquest all the law they know:
Subordinate they one by one succeed;
And one among them always takes the lead,
Is ever foremost wheresoe'er they stray;
Allowed precedence, undisputed sway;
With jealous pride her station is maintain'd,
For many a broil that post of honour gain'd.
At home, the yard affords a grateful scene:
For Spring makes e'en a miry cow-yard clean.
Thence from its chalky bed behold convey'd
The rich manure that drenching winter made,
Which piled near home, grows green with many a weed,
A promised nutriment for autumn's seed.
Forth comes the maid, and like the morning smiles;
The mistress, too, and followed close by Giles.
A friendly tripod forms their humble seat,
With pails bright scour'd and delicately sweet.
Where shadowing elms obstruct the morning ray,
Begins their work, begins the simple lay;

The full-charged udder yields its willing streams,
While Mary sings some lover's amorous dreams;
And crouching Giles beneath a neighbouring tree
Tugs o'er his pail, and chants with equal glee.
Whose hat with tatter'd brim, of nap so bare,
From the cow's side purloins a coat of hair,
A mottled ensign of his harmless trade,
An unambitious, peaceable cockade.
As unambitious too that cheerful aid
The mistress yields beside her rosy maid;
With joy she views her plenteous reeking store,
And bears a brimmer to the dairy door;
Her cows dismiss'd, the luscious mead to roam,
Till eve again recall them loaded home.
And now the *Dairy* claims her choicest care,
And half her household find employment there;
Slow rolls the churn, its load of clogging cream
At once foregoes its quality and name;
From knotty particles first floating wide
Congealing butter's dash'd from side to side;
Streams of new milk through flowing coolers stray,
And snow-white curd abounds, and wholesome whey.
Due north th'unglazed windows, cold and clear,
For warming sunbeams are unwelcome here.
Brisk goes the work beneath each busy hand,
And Giles must trudge, whoever gives command;
A Gibeonite, that serves them all by turns:
He drains the pump, from him the faggot burns:
From him the noisy hogs demand their food;
While at his heels run many a chirping brood,
Or down his path in expectation stand,
With equal claims upon his strewing hand.
Thus wastes the morn, till each with pleasure sees
The bustle o'er, and press'd the new-made cheese.

ROBERT BLOOMFIELD

MOLE CATCHER

With coat like any mole's, as soft and black,
And hazel boughs bundled beneath his arm,
With long-helved spade and rush bag on his back,
The trapper plods alone about the farm:
And spies new mounds in the ripe pasture-land,
And where the lob-worms writhe up in alarm
And easy sinks the spade, he takes his stand
Knowing the moles' dark highroad runs below:
Then sharp and square he chops the turf, and day
Gloats on the opened turnpike through the clay.

Out from his wallet hurry pin and prong,
And trap, and noose to tie it to the bow;
And then his grand arcanum, oily and strong,
Found out by his forefather years ago
To scent the peg and witch the moles along.
The bow is earthed and arched ready to shoot
And snatch the death-knot fast round the first mole
Who comes and snuffs well pleased and tries to root
Past the sly nose peg; back again is put
The mould, and death left smirking in the hole.
The old man goes and tallies all his snares
And finds the prisoners there and takes his toll.

And moles to him are only moles: but hares
See him afield and scarcely cease to nip
Their dinners, for he harms not them; he spares
The drowning fly that of his ale would sip
And throws the ant the crumbs of comradeship.
And every time he comes into his yard
Grey linnet knows he brings the groundsel sheaf,
And clatters round the cage to be unbarred,
And on his finger whistles twice as hard. –
What his old vicar says, is his belief,

In the side pew he sits and hears the truth;
And never misses once to ring his bell
On Sundays night and morn, nor once since youth
Has heard the chimes afield, but has heard tell
There's not a peal in England sounds so well.

EDMUND BLUNDEN

THE PLOUGHER

Sunset and silence! A man: around him earth savage, earth
    broken;
Beside him two horses – a plough!

Earth savage, earth broken, the brutes, the dawn, man there
    in the sunset,
And the Plough that is twin to the Sword, that is founder of
    Cities!

'Brute-tamer, plough-maker, earth-breaker! Can'st hear?
    There are ages between us.
Is it praying you are as you stand there alone in the sunset?

'Surely our sky-born gods can be naught to you, earth-child
    and earth-master?
'Surely your thoughts are of Pan, or of Wotan, or Dana?

'Yet why give thought to the gods? Has Pan led your brutes
    where they stumble?
'Has Dana numbed pain of the child-bed, or Wotan put
    hands to your plough?

'What matter your foolish reply! O man, standing lone and
    bowed earthward,
'Your task is a day near its close. Give thanks to the night-
    giving God.'

Slowly the darkness falls, the broken lands blend with the
    savage;
The brute-tamer stands by the brutes, a head's breadth only
    above them.

A head's breadth? Ay, but therein is hell's depth, and the
    height up to heaven,
And the thrones of the gods and their halls, their chariots,
    purples, and splendours.

PADRAIC COLUM

From KING HENRY VI

KING HENRY

> Oh God! me thinkes it were a happy life,
> To be no better than a homely Swaine —
> To sit upon a hill, as I do now,
> To carve out Dialls queintly, point by point,
> Thereby to see the Minutes how they runne:
> How many makes the Houre full compleate,
> How many Houres brings about the Day,
> How many Dayes will finish up the Yeare,
> How many Yeares, a Mortall man may live.
> When this is knowne, then to divide the Times:
> So many Houres, must I tend my Flocke;
> So many Houres, must I take my Rest;
> So many Houres, must I Contemplate:
> So many Houres, must I Sport my selfe:
> So many Dayes, my Ewes have bene with yong;
> So many weekes, ere the poore Fooles will Eane:
> So many yeares, ere I shall sheere the Fleece:
> So Minutes, Houres, Dayes, Months, and Yeares,
> Past over to the end they were created,
> Would bring white haires, unto a Quiet grave.
> Ah! what a life were this! How sweet! how lovely!
> Gives not the Hawthorne bush a sweeter shade
> To Shepheards, looking on their silly Sheepe,
> Than doth a rich Imbroider'd Canopie
> To Kings, that feare their Subject's treacherie?
> Oh yes, it doth, a thousandfold it doth.
> And to conclude, the Shepherd's homely Curds,
> His cold thinne drinke out of his Leather Bottle,
> His wonted sleepe, under a fresh tree's shade,
> All which secure, and sweetly he enjoyes,
> Is farre beyond a Prince's Delicates,
> His Viands sparkling in a Golden Cup,
> His bodie couched in a curious bed,
> When Care, Mistrust, and Treason waits on him.

WILLIAM SHAKESPEARE

Spring

From SUMMER'S LAST WILL AND TESTAMENT: SONG

Spring, the sweete spring, is the yeres pleasant King,
Then bloomes eche thing, then maydes daunce in a ring,
Cold doeth not sting, the pretty birds doe sing,
    Cuckow, jugge, jugge, puwe, towittawoo.

The Palme and May make countrey houses gay.
Lambs friske and play, the Shepherds pype all day,
And we heare aye birds tune this merry lay,
    Cuckow, jugge, jugge, puwe, towittawoo.

The fields breathe sweete, the dayzies kisse our feete,
Young lovers meete, old wives a-sunning sit:
In every streete, these tunes our earse doe greete,
    Cuckow, jugge, jugge, puwe, towittawoo.
      Spring the sweete spring.

THOMAS NASH

SAINT VALENTINE'S DAY

Well dost thou, Love, thy solemn Feast to hold
In vestal February;
Not rather choosing out some rosy day
From the rich coronet of the coming May,
When all things meet to marry!
   O quick, praevernal Power
That signall'st punctual through the sleepy mould
The Snowdrop's time to flower,
Fair as the rash oath of virginity
Which is first-love's first cry;
O, Baby spring,
That flutter'st sudden 'neath the breast of Earth
A month before the birth;
Whence is the peaceful poignancy,
The joy contrite,
Sadder than sorrow, sweeter than delight,
That burthens now the breath of everything,
Though each one sighs as if to each alone
The cherish'd pang were known?
At dusk of dawn, on his dark spray apart,
With it the Blackbird breaks the young Day's heart;
In evening's hush
About it talks the heavenly-minded Thrush;
The hill with like remorse
Smiles to the Sun's smile in his westering course;
The fisher's drooping skiff
In yonder sheltering bay;
The choughs that call about the shining cliff;
The children, noisy in the setting ray;
Own the sweet season, each thing as it may;
Thoughts of strange kindness and forgotten peace
In me increase;
And tears arise
Within my happy, happy Mistress' eyes,

And, lo, her lips, averted from my kiss,
Ask from Love's bounty, ah, much more than bliss!
   Is't the sequester'd and exceeding sweet
Of dear Desire electing his defeat?
Is't the waked Earth now to yon purpling cope
Uttering first-love's first cry,
Vainly renouncing, with a seraph's sigh,
Love's natural hope?
Fair-meaning Earth, foredoom'd to perjury!
Behold, all amorous May,
With roses heap'd upon her laughing brows,
Avoids thee of thy vows!
Were it for thee, with her warm bosom near,
To abide the sharpness of the Seraph's sphere?
Forget thy foolish words;
Go to her summons gay,
Thy heart with dead, wing'd Innocencies filled,
Ev'n as a nest with birds
After the old ones by the hawk are kill'd.
   Well dost thou, Love, to celebrate
The noon of thy soft ecstasy,
Or e'er it be too late,
Or e'er the Snowdrop die!

COVENTRY PATMORE

From THE NIGHT OF FOREBEING
AN ODE AFTER EASTER

Cast wide the folding doorways of the East,
For now is light increased!
And the wind-besomed chambers of the air,
See they be garnished fair;
And look the ways exhale some precious odours,
And set ye all about wild-breathing spice,
Most fit for Paradise!
Now is no time for sober gravity,
Season enough has Nature to be wise;
But now discinct, with raiment glittering free,
Shake she the ringing rafters of the skies
With festal footing and bold joyance sweet,
And let the earth be drunken and carouse!
For lo, into her house
Spring is come home with her world-wandering feet,
And all things are made young with young desires;
And all for her is light increased
In yellow stars and yellow daffodils,
And East to West, and West to East,
Fling answering welcome-fires,
By dawn and day-fall, on the jocund hills.
And ye, winged minstrels of her fair meinie,
Being newly coated in glad livery,
Upon her steps attend,
And round her treading dance, and without end
Reel your shrill lutany.
What popular breath her coming does out-tell
The garrulous leaves among!
What little noises stir and pass
From blade to blade along the voluble grass!·
O Nature, never-done
Ungaped-at Pentecostal miracle,
We hear thee, each man in his proper tongue!
Break, elemental children, break ye loose

From the strict frosty rule
Of grey-beard Winter's school.
Vault, O young winds, vault in your tricksome courses
Upon the snowy steeds that reinless use
In cœrule pampas of the heaven to run;
Foaled of the white sea-horses,
Washed in the lambent waters of the sun.
Let even the slug-abed snail upon the thorn
Put forth a conscious horn!
Mine elemental co-mates, joy each one;
And ah, my foster-brethren, seem not sad –
No, seem not sad,
That my strange heart and I should be so little glad.
Suffer me at your leafy feast
To sit apart, a somewhat alien guest,
And watch your mirth,
Unsharing in the liberal laugh of earth;
Yet with a sympathy
Begot of wholly sad and half-sweet memory –
The little sweetness making grief complete . . .

A higher and a solemn voice
I heard through your gay-hearted noise;
A solemn meaning and a stiller voice
Sounds to me from far days when I too shall rejoice,
Nor more be with your jollity at strife.
O prophecy
Of things that are, and are not, and shall be!
The great-vanned Angel March
Hath trumpeted
His clangorous 'Sleep no more' to all the dead –
Beat his strong vans o'er earth, and air, and sea.
And they have heard;
Hark to the *Jubilate* of the bird
For them that found the dying way to life!
And they have heard,
And quicken to the great precursive word;

Green spray showers lightly down the cascade of the larch;
The graves are riven,
And the Sun comes with power amid the clouds of heaven!
Before his way
Went forth the trumpet of the March;
Before his way, before his way
Dances the pennon of the May!
O Earth, unchilded, widowed Earth, so long
Lifting in patient Pine and Ivy-tree
Mournful belief and steadfast prophecy,
Behold how all things are made true!
Behold your bridegroom cometh in to you,
Exceeding glad and strong.
Raise up your eyes, O raise your eyes abroad!
No more shall you sit sole and vidual,
Searching, in servile pall,
Upon the hieratic night the star-sealed sense of all:
Rejoice, O barren, and look forth abroad!
Your children gathered back to your embrace
See with a mother's face.
Look up, O mortals, and the portent heed;
In very deed,
Washed with new fire to their irradiant birth,
Reintegrated are the heavens and earth!
From sky to sod,
The world's unfolded blossom smells of God.

FRANCIS THOMPSON

DESCRIPTION OF SPRING, WHEREIN ECHE THING RENEWES, SAVE ONELIE THE LOVER

The soote season, that bud and blome furth bringes,
With grene hath clad the hill and eke the vale:
The nightingale with fethers new she singes:
The turtle to her mate hath tolde her tale:
Somer is come, for every spray nowe springs,
The hart hath hong his olde head on the pale:
The buck in brake his winter cote he flinges:
The fishes flote with new repaired scale:
The adder all her sloughe awaye she flinges:
The swift swalow pursueth the flyes smale:
The busy bee her honye now she minges:
Winter is worne that was the flowers bale:
And thus I see among these pleasant thinges
Eche care decayes, and yet my sorrow springes.

HENRY HOWARD, EARL OF SURREY

From IN EARLY SPRING

O Spring, I know thee! Seek for sweet surprise
    In the young children's eyes.
But I have learnt the years, and know the yet
    Leaf-folded violet.
Mine ear, awake to silence, can foretell
    The cuckoo's fitful bell.
I wander in a grey time that encloses
    June and the wild hedge-roses.
A year's procession of the flowers doth pass
    My feet, along the grass.
And all you wild birds silent yet, I know
    The notes that stir you so,
Your songs yet half devised in the dim dear
    Beginnings of the year.
In these young days, you meditate your part;
    I have it all by heart
I know the secrets of the seeds of flowers
    Hidden and warm with showers,
And how, in kindling Spring, the cuckoo shall
    Alter his interval.
But not a flower, or song I ponder is
    My own, but memory's.
I shall be silent in those days desired
    Before a world inspired.
O all brown birds, compose your old song-phrases,
    Earth, thy familiar daisies! . . .

ALICE MEYNELL

THE PALM WILLOW

See, whirling snow sprinkles the starvèd fields,
  The birds have stayed to sing;
No covert yet their fairy harbour yields.
    When cometh Spring?
Ah! in their tiny throats what songs unborn
    Are quenched each morn.

The lenten lilies, through the frost that push,
  Their yellow heads withhold:
The woodland willow stands a lonely bush
    Of nebulous gold;
There the Spring-goddess cowers in faint attire
    Of frightened fire.

ROBERT BRIDGES

SPRING'S MESSENGERS

Where slanting banks are always with the sun
  The daisy is in blossom even now;
And where warm patches by the hedges run
  The cottager when coming home from plough
Brings home a cowslip root in flower to set.
Thus ere the Christmas goes the spring is met
  Setting up little tents about the fields
In sheltered spots. – Primroses when they get
  Behind the wood's old roots, where ivy shields
Their crimpled, curdled leaves, will shine and hide.
Cart ruts and horses' footings scarcely yield
  A slur for boys, just crizzled and that's all.
Frost shoots his needles by the small dyke side,
  And snow in scarce a feather's seen to fall.

JOHN CLARE

THE SPRING

Now that the Winter's gone, the earth hath lost
Her snow-white robes; and now no more the frost
Candies the grass, or casts an icy cream
Upon the silver lake or crystal stream:
But the warm sun thaws the benumbed earth,
And makes it tender; gives a sacred birth
To the dead swallow; wakes in hollow tree
The drowsy cuckoo and the humble-bee.
Now do a choir of chirping minstrels bring
In triumph to the world the youthful Spring:
The valleys, hills, and woods in rich array
Welcome the coming of the long'd-for May
Now all things smile: only my love doth lour,
Nor hath the scalding noonday sun the power
To melt that marble ice which still doth hold
Her heart congeal'd, and makes her pity cold.
The ox, which lately did for shelter fly
Into the stall, doth now securely lie
In open fields; and love no more is made
By the fireside, but in the cooler shade
Amyntas now doth with his Chloris sleep
Under a sycamore, and all things keep
Time with the season: only she doth carry
June in her eyes, in her heart January.

THOMAS CAREW

From LOVE'S LABOUR LOST

SONG

SPRING

When Daisies pied and Violets blew,
  And Lady-smockes all silver white,
And Cuckow-buds of yellow hew:
  Do paint the Meadowes with delight:
The Cuckow then on everie tree,
Mockes married men, for thus sings he,
Cuckow.
Cuckow, cuckow: O word of feare,
  Unpleasing to a married eare.

When Shepheards pipe on Oaten strawes,
  And merrie Larkes are Ploughmen's clockes:
When Turtles tread, and Rookes and Dawes,
  And Maidens bleach their summer smockes:
The Cuckow then on everie tree
Mockes married men; for thus sings he,
Cuckow.
Cuckow, cuckow: O word of feare,
  Unpleasing to a married eare.

WINTER

When Isicles hang by the wall,
  And Dick the Shepheard blowes his naile;
And Tom beares Logges into the hall,
  And Milke comes frozen home in paile;
When blood is nipt, and waies be fowle
Then nightly sings the staring Owle
Tu-whit
Tu-who: A merrie note,
While greasie Jone doth keele the pot.

87

When all aloud the winde doth blow,
   And coffing drownes the Parson's saw:
And birds sit brooding in the snow,
   And Marrian's nose looks red and raw:
When roasted Crabs hissed in the bowle,
Then nightly sings the staring Owle,
           Tu-whit
Tu-who: A merrie note,
While greasie Jone doth keele the pot.

WILLIAM SHAKESPEARE

YOUNG LAMBS

The spring is coming by a many signs;
   The trays are up, the hedges broken down,
That fenced the haystack, and the remnant shines
   Like some old antique fragment weathered brown.
And where suns peep, in every sheltered place,
   The little early buttercups unfold
A glittering star or two — till many trace
   The edges of the blackthorn clumps in gold.
And then a little lamb bolts up behind
   The hill and wags his tail to meet the yoe,
And then another, sheltered from the wind,
   Lies all his length as dead — and lets me go
Close bye and never stirs but baking lies,
With legs stretched out as though he could not rise.

JOHN CLARE

MARCH HARES

I made myself as a tree,
No withered leaf twirling on me;
No, not a bird that stirred my boughs,
As looking out from wizard brows
I watched those lithe and lovely forms
That raised the leaves in storms.

I watched them leap and run,
Their bodies hollowed in the sun
To thin transparency,
That I could clearly see
The shallow colour of their blood
Joyous in love's full flood.

I was content enough,
Watching that serious game of love,
That happy hunting in the wood
Where the pursuer was the more pursued,
To stand in breathless hush
With no more life myself than tree or bush.

ANDREW YOUNG

THE LIKENESS

When I came forth this morn I saw
   Quite twenty cloudlets in the air;
And then I saw a flock of sheep,
   Which told me how those clouds came there.

That flock of sheep, on that green grass,
   Well might it lie so still and proud!
Its likeness had been drawn in heaven,
   On a blue sky, in silvery cloud.

I gazed me up, I gazed me down,
   And swore, though good the likeness was,
'Twas a long way from justice done
   To such white wool, such sparkling grass.

W. H. DAVIES

SPRING

Frost-locked all the winter,
Seeds, and roots, and stones of fruits,
What shall make their sap ascend
That they may put forth shoots?
Tips of tender green,
Leaf, or blade, or sheath;
Telling of the hidden life
That breaks forth underneath,
Life nursed in its grave by Death.

Blows the thaw-wind pleasantly,
Drips the soaking rain,
By fits looks down the waking sun:
Young grass springs on the plain;
Young leaves clothe early hedgerow trees;
Seeds, and roots, and stones of fruits,
Swoln with sap put forth their shoots;
Curled-headed ferns sprout in the lane;
Birds sing and pair again.

There is no time like Spring,
When life's alive in everything,
Before new nestlings sing,
Before cleft swallows speed their journey back
Along the trackless track —
God guides their wing,
He spreads their table that they nothing lack, —
Before the daisy grows a common flower,
Before the sun has power
To scorch the world up in his noontide hour.

There is no time like Spring,
Like Spring that passes by;
There is no life like Spring-life born to die, —
Piercing the sod,
Clothing the uncouth clod,

Hatched in the nest,
Fledged on the windy bough,
Strong on the wing:
There is no time like Spring that passes by,
Now newly born, and now
Hastening to die.

CHRISTINA ROSSETTI

TO SPRING

O thou with dewy locks, who lookest down
Thro' the clear windows of the morning, turn
Thine angel eyes upon our western isle,
Which in full choir hails thy approach, O Spring!

The hills tell each other, and the list'ning
Vallies hear; all our longing eyes are turned
Up to thy bright pavillions: issue forth,
And let thy holy feet visit our clime.

Come o'er the eastern hills, and let our winds
Kiss thy perfumed garments; let us taste
Thy morn and evening breath: scatter thy pearls
Upon our love-sick land that mourns for thee.

O deck her forth with thy fair fingers; pour
Thy soft kisses on her bosom; and put
Thy golden crown upon her languish'd head,
Whose modest tresses were bound up for thee!

WILLIAM BLAKE

With dalliance rude young Zephyr woos
Coy May. Full oft with kind excuse
The boisterous boy the fair denies,
Or with a scornful smile complies.
  Mindful of disaster past,
And shrinking at the northern blast,
The sleety storm returning still,
The morning hoar, and evening chill;
Reluctant comes the timid Spring.
Scarce a bee, with airy ring,
Murmurs the blossom'd boughs around,
That clothe the garden's southern bound:
Scarce a sickly straggling flower
Decks the rough castle's rifted tower:
Scarce the hardy primrose peeps
From the dark dell's entangled steeps:
O'er the field of waving broom
Slowly shoots the golden bloom;
And, but by fits, the furze-clad dale
Tinctures the transitory gale.
While from the shrubbery's naked maze,
Where the vegetable blaze
Of Flora's brightest 'broidery shone,
Every chequer'd charm is flown;
Save that the lilac hangs to view
Its bursting gems in clusters blue.
  Scant along the ridgy land
The beans their new-born ranks expand:
The fresh-turn'd soil with tender blades
Thinly the sprouting barley shades:
Fringing the forest's devious edge,
Half robed appears the hawthorn hedge;
Or to the distant eye displays
Weakly green its budding sprays.

The swallow, for a moment seen,
Skims in haste the village green:
From the gray moor, on feeble wing,
The screaming plovers idly spring:
The butterfly, gay painted soon,
Explores awhile the tepid noon;
And fondly trusts its tender dyes
To fickle suns, and flattering skies.

Fraught with a transient, frozen shower,
If a cloud should haply lower,
Sailing o'er the landscape dark,
Mute on a sudden is the lark;
But when gleams the sun again
O'er the pearl-besprinkled plain,
And from behind his watery vail
Looks through the thin descending hail;
She mounts, and, lessening to the sight,
Salutes the blithe return of light,
And high her tuneful track pursues
Mid the dim rainbow's scatter'd hues.

Where in venerable rows
Widely-waving oaks enclose
The moat of yonder antique hall,
Swarm the rooks with clamorous call;
And to the toils of nature true,
Wreath their capacious nests anew.

Musing through the lawny park,
The lonely poet loves to mark
How various greens in faint degrees
Tinge the tall groups of various trees;
While, careless of the changing year,
The pine cerulean, never sere,
Towers distinguish'd from the rest,
And proudly vaunts her winter vest.

Within some whispering osier isle,
Where Glym's low banks neglected smile;

And each trim meadow still retains
The wintry torrent's oozy stains:
Beneath a willow, long forsook,
The fisher seeks his custom'd nook;
And bursting through the crackling sedge,
That crowns the current's cavern'd edge,
He startles from the bordering wood
The bashful wild-duck's early brood.

O'er the broad downs, a novel race,
Frisk the lambs with faltering pace,
And with eager bleatings fill
The fosse that skirts the beacon'd hill.

His free-born vigour yet unbroke
To lordly man's usurping yoke,
The bounding colt forgets to play,
Basking beneath the noontide ray,
And stretch'd among the daisies pied
Of a green dingle's sloping side:
While far beneath, where Nature spreads
Her boundless length of level meads,
In loose luxuriance taught to stray,
A thousand tumbling rills inlay
With silver veins the vale, or pass
Redundant through the sparkling grass.

Yet, in these presages rude,
Midst her pensive solitude,
Fancy, with prophetic glance,
Sees the teeming months advance;
The field, the forest, green and gay,
The dappled slope, the tedded hay;
Sees the reddening orchard blow,
The harvest wave, the vintage flow;
Sees June unfold his glossy robe
Of thousand hues o'er all the globe;
Sees Ceres grasp her crown of corn,
And Plenty load her ample horn.

THOMAS WARTON

HOME-THOUGHTS FROM ABROAD

Oh, to be in England
Now that April's there,
And whoever wakes in England
Sees, some morning, unaware,
That the lowest boughs and the brush-wood sheaf
Round the elm-tree bole are in tiny leaf,
While the chaffinch sings on the orchard bough,
In England – now!

And after April, when May follows,
And the whitethroat builds, and all the swallows!
Hark, where my blossomed pear-tree in the hedge
Leans to the field and scatters on the clover
Blossoms and dewdrops – at the bent spray's edge –
That's the wise thrush; he sings each song twice over,
Lest you should think he never could recapture
The first fine careless rapture!
And though the fields look rough with hoary dew,
All will be gay when noontide wakes anew
The buttercups, the little children's dower
– Far brighter than this gaudy melon-flower!

ROBERT BROWNING

I WANDERED LONELY AS A CLOUD

I wandered lonely as a cloud
That floats on high o'er vales and hills,
When all at once I saw a crowd,
A host, of golden daffodils;
Beside the lake, beneath the trees,
Fluttering and dancing in the breeze.

Continuous as the stars that shine
And twinkle on the milky-way,
They stretched in never-ending line
Along the margin of a bay:
Ten thousand saw I at a glance,
Tossing their heads in sprightly dance.

The waves beside them danced; but they
Out-did the sparkling waves in glee:
A poet could not but be gay,
In such a jocund company:
I gazed – and gazed – but little thought
What wealth the show to me had brought.

For oft, when on my couch I lie
In vacant or in pensive mood,
They flash upon that inward eye
Which is the bliss of solitude;
And then my heart with pleasure fills,
And dances with the daffodils.

WILLIAM WORDSWORTH

From SYLVIA, OR THE MAY QUEEN
MID-DAY

Deep in a wild sequester'd nook,
Where Phebus casts no scorching look,
But Earth's soft carpet, moist and green,
Freckled with golden spots is seen;
Where with the wind that swayeth him
The pine spins slowly round his stem;
The willow weeps as in despair
Amid her green dishevelled hair;
And long-arm'd elms and beeches hoar,
Spread a huge vault of umbrage o'er:
Yet not so thick but yellow day
Makes through the leaves his splendid way;
And though in solemness of shade,
The place is silent, but not sad:
Here as the Naiad of the spring
Tunes her deep-sounding liquid string,
And o'er the streamlet steals her song,
Leading its sleepy waves along, —
How rich to lay your limbs at ease
Under the humming trellises,
Bow'd down with clustering blooms and bees!
And leaning o'er some antique root
Murmur as old a ditty out,
To suit the low incessant roar,
The echo of some distant shore,
Where the sweet-bubbling waters run
To spread their foamy tippets on:
Or mid the dim green forest aisles
Still haughtier than cathedral piles,
Enwrapt in a fine horror stand
Musing upon the darkness grand.
Now looking sideways through the glooms
At ivied trunks shap'd into tombs;

Now up the pillaring larches bare
Arching their Gothic boughs in air:
Perchance you wander on, in pain
To catch green glimpses of the plain,
Half glad to see the light again!
And wading through the seeded grass
Out to a sultry knoll you pass;
There with cross'd arms, in moral mood,
Dreadless admire the cloister'd wood,
Returning your enhancèd frown,
Darker than night, stiller than stone.
But now the Sun with dubious eye
Measures the downfall of the sky,
And pauses, trembling, on thy brow,
Olympus, ere he plunge below
Where ever-thundering Ocean lies
Spread out in blue immensities.
No stir the forest dames among,
No aspen wags a leafy tongue,
Absorb'd in meditation stands
The cypress with her swathèd hands,
And even the restless Turin-tree
Seems lost in a like reverie;
Zephyr hath shut his scented mouth,
And not a cloud moves from the south;
The hoary thistle keeps his beard,
Chin-deep amid the sea-green sward,
And sleeps unbrushed by any wing
Save of that gaudy flickering thing
Too light to wake the blue-hair'd king;
Alone of the bright-coated crowd
This vanity is seen abroad,
Sunning his ashy pinnions still
On flowery bank or ferny hill:
Now not a sole wood-note is heard,
The wild reed breathes no trumpet-word,

Ev'n the home-happy cushat quells
Her note of comfort in the dells; —
'Tis noon! — and in the shadows warm
You only hear the grey-flies swarm.
You gaze between the earth and sky,
With wide, unconscious, dizzy eye,
And like the listless willow seem
Dropping yourself into a dream.

GEORGE DARLEY

From THE BOOK OF THE DUCHESS

I loked forth, for I was waked
With smale foules a gret hepe,
That had affrayed me out of slepe
Through noyse and swetnesse of hir song;
And, as me mette, they sate among,
Upon my chambre-roof withoute,
Upon the tyles, al a-boute,
And songen, everich in his wyse,
The most solempne servyse
By note, that ever man, I trowe,
Had herd; for som of hem song lowe,
Som hye, and al of oon acorde
To telle shortly, at oo worde,
Was never y-herd so swete a steven,
But hit had be a thing of heven.

CHAUCER

SONG

Surcharged with discontent,
To Sylvane's boure I went
To ease my hevy grief-oppressèd hart,
And trie what comfort winged creatures
Coulde yeelde unto my inwarde troubled smarte,
By modulating their delightfull mesurs
To my eares pleasing ever.
Of straines so sweet, sweete birdes deprive us never.

The Thrush did pipe full cleare,
And eke with very merry cheare
The Lenite lifted up her pleasant voyce.
The Goldfinch chirpid and the Pie did chatter,
The Blackebirde whistled and bed mee rejoyce,
The Stocke dove mormerd with a solemne flatter.
The little daw, ka-ka he cride;
The hic-quaile he beside
Tickled his part in a partie-coloured coate
The Jay did blow his how-boy gallantly.

The wren did treble many a pretty note.
The woodpecker did hamer melowdie.
The kite, tiw-whiw, full oft
Cride, soring up aloft,
And downe againe returnèd presently.
To whom the heralde of Cornutoes all sung cockoo
Ever, whilst poor Margery cried: Who
Did ring nightes 'larum bell?
Withall all did do well.
O might I heare them ever.
Of straines so sweet, sweete birds deprive us never.

        Then Hesperus on high
       Brought cloudy night in skie,
When loe, the thicket-keeping company
      Of fethered singers left their madrigals,
Sonets and elegies, and presently
     Shut them within their mossie severals,
And I came home and vowde to love them ever.
Of straines so sweet, sweet birdes deprive us never.

ANON.

From POLY-OLBION

When *Phœbus* lifts his head out of the Winteres wave
No sooner doth the Earth her flowerie bosome brave,
At such time as the Yeare brings on the pleasant Spring,
But Hunts-up to the Morne the feath'red *Sylvans* sing:
And in the lower Grove as on the rising Knole,
Upon the highest spray of every mounting pole,
Those Quiristers are pearcht with many a speckled breast.
Then from her burnisht gate the goodly glittring East
Gilds every lofty top which late the humorous Night
Bespangled had with pearle to please the Mornings sight:
On which the mirthfull Quires, with their cleere open throats
Unto the joyfull Morne so straine their warbling notes
That Hills and Valleys ring, and even the echoing Ayre
Seems all compos'd of sounds about them everywhere.
The *Throstell* with shrill sharps, as purposely he song
T' awake the lustlesse Sunne, or chiding that so long
He was in comming forth that should the thickets thrill:
The *Woosell* nere at hand that hath a golden bill;
As Nature him had markt of purpose, t' let us see
That from all other Birds his tunes should different bee:
For, with their vocall sounds they sing to pleasant May,
Upon his dulcet pype the *Merle* doth onely play.[1]
When in the lower Brake the *Nightingale* hard-by
In such lamenting straines the joyfull howres doth ply,
As though the other Birds shee to her tunes would draw:
And, but that Nature (by her all-constraining law)
Each Bird to her owne kind this season doth invite,
They else, alone to hear that Charmer of the Night
(The more to use their eares) their Voyces sure would spare
That moduleth her tunes so admirably rare,
As man to set in Parts, at first had learn'd of her.

MICHAEL DRAYTON

[1] Of all Birds, only the *Blackbird* whistleth.

From THE BIRD

Hither thou com'st; the busie wind all night
Blew through thy lodging, where thy own warm wing
Thy pillow was. Many a sullen storm
(For which coarse man seems much the fitter born)
    Rain'd on thy bed
    And harmless head.
And now as fresh and chearful as the light,
Thy little heart in early hymns doth sing
Unto, that *providence*, whose unseen arm
Curb'd them, and cloath'd thee well and warm.
    All things that be, praise Him; and had
    Their lesson taught them, when first made.

So hills and valleys into singing break;
And though poor stones have neither speech nor tongue,
While active winds and streams both run and speak,
Yet stones are deep in admiration.
Thus Praise and Prayer here beneath the sun
Make lesser mornings, when the great are done.

For each enclosed spirit is a star
Inlightning his own little sphere,
Whose light, though fetcht and borrowed from afar,
Both mornings makes and evenings there.

HENRY VAUGHAN

SPRING

What bird so sings, yet so does wail?
O 'tis the ravish'd nightingale.
Jug, jug, jug, jug, tereu! she cries,
And still her woes at midnight rise.
Brave prick-song! Who is't now we hear?
None but the lark so shrill and clear;
Now at heaven's gate she claps her wings,
The morn not waking till she sings.
Hark, hark, with what a pretty throat
Poor robin redbreast tunes his note!
Hark how the jolly cuckoos sing
Cuckoo! to welcome in the spring!
Cuckoo! to welcome in the spring!

JOHN LYLY

From MILTON

Thou hearest the Nightingale begin the Song of Spring:
The Lark sitting upon his earthy bed, just as the morn
Appears, listens silent: then springing from the waving Corn-
    field loud
He leads the Choir of Day; trill, trill, trill, trill:
Mounting upon the wings of light into the Great Expanse;
Re-echoing against the lovely blue and shining heavenly
    Shell:
His little throat labours with inspiration; every feather
On throat and breast and wings vibrates with the effluence
    Divine.
All Nature listens silent to him, and the awful Sun
Stands still upon the Moutnain looking on this little Bird
With eyes of soft humility, and wonder, love, and awe.
Then loud from their green covert all the Birds begin their
    Song,
The Thrush, the Linnet, and the Goldfinch, Robin and the
    Wren
Awake the Sun from his sweet reverie upon the Mountain:
The Nightingale again assays his song, and through the day
And through the night warbles luxuriant; every Bird of
    Song
Attending his loud harmony with admiration and love.

WILLIAM BLAKE

SONG

A sunny shaft did I behold,
  From sky to earth it slanted:
And poised therein a bird so bold —
  Sweet bird, thou wert enchanted!
He sank, he rose, he twinkled, he trolled
  Within that shaft of sunny mist;
His eyes of fire, his beak of gold,
  All else of amethyst!

And thus he sang: 'Adieu! adieu!
Love's dreams prove seldom true.
The blossoms, they make no delay:
The sparkling dew-drops will not stay.
      Sweet month of May,
        We must away;
      Far, far away!
          To-day! to-day!'

S. T. COLERIDGE

From THE RAINBOW

Still young and fine! but what is still in view
We slight as old and soil'd, though fresh and new.
How bright wert thou, when *Shem's* admiring eye
Thy burnished, flaming *Arch* did first descry!
When *Terah, Nahor, Haran,* Abram, Lot,
The youthful world's grey fathers in one knot,
Did with intentive looks watch every hour
For thy new light, and trembled at each shower!
When thou dost shine, darkness looks white and fair,
Storms turn to music, clouds to smiles and air:
Rain gently spends his honey-drops, and pours
Balm on the cleft earth, milk on grass and flowers.
Bright pledge of peace and sunshine! The sure tye
Of thy Lord's hand, the object of his eye!
When I behold thee, though my sight be dim,
Distant and low, I can in thine see Him,
Who looks upon thee from His glorious throne,
And mindes the Covenant 'twixt *All* and *One*.

HENRY VAUGHAN

A GREAT TIME

Sweet chance, that led my steps abroad,
   Beyond the town, where wild flowers grow —
A rainbow and a cuckoo, Lord,
   How rich and great the times are now!
       Know, all ye sheep
       And cows, that keep
On staring that I stand so long
   In grass that's wet from heavy rain -
A rainbow and a cuckoo's song
   May never come together again;
       May never come
       This side the tomb.

W. H. DAVIES

TO THE CUCKOO

O blithe New-comer! I have heard,
I hear thee and rejoice.
O Cuckoo! shall I call thee Bird,
Or but a wandering Voice?

While I am lying on the grass
Thy twofold shout I hear;
From hill to hill it seems to pass,
At once far off and near.

Though babbling only, to the Vale,
Of sunshine and of flowers,
Thou bringest unto me a tale
Of visionary hours.

Thrice welcome, darling of the Spring!
Even yet thou art to me
No bird: but an invisible Thing,
A voice, a mystery;

The same whom in my School-boy days
I listened to; that Cry
Which made me look a thousand ways
In bush, and tree, and sky.

To seek thee did I often rove
Through woods and on the green;
And thou wert still a hope, a love;
Still longed for, never seen.

And I can listen to thee yet;
Can lie upon the plain
And listen, till I do beget
That golden time again.

O blessèd Bird! the earth we pace
Again appears to be
An unsubstantial, faery place;
That is fit home for Thee!

WILLIAM WORDSWORTH

TO THE CUCKOO

Hail, beauteous stranger of the grove!
    Thou messenger of Spring!
Now Heaven repairs thy rural seat,
    And woods thy welcome sing.

What time the daisy decks the green,
    Thy certain voice we hear;
Hast thou a star to guide thy path,
    Or mark the rolling year?

Delightful visitant! with thee
    I hail the time of flowers,
And hear the sound of music sweet
    From birds among the bowers.

The schoolboy, wandering thro' the wood
    To pull the primrose gay,
Starts, the new voice of Spring to hear,
    And imitates thy lay.

What time the pea puts on the bloom
    Thou fliest thy vocal vale,
An annual guest in other lands,
    Another Spring to hail.

Sweet bird! thy bower is ever green,
    Thy sky is ever clear;
Thou hast no sorrow in thy song,
    No winter in thy year!

O could I fly, I'd fly with thee!
    We'd make, with joyful wing,
Our annual visit o'er the globe,
    Companions of the Spring.

JOHN LOGAN OR MICHAEL BRUCE

THE CROW

With rakish eye and plenished crop,
   Oblivious of the farmer's gun,
Upon the naked ash-tree top
   The Crow sits basking in the sun.

An old ungodly rogue, I wot!
For, perched in black against the blue,
His feathers, torn with beak and shot,
   Let woful glints of April through.

The year's new grass, and, golden-eyed,
   The daisies sparkle underneath,
And chestnut-trees on either side
   Have opened every ruddy sheath.

But doubtful still of frost and snow,
   The ash alone stands stark and bare,
And on its topmost twig the Crow
   Takes the glad morning's sun and air.

WILLIAM CANTON

THE GREEN WOODPECKER

Whether that popinjay
   Screamed now at me or at his mate
I could not rightly say,
   Not knowing was it love or was it hate.

I hoped it was not love
   But hate that roused that gaudy bird;
For earth I love enough
   To crave of her at least an angry word.

ANDREW YOUNG

THE STOCKDOVES

They rose up in a twinkling cloud
And wheeled about and bowed
To settle on the trees
Perching like small clay images.

Then with a noise of sudden rain
They clattered off again
And over Ballard Down
They circled like a flying town.

Though one could sooner blast a rock
Than scatter that dense flock
That through the winter weather
Some iron rule has held together.

Yet in another month from now
Love like a spark will blow
Those birds the country over
To drop in trees, lover by lover.

ANDREW YOUNG

THE SCARECROW

Shouting, and flourishing a crowd
Of the mountainous snows of cloud,
Over the hillside stalks the wind,
And like a breath of Impulse sweeps
Bright panic through the landscape's mind.

Birch and aspen bent from the root
Flounce in a radiant dispute,
While forests, drumming like an ocean,
Down to their stiff foundations sway;
Miles of pasture all agleam
Set out for the horizon's rim,
And the mountains are in motion:
Till the whole earth its shackles slips
And, as a hare, fleet-thudding flies
To outwit the harrier of the skies.

But still the thwarted wind all day
With many a thrust and subtle grapple
Strains every thew to overtopple
That agèd, rusty-ragg'd scarecrow
Who shakes his fist to warn away
The flocks that flurry around or, bolder,
Settle pattering on his shoulder:
Strippings of some forsaken bough.

STANLEY SNAITH

THE EMBRYO

That grey-green river pouring past,
The moorhen and the vole,
Though spring was dark above,
Will always haunt my soul.

Old thorny plum-trees running wild
Beside the river donned
White bloom – ah, not too old for love,
Though day looked stone beyond.

No one yet crossed the muddy plank
That bridged the full creak round,
Nor on the flood-strewn isle
Sought summer's camping-ground;

Where, to be sure, a drowned sheep lodged
In a black holt of alders,
Its poor fleece brown and vile,
To shudder young beholders.

Surly the day leaned down, its breath
Bit; yet through frown and chill
This otter's-home, this stream
Full-marching to the mill,

The claw-like trees, the cryptic gloom
Enwombed a joy that drew
Through grey-green depths the bream,
The swans through air anew.

EDMUND BLUNDEN

THE DAISY

And as for me, though that I konne but lyte,
On bokės for to rede I me delyte,
And to hem yive I feyth and ful credence,
And in myn herte have hem in reverence
So hertėly, that there is gamė noon
That fro my bokės maketh me to goon,
But it be seldom on the holyday,
Save, certently, when that the month of May
Is comen, and that I hear the foulės synge,
And that the flourės gymnen for to sprynge, –
Farewel my boke, and my devocion!

Now have I thanne suche a condicion,
Thát of alle the flourės in the mede,
Than love I most thise flourės white and rede,
Suche as men callen daysyes in our toun.
To hem have I so grete affeccioun,
As I seyde erst, when comen is the May,
That in my bed ther daweth me no day,
That I nam up and walkyng in the mede,
To seen this floure agein the sonné sprede,
Whan it uprysith erly by the morwe;
That blisful sightė softneth al my sorwe,
So glad am I, whan that I have presence
Of it, to doon it allė reverence,
As she that is of allė floures flour,
Fulfillėd of al vertue and honour,
And evere ilikė faire, and fresshe of hewe.
And I love it, and evere ylikė newe,
And ever shal, til that myn hertė dye;
I swere I nat, of this I wol nat lye;
Ther lovėd no wight hotter in his lyve.

And, whan that it is eve, I rennė blyve,
As sone as evere the sonnė gynneth weste,
To seen this flour, how it wol go to reste,

For fere of nyght, so hateth she derknesse!
Hir chere is pleynly sprad in the brightnesse
Óf the sonne, for ther it wol unclose.
Allas, that I ne had Englyssh, ryme or prose,
Súffisant this flour to preyse aryght!

GEOFFREY CHAUCER

TO DAFFADILLS

Faire Daffadills, we weep to see
    You haste away so soone:
As yet the early-rising Sun
    Has not attain'd his Noone.
            Stay, stay,
        Untill the hasting day
            Has run
        But to the Even-song;
And, having pray'd together, we
    Will goe with you along.

We have short time to stay, as you,
    We have as short a Spring;
As quick a growth to meet Decay,
    As you, or any thing.
            We die,
        As your hours doe, and drie
            Away,
        Like to the Summers raine;
Or as the pearles of Mornings dew
    Ne'r to be found againe.

ROBERT HERRICK

TO VIOLETS

Welcome Maids of Honour,
    You doe bring
    In the Spring;
And wait upon her.

She has Virgins many
    Fresh and faire;
    Yet you are
More sweet than any.

Y'are the Maiden Posies,
    And so grac't,
    To be plac't,
'Fore Damask Roses.

Yet though thus respected,
    By and by
    Ye doe lie,
Poore Girles, neglected.

ROBERT HERRICK

First came the primrose,
On the bank high,
Like a maiden looking forth
From the window of a tower
When the battle rolls below,
So looked she,
And saw the storms go by.

Then came the wind-flower
In the valley left behind,
As a wounded maiden pale
With purple streaks of woe
When the battle has rolled by
Wanders to and fro,
So tottered she,
Dishevelled in the wind.

Then came the daisies,
On the first of May,
Like a bannered show's advance
While the crowd runs by the way,
With ten thousand flowers about them they
   came trooping through the fields

As a happy people come.
So came they,
As a happy people come,
When the war has rolled away,
With dance and tabor, pipe and drum,
And all make holiday.

Then came the cowslip,
Like a dancer in the fair,
She spread her little mat of green,
And on it danced she.
With a fillet bound about her brow,
A fillet round her happy brow,
A golden fillet round her brow,
And rubies in her hair.

SYDNEY DOBELL

TO BLOSSOMS

Faire pledges of a fruitfull Tree,
    Why do yee fall so fast?
    Your date is not so past;
But you may stay yet here a while,
    To blush and gently smile;
        And go at last.

What, were yee borne to be
    An houre or half's delight;
    And so to bid goodnight?
'Twas pitie Nature brought yee forth
    Meerly to shew your worth,
        And lose you quite.

But you are lovely Leaves, where we
    May read how soon things have
    Their end, though ne'er so brave:
And after they have shown their pride,
    Like you a while: They glide
        Into the Grave.

ROBERT HERRICK

THE BOTANIST'S VISION

The sun that in Breadalbane's lake doth fall
Was melting to the sea down golden Tay,
When a cry came along the peopled way,
'Sebastopol is ours!' From that wild call
I turned, and leaning on a time-worn wall
Quaint with the touch of many an ancient day,
The mappèd mould and mildewed marquetry
Knew with my focussed soul; which bent down all
Its sense, power, passion, to the sole regard
Of each green minim, as it were but born
To that one use. I strode home stern and hard;
In my hot hands I laid my throbbing head,
And all the living world and all the dead
Began a march which did not end at morn.

SYDNEY DOBELL

THE WOODSPURGE

The wind flapped loose, the wind was still,
Shaken out dead from tree and hill:
I had walked on at the wind's will, —
I sat now, for the wind was still.

Between my knees my forehead was, —
My lips, drawn in, said not Alas!
My hair was over in the grass,
My naked ears heard the day pass.

My eyes, wide open, had the run
Of some ten weeds to fix upon;
Among those few, out of the sun:
The woodspurge flowered, three cups in one.

From perfect grief there need not be
Wisdom or even memory:
One thing then learnt remains to me, —
The woodspurge has a cup of three.

DANTE GABRIEL ROSSETTI

THE WIFE OF LLEW

And Gwydion said to Math, when it was Spring:
'Come now and let us make a wife for Llew.'
And so they broke broad boughs yet moist with dew,
And in a shadow made a magic ring:
They took the violet and the meadow-sweet
To form her pretty face, and for her feet
They built a mound of daisies on a wing,
And for her voice they made a linnet sing
In the wide poppy blowing for her mouth.
And over all they chanted twenty hours.
And Llew came singing from the azure south
And bore away his wife of birds and flowers.

FRANCIS LEDWIDGE

HAWTHORN

Beneath that hawthorn shade the grass will hardly grow,
So many babes have played and kept the bare clay so,
So many loves delayed in the moonlight's ebb and flow –
     Daisy-chains and May beginnings,
     Fail not till I pass below.

The roots of this same thorn are polished like a stool,
 Each grey and goblin horn grown craftwise beautiful,
And sometimes to adorn is left a tuft of wool –
     I envy still the merry runnings
     Of those that pass that way from school.

The moonlight through the may and the whisper fluttering
                         there,
Like angels on their way to the lamp of pain and prayer,
Gleams and ripplings play, and we lay our forehead bare,
     For here the coolest, cleverest cunnings
     Know the unknown's wingèd air.

Come, little tiny child, here's white violets for thee,
Come, smiling beauty wild, love's the dryad of this tree,
And thou, baptizèd mild, this thorny chapel see,
     And may I for all my sinnings
     Sit in this same sanctuary.

EDMUND BLUNDEN

THE KNOTTED ASH

Is this a lovers' vow?
Who else should tie it and for what,
This olive-coloured sapling in a knot,
Till now spring's sap must stoop
And bend back in a gouty loop
Rising from root to sooty-budded bough?

They may be tired of love,
Who found it not enough
To twine the glances of their eyes
Like kissing brimstone butterflies;
But death itself cannot untwist
This piteous tree-contortionist.

ANDREW YOUNG

From A SHROPSHIRE LAD

Loveliest of trees, the cherry now
Is hung with bloom along the bough,
And stands about the woodland ride
Wearing white for Eastertide.

Now, of my threescore years and ten,
Twenty will not come again,
And take from seventy springs a score,
It only leaves me fifty more.

And since to look at things in bloom
Fifty springs are little room,
About the woodlands I will go
To see the cherry hung with snow.

A. E. HOUSMAN

MAY

May! queen of blossoms,
  And fulfilling flowers,
With what pretty music
  Shall we charm the hours?
Wilt thou have pipe and reed,
Blown in the open mead?
Or to the lute give heed
  In the green bowers?

Thou hast no need of us,
  Or pipe or wire;
Thou hast the golden bee
  Ripen'd with fire;
And many thousand more
Songsters, that thee adore,
Filling earth's grassy floor
  With new desire.

Thou hast thy mighty herds,
Tame and free-livers;
Doubt not, thy music too
  In the deep rivers;
And the whole plumy flight
Warbling the day and night –
Up at the gates of light,
See, the lark quivers!

LORD THURLOW

Is not thilke the merry month of May,
When love-lads masken in fresh array?
How falls it, then, we no merrier been,
Ylike as others, girt in gaudy green
Our blanket liveries been all too sad
For thilke same season, when all is yclad
With pleasaunce; the ground with grass, the woods
With green leaves, the bushes with blossoming buds.
Young folk now flocken in every where
To gather May buskets and smelling brere;
And home they hasten the postes to dight,
And all the kirk-pillars ere day-light,
With hawthorne buds and sweet eglantine,
And garlands of roses and sops-in-wine.

EDMUND SPENSER

ON A BANK AS I SATE FISHING

A description of the SPRING

And now all *Nature* seem'd in *love*;
The lusty *sap* began to move;
New *juice* did stir th' embracing *Vines*;
And *Birds* had drawn their *Valentines*:
The *jealous Trout*, that low did lie,
Rose at a well-dissembled *flie*:
There stood my Friend, with patient skill
Attending of his trembling *quill*.
Already were the *Eaves* possest
With the swift *Pilgrims* daubed nest.
The *Groves* already did rejoyce
In *Philomels* triumphing *voice*.

The *showers* were short, the *weather* mild,
The morning fresh, the evening smil'd.

Jone takes her neat-rub'd Pale, and now
She trips to milk the Sand-red *Cow*;
Where for some sturdy foot-ball *Swain*,
Jone strokes a *sillabub* or twain.

The *Fields* and *Gardens* were beset
With *Tulip, Crocus, Violet*:
And now, though late, the *modest Rose*
Did more than half a blush disclose.
Thus all look'd *gay*, all full of *chear*,
To welcome the New-livery'd *year*.

SIR HENRY WOTTON

From RURAL SPORTS: A GEORGIC

... When floating clouds their spongy fleeces drain,
Troubling the streams with swift-descending rain,
And waters tumbling down the mountain's side,
Bear the loose soil into the swelling tide;
Then, soon as vernal gales begin to rise,
And drive the liquid burthen thro' the skies,
The fisher to the neighb'ring current speeds,
Whose rapid surface purles unknown to weeds;
Upon a rising border of the brook
He sits him down, and ties the treach'rous hook;
Now expectation chears his eager thought,
His bosom glows with treasures yet uncaught,
Before his eyes a banquet seems to stand,
Where ev'ry guest applauds his skilful hand.

   Far up the stream the twisted hair he throws,
Which down the murm'ring current gently flows;
When if or chance or hunger's pow'rful sway
Directs the roving trout this fatal way,
He greedily sucks in the twining bait,
And tugs and nibbles the fallacious meat:
Now, happy fisherman, now twitch the line!
How the rod bends! behold, the prize is thine!
Cast on the bank, he dies with gasping pains,
And trickling blood his silver mail distains.

   You must not ev'ry worm promiscuous use,
Judgment will tell thee proper bait to chuse;
The worm that draws a long immod'rate size
The trout abhors, and the rank morsel flies;
And if too small, the naked fraud's in sight,
And fear forbids, while hunger does invite.
Those baits will best reward the fisher's pains
Whose polish'd tails a shining yellow stains:
Cleanse them from filth, to give a tempting gloss,
Cherish the sully'd reptile race with moss;

Amid the verdant bed they twine, they toil,
And from their bodies wipe their native soil.
  But when the sun displays his glorious beams,
And shallow rivers flow with silver streams,
Then the deceit the scaly breed survey,
Bask in the sun, and look into the day.
You now a more delusive art must try,
And tempt their hunger with the curious fly.
  To frame the little animal, provide
All the gay hues that wait on female pride,
Let nature guide thee; sometimes golden wire
The shining bellies of the fly require;
The peacock's plumes thy tackle must not fail,
Nor the dear purchase of the sable's tail.
Each gaudy bird some slender tribute brings,
And lends the growing insect proper wings:
Silks of all colours must their aid impart,
And ev'ry fur promote the fisher's art.
So the gay lady, with expensive care,
Borrows the pride of land, of sea, and air,
Furs, pearls, and plumes, the glittering thing displays,
Dazles our eyes, and easie hearts betrays.
  Mark well the various seasons of the year,
How the succeeding insect race appear;
In this revolving moon one colour reigns,
Which in the next the fickle trout disdains,
Oft' have I seen a skilful angler try
The various colours of the treach'rous fly;
When he with fruitless pain hath skim'd the brook,
And the coy fish rejects the skipping hook,
He shakes the boughs that on the margin grow,
Which o'er the stream a waving forrest throw;
When if an insect fall (his certain guide)
He gently takes him from the whirling tide;
Examines well his form with curious eyes,
His gaudy vest, his wings, his horns and size.

Then round his hook the chosen fur he winds,
And on the back a speckled feather binds,
So just the colours shine thro' ev'ry part,
That nature seems to live again in art.
Let not thy wary step advance too near,
While all thy hope hangs on a single hair;
The new-form'd insect on the water moves,
The speckled trout the curious snare approves;
Upon the curling surface let it glide
With nat'ral motion from thy hand supply'd,
Against the stream now gently let it play,
Now in the rapid eddy roll away.
The scaly shoals float by, and seiz'd with fear
Behold their fellows tost in thinner air;
But soon they leap, and catch the swimming bait,
Plunge on the hook, and share an equal fate.

JOHN GAY

EAGER SPRING

Whirl, snow, on the blackbird's chatter;
You will not hinder his song to come.
East wind, Sleepless, you cannot scatter
Quince-bud, almond-bud,
Little grape-hyacinth's
Clustering brood,
Nor unfurl the tips of the plum.
No half born stalk of a lily stops;
There is sap in the storm-torn bush;
And, ruffled by gusts in a snow-blurred copse,
'Pity to wait' sings a thrush.

Love, there are few springs left for us;
They go, and the count of them as they go
Makes surer the count that is left for us.
More than the East wind, more than the snow,
I would put back these hours that bring
Buds and bees and are lost;
I would hold the night and the frost,
To save for us one more Spring.

GORDON BOTTOMLEY

Morning

MORNING

To find the Western path,
Right thro' the Gates of Wrath
I urge my way;
Sweet Mercy leads me on
With soft repentant moan:
I see the break of day.

The war of swords and spears,
Melted by dewy tears,
Exhales on high;
The Sun is freed from fears,
And with soft grateful tears
Ascends the sky.

WILLIAM BLAKE

From THE FAITHFUL SHEPHERDESSE

Shepherds, rise and shake off sleepe,
See the blushing Morne doth peepe
Through the windowes, whilst the Sunne
To the mountaine tops is runne,
Gilding all the Vales below
With his rising flames, which grow
Greater by his climbing stil.
Up ye lazie groomes, and fill
Bagg and Bottle for the field;
Claspe your cloakes fast, lest they yeeld
To the bitter Northeast wind.
Call the Maydens up, and find
Who lay longest, that she may
Go without a friend all day;
Then reward your dogs, and pray
Pan to keepe you from decay:
So unfold and then away.

JOHN FLETCHER

THE MORNING QUATRAINS

I

The Cock has crow'd an hour ago,
'Tis time we now dull sleep forgo;
Tir'd Nature is by sleep redress'd,
And Labour's overcome by Rest.

II

We have out-done the work of Night,
'Tis time we rise t'attend the Light,
And e'er he shall his Beams display,
To plot new bus'ness for the day.

III

None but the slothfull, or unsound,
Are by the Sun in Feathers found,
Nor, without rising with the Sun,
Can the World's bus'ness e'er be done.

IV

Hark! Hark! the watchfull Chanticler,
Tells us the day's bright Harbinger
Peeps o'er the Eastern Hills, to awe
And warn night's sov'reign to withdraw.

V

The Morning Curtains now are drawn,
And now appears the blushing dawn;
Aurora has her Roses shed,
To strew the way *Sol's* steeds must tread.

VI

Xanthus and *Æthon* harness'd are,
To roll away the burning Carr,
And, snorting flame, impatient bear
The dressing of the Chariotier.

VII

The sable Cheeks of sullen Night
Are streak'd with Rosie streams of light,
Whilst she retires away in fear,
To shade the other Hemisphere.

VIII

The merry Lark now takes her wings,
And long'd-for day's loud wellcome sings,
Mounting her body out of sight,
As if she meant to meet the light.

IX

Now doors and windows are unbar'd,
Each where are chearfull voices heard,
And round about Good-morrows fly,
As if Day taught Humanity.

X

The Chimnies now to smoke begin,
And the old Wife sits down to spin,
Whilst *Kate*, taking her Pail, does trip
Mull's swoln and strad'ling Paps to strip.

XI

Vulcan now makes his Anvil ring,
Dick whistles loud, and *Maud* doth sing,
And *Silvio* with his Bugle Horn
Winds an Imprime unto the Morn.

XII

Now through the morning doors behold
Phœbus array'd in burning Gold,
Lashing his fiery Steeds, displays
His warm and all enlight'ning Rays.

XIII

Now each one to his work prepares,
All that have hands are Labourers,
And Manufactures of each trade
By op'ning Shops are open laid.

XIV

Hob yokes his Oxen to the Team,
The Angler goes unto the stream,
The Wood-man to the Purlews highs,
And lab'ring Bees to load their thighs.

XV

Fair *Amarillis* drives her Flocks,
All night safe folded from the Fox,
To flow'ry Downs, where *Collin* stays,
To court her with his Roundelays.

XVI

The Traveller now leaves his Inn,
A new day's Journey to begin,
As he would post it with the day,
And early rising makes good way.

XVII

The slick-fac'd School-boy Sachel takes,
And with slow pace small riddance makes;
For why, the haste we make, you know,
To Knowledge and to Vertue's slow.

XVIII

The Fore-horse gingles on the Road,
The Waggoner lugs on his Load,
The Field with busy People snies,[1]
The City rings with various cries.

[1] Snies = swarms

XIX

The World is now a busie swarm,
All doing good, or doing harm;
But let's take heed our Acts be true,
For Heaven's eye sees all we doe.

XX

None can that piercing sight evade,
It penetrates the darkest shade,
And sin, though it could scape the eye,
Would be discover'd by the Cry.

CHARLES COTTON

PLOUGHMAN SINGING

Here morning in the ploughman's songs is met
   Ere yet one footstep shows in all the sky,
And twilight in the east, a doubt as yet,
   Shows not her sleeve of grey to know her bye.
Woke early, I arose and thought that first
   In winter time of all the world was I.
The old owls might have hallooed if they durst,
   But joy just then was up and whistled bye
A merry tune which I had known full long,
   But could not to my memory wake it back,
Until the ploughman changed it to the song.
   O happiness, how simple is thy track.
 – Tinged like the willow shoots, the east's young brow
Glows red and finds thee singing at the plough.

JOHN CLARE

ON MAY MORNING

Now the bright morning Star, Day's harbinger,
Comes dancing from the East, and leads with her
The Flowry *May*, who from her green lap throws
The yellow Cowslip, and the pale Primrose.
Hail bounteous *May* that dost inspire
Mirth and youth and warm desire,
Woods and Groves are of thy dressing,
Hill and Dale doth boast thy blessing.
Thus we salute thee with our early Song,
And welcom thee, and wish thee long.

JOHN MILTON

SONG

Hearke, hearke, the Larke at Heaven's gate sings,
   And Phœbus gins arise,
His Steeds to water at those Springs
   On chalic'd Flowres that lyes:
And winking Mary-buds begin To ope their Golden eyes:
With every thing that pretty is, My lady sweet arise:
      Arise, arise.

WILLIAM SHAKESPEARE

From THE RAPE OF LUCRECE

Packe clowdes away, and welcome day
  With night we banish sorrow.
Sweete Ayre, blow soft; mount Larke aloft,
  To give my Love good-morrow:
Winges from the winde, to please her mind,
  Notes from the Larke ile borrow;
Bird prune thy wing, Nightingale sing:
  To give my Love good-morrow.
    To give my Love good-morrow
    Notes from them all I'le borrow.

Wake from thy nest, Robin red-brest,
  Sing Birdes in every Furrow,
And from each bill let Musicke shrill.
  Give my faire Love good-morrow:
Blacke-bird and Thrush, in every Bush,
  Stare, Linnet, and Cocke-sparrow,
You pritty elves, amongst your selves
  Sing my faire Love good-morrow.
    To give my Love good-morrow,
    Sing Birdes in every Furrow.

THOMAS HEYWOOD

From EPITHALAMION

Wake now, my love, awake! for it is time;
The Rosy Morne long since left Tithones bed,
All ready to her silver coche to clyme;
And Phœbus gins to shew his glorious hed.
Hark! how the cheerefull birds doe chaunt theyr laies
And carroll of Loves praise.
The merry Larke hir mattins sings aloft;
The thrush replyes; the Mavis descant playes:
The Ouzell shrills; the Ruddock warbles soft;
So goodly all agree, with sweet consent,
To this dayes merriment.
Ah! my deere love, why doe ye sleepe thus long,
When meeter were that ye should now awake,
T'awayt the comming of your joyous make,
And hearken to the birds love-learned song,
The deawy leaves among!
Now they of joy and pleasance to you sing,
That all the woods them answer, and theyr eccho ring.

EDMUND SPENSER

CORINNA'S GOING A MAYING

Get up, get up for shame, the Blooming Morne
Upon her wings presents the god unshorne.
  See how *Aurora* throwes her faire
  Fresh-quilted colours through the aire:
  Get up, sweet-Slug-a-bed, and see
  The Dew-bespangling Herbe and Tree.
Each flower has wept, and bow'd toward the East,
Above an houre since; yet you not drest,
  Nay! not so much as out of bed?
  When all the Birds have Mattens seyd,
  And sung their thankfull Hymnes: 'tis sin,
  Nay, profanation to keep in,
When as a thousand Virgins on this day,
Spring, sooner than the Lark, to fetch in May.

Rise; and put on your Foliage, and be seene
To come forth, like the Spring-time, fresh and greene;
  And sweet as *Flora*. Take no care
  For Jewels for your Gowne, or Haire:
  Fear not; the leaves will strew
  Gemms in abundance upon you:
Besides, the childhood of the Day has kept,
Against you come, some *Orient Pearls* unwept:
  Come, and receive them while the light
  Hangs on the Dew-locks of the night:
  And *Titan* on the Eastern hill
  Retires himselfe, or else stands still
Till you come forth. Wash, dresse, be briefe in praying:
Few Beads are best, when once we goe a Maying.

Come, my *Corinna*, come; and comming, marke
How each field turns a street; each street a Parke
  Made green, and trimm'd with trees: see how
  Devotion gives each House a Bough,
  Or Branch: Each Porch, each doore, ere this,
  An Arke a Tabernacle is

Made up of white-thorn neatly enterwove;
As if here were those cooler shades of love.
    Can such delights be in the street,
    And open fields, and we not see't?
    Come, we'll abroad; and let's obay
    The Proclamation made for May:
And sin no more, as we have done, by staying;
But my *Corinna*, come, let's goe a Maying.

There's not a budding Boy, or Girle, this day,
But is got up, and gone to bring in May.
    A deale of Youth, ere this, is come
    Back, and with *White-thorn* laden home.
    Some have dispatcht their Cakes and Creame,
    Before that we have left to dreame:
And some have wept, and woo'd, and plighted Troth,
And chose their Priest, ere we can cast off sloth:
    Many a green-gown has been given;
    Many a kisse, both odde and even:
    Many a glance too has been sent
    From out the eye, Loves Firmanent:
Many a jest told of the Keyes betraying
This night, and Locks pickt, yet w'are not a Maying.

Come, let us goe, while we are in our prime;
And take the harmlesse follie of the time.
    We shall grow old apace, and die
    Before we know our liberty.
    Our life is short; and our dayes run
    As fast away as do's the Sunne:
And as a vapour, or a drop of raine
Once lost, can ne'r be found againe:
    So when or you or I are made
    A fable, song, or fleeting shade;
    All love, all liking, all delight
    Lies drown'd with us in endlesse night.
Then while time serves, and we are but decaying;
Come, my *Corinna*, come, let's goe a Maying.

THE SUNNE RISING

Busie old foole, unruly Sunne,
Why dost thou thus,
Through windowes, and through curtaines call on us?
Must to thy motions lovers seasons run?
Sawcy pedantique wretch, goe chide
Late schoole-boyes, and sowre prentices,
Goe tell Court-huntsmen, that the King will ride,
Call countrey ants to harvest offices;
Love, all alike, no season knowes, nor clyme,
Nor houres, dayes, moneths, which are the rags of time.

Thy beames, so reverend, and strong
Why shouldst thou thinke?
I could eclipse and cloud them with a winke,
But that I would not lose her sight so long:
If her eyes have not blinded thine,
Looke, and to morrow late, tell mee,
Whether both the 'India's of spice and Myne
Be where thou lefst them, or lie here with mee.
Aske for those Kings whom thou saw'st yesterday,
And thou shalt heare, All here in one bed lay.

She is all States, and all Princes, I,
Nothing else is.
Princes doe but play us; compar'd to this,
All honor's mimique; All wealth alchimie.
Thou sunne art halfe as happy as wee,
In that the world's contracted thus;
Thine age askes ease, and since thy duties bee
To warme the world, that's done in warming us.
Shine here to us, and thou art everywhere;
This bed thy center is, these walls, thy spheare.

JOHN DONNE

DAY-BREAK

Stay, *Phœbus*, stay, and cool thy flaming Head
In the Green bosom of thy liquid Bed:
 Betray not, with thine envious Light,
  Th' embraces of an happy Night;
For her fair blushes, if thou dar'st to rise,
Will, by Eclipse, hoodwink thy sawcy Eyes.

Lest Lovers do upbraid thy beamy *Car*,
With the pale glory of th' inferiour *Star*,
 And henceforth dare to say, in scorn,
  Sol's Ray is wain'd to *Phœbe's* horn,
And, for his Treason to a Lovers bliss,
Suffers *Actaeons Metamorphosis.*

Why should we rise t'adore the rising *Sun*,
And leave the Rites to greater Lights, undone?
 Or quit her warm, and spicy nest,
  Because the *Morn* peeps through *the East*,
To scortch in thy rude flames, to toyl, and sweat,
When in Loves fire we melt without thy heat?

When from my passionate Embraces she
Springs, as asham'd to be surpriz'd by thee,
 The pillows furrow'd brows descry
  A wrath for thy discovery,
Swell, and wax pale at thy insulting height,
For rage to be depriv'd of her dear weight.

Then stay, or lash thy Pamper'd Horses still,
To shew a swift obedience to her Will,
 And blushing, bow as low as Night,
  Lest I pursue thee, by thy Light,
And lock the Morning Doors to stop thy Race,
Imprisoning so in Clouds thy tell tale Face.

CHARLES COTTON

ON A DROP OF DEW

See how the Orient Dew,
Shed from the Bosom of the Morn
   Into the blowing Roses,
Yet careless of its Mansion new;
For the clear Region where t'was born
   Round in its self incloses:
And in its little Globes Extent,
Frames as it can its native Element.
   How it the purple flow'r does slight,
     Scarce touching where it lyes,
But gazing back upon the Skies,
  Shines with a mournful Light;
    Like its own Tear,
Because so long divided from the Sphear.
   Restless it roules and unsecure,
    Trembling lest it grow impure,
Till the warm sun pitty it's Pain,
   And to the Skies exhale it back again.
   So the Soul, that Drop, that Ray
Of the clear Fountain of Eternal Day,
   Could it within the humane flow'r be seen,
    Remembering still its former height,
Shuns the sweet leaves and blossoms green;
  And, recollecting its own light,
Does, in its pure and circling thoughts, express
The greater Heaven in an Heaven less.
   In how coy a Figure wound,
    Every way it turns away:
So the World excluding round,
   Yet receiving in the Day.
   Dark beneath, but bright above:
  Here disdaining, there in Love.

How loose and easie hence to go:
   How girt and ready to ascend.
Moving but on a point below,
   It all about does upwards bend,
Such did the Manna's sacred Dew destil;
White and intire, though congeal'd and chill.
Congeal'd on Earth: but does, dissolving, run
Into the Glories of th' Almighty Sun.

ANDREW MARVELL

ON A FOULE MORNING, BEING THEN TO TAKE A JOURNEY

Where art thou *Sol*, while thus the blind-fold Day
Staggers out of the East, loses her way
Stumbling on night? Rouze thee Illustrious Youth,
And let no dull mists choake the Light's faire growth.
Point here thy beames; O glance on yonder flocks,
And make their fleeces Golden as thy locks.
Unfold thy faire front, and there shall appeare
Full glory, flaming in her owne free spheare.
Gladnesse shall cloath the Earth, we will instile
The face of things, an universall smile.
Say to the Sullen Morne, thou com'st to court her;
And wilt command proud *Zephirus* to sport her
With wanton gales: his balmy breath shall licke
The tender drops which tremble on her cheeke;
Which rarified, and in a gentle raine
On those delicious bankes distill'd againe,
Shall rise in a sweet Harvest, which discloses
To every blushing Bed of new-borne Roses.
Hee'l fan her bright locks, teaching them to flow,
And friske in curl'd *Maenders*; Hee will throw
A fragrant Breath suckt from the spicy nest
O' th' pretious *Phoenix*, warme upon her Breast.
Hee with a dainty and soft hand will trim,
And brush her Azure Mantle, which shall swim
In silken Volumes; wheresoe're shee'l tread,
Bright clouds like Golden fleeces shall be spread.
Rise then (faire blew-ey'd Maid) rise and discover
Thy silver brow, and meet thy Golden lover.
See how hee runs, with what a hasty flight,
Into thy bosome, bath'd with liquid Light.
Fly, fly prophane fogs, farre hence fly away,
Taint not the pure streames of the springing Day,
With your dull influence, it is for you,
To sit and scoule upon Night's heavy brow;

Not on the fresh cheekes of the virgin Morne,
Where nought but smiles, and ruddy joyes are worne.
Fly then, and doe not thinke with her to stay;
Let it suffice, shee'l weare no maske to-day.
RICHARD CRASHAW

VERTUE

Sweet day, so cool, so calm, so bright,
The bridall of the earth and skie,
The dew shall weep thy fall to-night;
      For thou must die.

Sweet rose, whose hue angrie and brave
Bids the rash gazer wipe his eye,
Thy root is ever in its grave,
      And thou must die.

Sweet spring, full of sweet days and roses,
A box where sweets compacted lie,
My musick shows ye have your closes,
      And all must die.

Onely a sweet and vertuous soul,
Like season'd timber, never gives;
But though the whole world turn to coal,
      Then chiefly lives.

GEORGE HERBERT

Summer

NOON QUATRAINS

I

The day grows hot, and darts his Rays
From such a sure and killing place,
That this half World are fain to fly
The danger of his burning eye.

II

His early Glories were benign,
Warm to be felt, bright to be seen,
And all was comfort, but who can
Endure him when *Meridian*?

III

Of him we as of Kings complain,
Who mildly do begin to reign,
But to the *Zenith* got of pow'r,
Those whom they should protect devour.

IV

Has not another *Phaethon*
Mounted the Chariot of the Sun,
And, wanting Art to guide his Horse,
Is hurri'd from the Sun's due course.

V

If this hold on, our fertile Lands,
Will soon be turn'd to parched Sands,
And not an Onion that will grow
Without a *Nile* to overflow.

VI

The grazing Herds now droop and pant,
E'en without labour fit to faint,
And willingly forsook their Meat
To seek out cover from the heat.

The lagging Ox is now unbound,
From larding the new turn'd up ground,
Whilst *Hobbinal* alike o'er-laid,
Takes his course dinner to the shade.

VIII

Cellars and Grottos now are best
To eat and drink in, or to rest,
And not a Soul above is found
Can find a refuge under ground.

IX

When Pagan Tyranny grew hot,
Thus persecuted Christians got
Into the dark but friendly Womb
Of unknown Subterranean *Rome.*

X

And as that heat did cool at last,
So a few scorching hours o'er pass'd,
In a more mild and temp'rate Ray
We may again enjoy the day.

CHARLES COTTON

A SUMMER DAY

O perfect Light, which shaid[1] away
  The darkness from the light,
And set a ruler o'er the day,
  Another o'er the night —

Thy glory, when the day forth flies,
  More vively doth appear
Than at mid day unto our eyes
  The shining sun is clear.

The shadow of the earth anon
  Removes and drawis by
While in the East, when it is gone,
  Appears a clearer sky.

Which soon perceive the little larks,
  The lapwings and the snipe,
And tune their songs, like Nature's clerks,
  O'er meadow, muir, and stripe.[2]

Our hemisphere is polisht clean,
  And lighten'd more and more,
While everything is clearly seen
  Which seemit dim before:

Except the glistering astres bright,
  Which all the night were clear,
Offuskit[3] with a greater light
  No longer do appear.

The golden globe incontinent
  Sets up his shining head,
And o'er the earth and firmanent
  Displays his beams abread.

[1] parted   [2] rill   [3] darkened

For joy the birds with boulden[1] throats
 Against his visage sheen[2]
Take up their kindly musick notes
 In woods and gardens green.

The dew upon the tender crops,
 Like pearlis white and round,
Or like to melted silver drops,
 Refreshis all the ground.

The misty reek, the clouds of rain,
 From tops of mountains skails,[3]
Clear are the highest hills and plain,
 The vapours take the vales.

The ample heaven of fabrick sure
 In cleanness does surpass
The crystal and the silver pure,
 Or clearest polisht glass.

The time so tranquil is and still
 That nowhere shall ye find,
Save on a high and barren hill,
 An air of peeping wind.

All trees and simples,[4] great and small,
 That balmy leaf do bear,
Than they were painted on a wall
 No more they move or steir.

Calm is the deep and purple sea,
 Yea, smoother than the sand;
The waves that weltering wont to be
 Are stable like the land.

So silent is the cessile[5] air
 That every cry and call
The hills and dales and forest fair
 Again repeats them all.

[1] swollen   [2] bright   [3] clears   [4] herbs   [5] yielding

164

The flourishes[1] and fragrant flowers,
 Through Phoebus' fostering heat,
Refresht with dew and silver showers
 Cast up an odour sweet.

The cloggit busy humming bees,
 That never think to drone,
On flowers and flourishes of trees
 Collect their liquor brown.

The Sun, most like a speedy post
 With ardent course ascends;
The beauty of the heavenly host
 Up to our zenith tends.

The burning beams down from his face
 So fervently can beat,
That man and beast now seek a place
 To save them from the heat.

The herds beneath some leafy tree
 Amidst the flowers they lie;
The stable ships upon the sea
 Tend up their sails to dry.

With gilded eyes and open wings
 The cock his courage shows;
With claps of joy his breast he dings,
 And twenty times he crows.

The dove with whistling wings so blue
 The winds can fast collect;
Her purple pens turn many a hue
 Against the sun direct.

Now noon is went; gone is midday,
 The heat doth slake at last;
The sun descends down West away,
 For three of clock is past.

[1] blossoms
165

The rayons of the sun we see
    Diminish in their strength;
The shade of every tower and tree
    Extendit is in length.

Great is the calm, for everywhere
    The wind is setting down;
The reek throws right up in the air
    From every tower and town.

The gloming comes; the day is spent;
    The sun goes out of sight;
And painted is the occident
    With purple sanguine bright.

Our west horizon circular
    From time the sun be set
Is all with rubies, as it were,
    Or roses red o'erfret.

What pleasure were to walk and see,
    Endlong a river clear,
The perfect form of every tree
    Within the deep appear.

O then it were a seemly thing,
    While all is still and calm,
The praise of God to play and sing
    With cornet and with shalm!

All labourers draw home at even,
    And can to other say,
Thanks to the gracious God of heaven,
    Which sent this summer day.

ALEXANDER HUME

THE KINGFISHER

It was the Rainbow gave thee birth,
   And left thee all her lovely hues;
And, as her mother's name was Tears,
   So runs it in thy blood to choose
For haunts the lonely pools, and keep
In company with trees that weep.

Go you and, with such glorious hues,
   Live with proud Peacocks in green parks;
On lawns as smooth as shining glass,
   Let every feather show its mark;
Get thee on boughs and clap thy wings
Before the windows of proud kings.

Nay, lovely Bird, thou art not vain;
   Thou hast no proud ambitious mind;
I also love a quiet place
   That's green, away from all mankind;
A lonely pool, and let a tree
Sigh with her bosom over me.

W. H. DAVIES

WATER MOMENT

The silver eel slips through the waving weeds,
And in the tunnelled shining stone recedes;
The earnest eye surveys the crystal pond
And guards the cave: the sweet shoals pass beyond.
The watery jewels that these have for eyes,
The tiger streaks of him that hindmost plies,
The red-gold wings that smooth their daring paces,
The sunlight dancing about their airs and graces,
Burn that strange watcher's heart; then the sly brain
Speaks, all the dumb shoal shrieks, and by the stone
The silver death writhes with the chosen one.

EDMUND BLUNDEN

And now to the Abbyss I pass
Of that unfathomable Grass,
Where Men like Grasshoppers appear,
But Grasshoppers are Gyants there:
They, in their squeking Laugh, contemn
Us as we walk more low then them:
And, from the Precipices tall
Of the green spir's, to us do call.

To see Men through this Meadow Dive,
We wonder how they rise alive.
As, under Water, none does know
Whether he fall through it or go.
But, as the Marriners that sound,
And show upon their Lead the Ground,
They bring up Flow'rs so to be seen,
And prove they've at the Bottom been.

No Scene that turns with Engines strange
Does oftner then these Meadows change.
For when the Sun the Grass hath vext,
The tawny Mowers enter next;
Who seem like Israelites to be,
Walking on foot through a green Sea.
To them the Grassy Deeps divide,
And crowd a Lane to either Side.

With whistling Sithe, and Elbow strong,
These Massacre the Grass along:
While one, unknowing, carves the Rail,
Whose yet unfeather'd Quils her fail.
The Edge all bloody from its Brest
He draws, and does his stroke detest;
Fearing the Flesh untimely mow'd
To him a Fate as black forbode.

But bloody Thestylis, that waites
To bring the mowing Camp their Cates,
Greedy as Kites has trust it up,
And forthwith means on it to sup:
When on another quick She lights,
And cryes, he call'd us Israelites;
But now, to make his saying true,
Rails rain for Quails, for Manna Dew.

Unhappy Birds! what does it boot
To build below the Grasses Root;
When Lowness is unsafe as Hight,
And Chance o'retakes what scapeth spight?
And now your Orphan Parents Call
Sounds your untimely Funeral.
Death-Trumpets creak in such a Note,
And 'tis the Sourdine in their Throat.

Or sooner hatch or higher build:
The Mower now commands the Field;
In whose new Traverse seemeth wrought
A Camp of Battail newly fought:
Where, as the Meads with Hay, the Plain
Lyes quilted ore with Bodies slain:
The Women that with forks it fling,
Do represent the Pillaging.

And now the careless Victors play,
Dancing the Triumphs of the Hay;
Where every Mowers wholesome Heat
Smells like an Alexanders sweat.
Their Females fragrant as the Mead
Which they in Fairy Circles tread:
When at their Dances End they kiss,
Their new-made Hay not sweeter is.

When after this 'tis pil'd in Cocks,
Like a calm Sea it shews the Rocks:
We wondring in the River near
How Boats among them safely steer.
Or, like the Desert Memphis Sand,
Short Pyramids of Hay do stand.
And such the Roman Camps do rise
In Hills for Soldiers Obsequies.

This Scene again withdrawing brings
A new and empty Face of things;
A levell'd space, as smooth and plain,
As Clothes for Lilly strecht to stain.
The World when first created sure
Was such a Table rase and pure.
Or rather such is the Toril
Ere the Bulls enter at Madril.

For to this naked equal Flat,
Which Levellers take Pattern at,
The Villagers in common chase
Their Cattle, which it closer rase;
And what below the Sith increast
Is pincht yet nearer by the Breast.
Such in the painted World, appear'd
Davenant with th' Universal Heard.

They seem within the polisht Grass
A Landskip drawen in Looking-Glass.
And shrunk in the huge Pasture show
As Spots, so shap'd, on Faces do.
Such Fleas, ere they approach the Eye,
In Multiplying Glasses lye.
They feed so wide, so slowly move,
As Constellations do above.

Then, to conclude these pleasant Acts,
Denton sets ope its Cataracts;
And makes the Meadow truly be
(What it but seem'd before) a Sea.
For, jealous of its Lords long stay,
It try's t'invite him thus away.
The River in it self is drown'd,
And Isl's th' astonish Cattle round.

Let others tell the Paradox,
How Eels now bellow in the Ox,
How Horses at their Tails do kick,
Turn'd as they hang to Leeches quick;
How Boats can over Bridges sail;
And Fishes do the Stables scale.
How Salmons trespassing are found;
And Pikes are taken in the Pound.

But I, retiring from the Flood,
Take Sanctuary in the Wood;
And, while it lasts, my self imbark
In this yet green, yet growing Ark;
Where the first Carpenter might best
Fit Timber for his Keel have Prest.
And where all Creatures might have shares;
Although in Armies, not in Paires.

The double Wood of ancient Stocks
Link'd in so thick, an Union locks,
It like two Pedigrees appears,
On one hand Fairfax, th' other Veres:
Of whom though many fell in War,
Yet more to Heaven shooting are:
And, as they Natures Cradle deckt,
Will in green Age her Hearse expect.

When first the Eye this Forrest sees
It seems indeed as Wood not Trees:
As if their Neighbourhood so old
To one great Trunk them all did mold.
There the huge Bulk takes place, as ment
To thrust up a Fifth Element;
And stretches still so closely wedg'd
As if the Night within were hedg'd.

Dark all without it knits; within
It opens passable and thin;
And in as loose an order grows,
As the Corinthean Porticoes.
The arching Boughs unite between
The Columnes of the Temple green;
And underneath the winged Quires
Echo about their tuned Fires.

The Nightingale does here make choice
To sing the Tryals of her Voice.
Low Shrubs she sits in, and adorns
With Musick high the squatted Thorns.
But highest Oakes stoop down to hear,
And listning Elders prick the Ear.
The Thorn, lest it should hurt her, draws
Within the Skin its shrunken claws.

But I have for my Musick found
A Sadder, yet more pleasing Sound:
The Stock-doves, whose fair necks are grac'd
With Nuptial Rings their Ensigns chast;
Yet always, for some Cause unknown,
Sad pair unto the Elms they moan.
O why should such a Couple mourn,
That in so equal Flames do burn!

Then as I careless on the Bed
of gelid Straw-berryes do tread,
And through the Hazles thick espy
The hatching Throstles shining Eye;
The Heron from the Ashes top,
The eldest of its young lets drop,
As if it Stork-like did pretend
That Tribute to its Lord to send.

But most the Hewel's wonders are,
Who here has the Hold-felsters care.
He walks still upright from the Root,
Meas'ring the Timber with his Foot;
And all the way, to keep it clean,
Doth from the Bark the Wood-moths glean.
He, with his Beak, examines well
Which fit to stand and which to fell.

The good he numbers up, and hacks;
As if he mark'd them with the Ax.
But where he, tinkling with his Beak,
Does find the hollow Oak to speak,
That for his building he designs,
And through the tainted Side he mines.
Who could have thought the tallest Oak
Should fall by such a feeble Strok'!

Nor would it, had the Tree not fed
A Traitor-worm, within it bred,
As first our Flesh corrupt within
Tempts impotent and bashful Sin.
And yet that Worm triumphs not long,
But serves to feed the Hewels young.
While the Oake seems to fall content,
Viewing the Treason's punishment.

Thus I, easie Philosopher,
Among the Birds and Trees confer:
And little now to make me, wants
Or of the Fowles, or of the Plants.
Give me but Wings as they, and I
Streight floting on the Air shall fly:
Or turn me but, and you shall see
I was but an inverted Tree.

Already I begin to call
In their most learned Original:
And where I language want, my Signs
The Bird upon the Bough divines;
And more attentive there does sit
Then if She were with Lime-twigs knit.
No Leaf does tremble in the Wind
Which I returning cannot find.

Out of these scatter'd Sibyls Leaves
Strange Prophecies my Phancy weaves:
And in one History consumes,
Like Mexique Paintings, all the Plumes.
What Rome, Greece, Palestine, ere said
I in this light Mosaick read.
Thrice happy he who, not mistook,
Hath read in Natures mystick Book.

And see how Chance's better Wit
Could with a Mask my studies hit!
The Oak-Leaves me embroyder all,
Between which Caterpillars crawl:
And Ivy, with familiar trails,
Me licks, and clasps, and curles, and hales.
Under this antick Cope I move
Like some great Prelate of the Grove.

Then, languishing with ease, I toss
On Pallets swoln of Velvet Moss;
While the Wind, cooling through the Boughs,
Flatters with Air my panting Brows.
Thanks for my Rest ye Mossy Banks,
And unto you cool Zephyr's Thanks,
Who, as my Hair, my Thoughts too shed,
And winnow from the Chaff my Head.

How safe, methinks, and strong, behind
These Trees have I incamp'd my Mind;
Where Beauty, aiming at the Heart,
Bends in some Tree its useless Dart;
And where the World no certain Shot
Can make, or me it toucheth not.
But I on it securely play,
And gaul its Horsemen all the Day.

Bind me ye Woodbines in your 'twines,
Curle me about ye gadding Vines,
And Oh so close your Circles lace,
That I may never leave this Place:
But, lest your Fetters prove too weak,
Ere I your Silken Bondage break,
Do you, O Brambles, chain me too,
And courteous Briars nail me through.

Here in the Morning tye my Chain,
Where the two Woods have made a Lane;
While, like a Guard on either side,
The Trees before their Lord divide;
This, like a long and equal Thread,
Betwixt two Labyrinths does lead.
But, where the Floods did lately drown,
There at the Ev'ning stake me down.

For now the Waves are fal'n and dry'd,
And now the Meadows fresher dy'd;
Whose Grass, with moister colour dasht,
Seems as green Silks, but newly washt.
No Serpent new nor Crocodile
Remains behind our little Nile;
Unless it self you will mistake,
Among these Meads the only Snake.

See in what wanton harmless folds
It ev'ry where the Meadow holds;
And its yet muddy back doth lick,
Till as a Chrystal Mirrour slick;
Where all things gaze themselves, and doubt
If they be in it or without.
And for his shade which therein shines,
Narcissus like, the Sun too pines.

ANDREW MARVELL

From THE SEASONS (SUMMER)

SHEEP-DIPPING AND SHEARING

Or rushing thence, in one diffusive Band,
They drive the troubled Flocks, by many a Dog
Compell'd, to where the mazy-running Brook
Forms a deep Pool; this Bank abrupt and high,
And That, fair-spreading in a pebbled shore.
Urg'd to the giddy Brink, much is the Toil,
The Clamour much, of Men, and Boys, and Dogs,
Ere the soft fearful People to the Flood
Commit their woolly Sides. And oft the Swain,
On some impatient seizing, hurls them in:
Embolden'd then, nor hesitating more,
Fast, fast, they plunge amid the flashing Wave,
And panting labour to the farther Shore.
Repeated This, till deep the well-wash'd Fleece
Has drunk the Flood, and from his lively Haunt
The Trout is banish'd by the sordid Stream;
Heavy, and dripping, to the breezy Brow
Slow-move the harmless Race: where, as they spread
Their swelling Treasures to the sunny Ray,
Inly disturb'd, and wondering what this wild
Outrageous Tumult means, their loud complaints
The Country fill; and, toss'd from Rock to Rock,
Incessant Bleatings run around the Hills.
At last, of snowy White, the gather'd Flocks
Are in the wattled Pen innumerous press'd,
Head above Head; and, rang'd in lusty Rows,
The Shepherds sit, and wet the sounding Shears.
The Housewife waits to roll her fleecy Stores,
With all her gay-drest Maids attending round.
One, chief, in gracious Dignity inthron'd,
Shines o'er the Rest, the pastoral Queen, and rays
Her Smiles, sweet-beaming, on her Shepherd-King;
While the glad Circle round them yield their Souls
To festive Mirth, and Wit that knows no Gall.

Meantime, their joyous Task goes on apace:
Some mingling stir the melted Tar, and Some,
Deep on the new-shorn Vagrant's heaving Side,
To stamp his Master's Cipher ready stand;
Others th' unwilling Wether drag along;
And, glorying in his Might, the sturdy Boy
Holds by the twisted Horns th' indignant Ram.
Behold where bound, and of its Robe bereft,
By needy Man, that all-depending Lord,
How meek, how patient, the mild Creature lies!
What Softness in its melancholy Face,
What dumb complaining Innocence appears!
Fear not, ye gentle Tribes, 'tis not the Knife
Of horrid Slaughter that is o'er you waved;
No, 'tis the tender Swain's well-guided Shears,
Who having now, to pay his annual Care,
Borrow'd your Fleece, to you a cumbrous Load,
Will send you bounding to your Hills again.

JAMES THOMSON

HAYMAKING

After night's thunder far away had rolled
The fiery day had a kernel sweet of cold,
And in the perfect blue the clouds uncurled,
Like the first gods before they made the world
And misery, swimming the stormless sea
In beauty and in divine gaiety.
The smooth white empty road was lightly strewn
With leaves – the holly's Autumn falls in June –
And fir cones standing stiff up in the heat.
The mill-foot water tumbled white and lit
With tossing crystals, happier than any crowd
Of children pouring out of school aloud.
And in the little thickets where a sleeper
For ever might lie lost, the nettle-creeper
And garden warbler sang unceasingly;
While over them shrill shrieked in his fierce glee
The swift with wings and tail as sharp and narrow
As if the bow had flown off with the arrow.
Only the scent of woodbine and hay new-mown
Travelled the road. In the field sloping down,
Park-like, to where its willows showed the brook,
Haymakers rested. The tosser lay forsook
Out in the sun; and the long waggon stood
Without its team, it seemed it never would
Move from the shadow of that single yew.
The team, as still, until their task was due,
Beside the labourers enjoyed the shade
That three squat oaks mid-field together made
Upon a circle of grass and weed uncut,
And on the hollow, once a chalk-pit, but
Now brimmed with nut and elder-flower so clean.
The men leaned on their rakes, about to begin,
But still. And all were silent. All was old,
This morning time, with a great age untold,

Older than Clare and Cobbett, Morland and Crome,
Than, at the field's far edge, the farmer's home,
A white house crouched at the foot of a great tree.
Under the heavens that know not what years be
The men, the beasts, the trees, the implements
Uttered even what they will in times far hence –
All of us gone out of the reach of change –
Immortal in a picture of an old grange.

EDWARD THOMAS

THE RUINED CHAPEL

From meadows with the sheep so shorn
They, not their lambs, seem newly born
Through the graveyard I pass,
Where only blue plume-thistle waves
And headstones lie so deep in grass
They follow dead men to their graves,
And as I enter by no door
This chapel where the slow moss crawls
I wonder that so small a floor
Can have the sky for roof, mountains for walls.

ANDREW YOUNG

THE FAIRY RING

Here the horse-mushrooms make a fairy ring,
  Some standing upright and some overthrown,
A small Stonehenge, where heavy black snails cling
  And bite away, like Time, the tender stone.

ANDREW YOUNG

From THE FARMER'S BOY
(MID-DAY REST)

. . . Just where the parting bough's light shadows play,
Scarce in the shade, nor in the scorching day,
Stretch'd on the turf he lies, a peopled bed,
Where swarming insects creep around his head.
The small dust-colour'd beetle climbs with pain
O'er the smooth plaintain leaf, a spacious plain!
Thence higher still, by countless steps convey'd,
He gains the summit of a shivering blade,
And flirts his filmy wings, and looks around,
Exulting in his distance from the ground.
The tender speckled moth here dancing seen,
The vaulting grasshopper of glossy green,
And all prolific Summer's sporting train,
Their little lives by various powers sustain.
But what can unassisted vision do?
What, but recoil where most it would pursue;
His patient gaze but finish with a sigh,
When music waking speaks the sky-lark nigh!
Just starting from the corn she cheerly sings,
And trusts with conscious pride her downy wings:
Still louder breathes, and in the face of day
Mounts up, and calls on Giles to mark her way.
Close to his eyes his hat he instant bends,
And forms a friendly telescope, that lends
Just aid enough to dull the glaring light,
And place the wandering bird before his sight,
Yet oft beneath a cloud she sweeps along,
Lost for awhile, yet pours her varied song:
He views the spot, and as the cloud moves by,
Again she stretches up the clear blue sky;
Her form, her motion, undistinguish'd quite,
Save when she wheels direct from shade to light:
The fluttering songstress a mere speck became,
Like fancy's floating bubbles in a dream;

He sees her yet, but yielding to repose,
Unwittingly his jaded eyelids close.
Delicious sleep! From sleep who could forbear
With no more guilt than Giles, and no more care?
Peace o'er his slumbers waves her guardian wing,
Nor conscience once disturbs him with a sting:
He wakes refresh'd from every trivial pain,
And takes his pole and brushes round again.

ROBERT BLOOMFIELD

THE SHEPHERD'S TREE

Huge elm, with rifted trunk all notched and scarred,
   Like to a warrior's destiny! I love
To stretch me often on thy shadowed sward,
   And hear the laugh of summer leaves above;
Or on thy buttressed roots to sit, and lean
   In careless attitude, and there reflect
On times, and deeds, and darings that have been –
   Old castaways, now swallowed in neglect;
While thou art towering in thy strength of heart,
   Stirring the soul to vain imaginings,
In which life's sordid being hath no part.
   The wind of that eternal ditty sings,
Humming of future things, that burn the mind
To leave some fragment of itself behind.

JOHN CLARE

TO MEDDOWES

Ye have been fresh and green,
  Ye have been fill'd with flowers:
And ye the Walks have been
  Where Maids have spent their houres.

You have beheld, how they
  With *Wicker Arks* did come
To kisse, and beare away
  The richer Couslips home.

Y'ave heard them sweetly sing,
  And seen them in a Round:
Each Virgin, like a Spring,
  With Hony-succles crown'd.

But now, we see, none here,
  Whose silv'rie feet did tread,
And with dishevell'd Haire,
  Adorn'd this smoother Mead.

Like Unthrifts, having spent,
  Your stock, and needy grown,
Y'are left here to lament
  Your poore estates, alone.

ROBERT HERRICK

From KING LEAR

Heere's the place: stand still: how fearefull
And dizzie 'tis, to cast one's eyes so low,
The Crowes and Choughes, that wing the midway ayre
Show scarce so grosse as Beetles. Halfe way downe
Hangs one that gathers Sampire: dreadful Trade:
Me thinkes he seemes no bigger than his head.
The Fishermen, that walke upon the beach
Appeare like Mice: and yond tall Anchoring Barke,
Diminish'd to her Cocke: her Cocke, a Buoy
Almost too small for sight. The murmuring Surge,
That on the unnumbred idle Pebbles chafes
Cannot be heard so high. Ile looke no more,
Least my braine turne, and the deficient sight
Topple downe headlong.

WILLIAM SHAKESPEARE

THE HEDGE-ROSE OPENS

How passionately it opens after rain,
    And oh, how like a prayer
To those great shining skies! Do they disdain
    A bride so small and fair?
See the imploring petals, how they part
    And utterly lay bare
The perishing treasures of that piteous heart
    In wild surrender there.
What? Would'st *thou*, too, drink up the Eternal bliss,
    Ecstatically dare,
O little bride of God, to invoke *His* kiss? –
    But oh, how like a prayer!

ALFRED NOYES

TO A SKYLARK

Ethereal Minstrel! Pilgrim of the sky!
Dost thou despise the earth where cares abound?
Or, while the wings aspire, are heart and eye
Both with thy nest upon the dewy ground?
Thy nest which thou canst drop into at will
Those quivering wings composed, that music still!

To the last point of vision, and beyond,
Mount, daring Warbler! that love-prompted strain,
('Twixt thee and thine a never-failing bond)
Thrills not the less the bosom of the plain:
Yet might'st thou seem, proud privilege! to sing
All independent of the leafy spring.

Leave to the Nightingale her shady wood;
A privacy of glorious light is thine;
Whence thou dost pour upon the world a flood
Of harmony, with instinct more divine;
Type of the wise who soar, but never roam;
True to the kindred points of Heaven and Home!

WILLIAM WORDSWORTH

TO A SKYLARK

Hail, to thee, blithe Spirit!
   Bird thou never wert! –
That from Heaven, or near it,
   Pourest thy full heart
In profuse strains of unpremeditated art.

Higher still and higher
   From the earth thou springest,
Like a cloud of fire;
   The blue deep thou wingest
And singing still dost soar, and soaring ever singest.

In the golden lightning
   Of the sunken sun,
O'er which clouds are bright'ning,
   Thou dost float and run;
Like an unbodied joy whose race is just begun.

The pale purple even
   Melts around thy flight;
Like a star of heaven,
   In the broad daylight
Thou art unseen, but yet I hear thy shrill delight –

Keen as are the arrows
   Of that silver sphere,
Whose intense lamp narrows
   In the white dawn clear,
Until we hardly see, we feel that it is there.

All the earth and air
   With thy voice is loud,
As, when night is bare,
   From one lonely cloud
The moon rains out her beams, and heav'n is overflowed.

What thou art we know not;
    What is most like thee?
From rainbow clouds there flow not
    Drops so bright to see,
As from thy presence showers a rain of melody.

Like a poet hidden
    In the light of thought,
Singing hymns unbidden,
    Till the world is wrought
To sympathy with hopes and fears it heeded not:

Like a high-born maiden
    In a palace tower,
Soothing her love-laden
    Soul in secret hour
With music sweet as love, which overflows her bower;

Like a glow-worm golden
    In a dell of dew,
Scattering unbeholden
    Its aerial hue
Among the flowers and grass, which screen it from the view:

Like a rose embowered
    In its own green leaves,
By warm winds deflowered,
    Till the scent it gives
Makes faint with too much sweet these heavy-wingèd thieves:

Sound of vernal showers
    On the twinkling grass,
Rain-awaken'd flowers –
    All that ever was
Joyous, and clear, and fresh, thy music doth surpass.

Teach us, Sprite or Bird,
  What sweet thoughts are thine:
I have never heard
  Praise of love or wine
That panted forth a flood of rapture so divine.

Chorus hymeneal,
  Or triumphal chant,
Matched with thine would be all
  But an empty vaunt,
A thing wherein we feel there is some hidden want.

What objects are the fountains
  Of thy happy strain?
What fields, or waves, or mountains?
  What shapes of sky or plain?
What love of thine own kind? what ignorance of pain?

With thy clear keen joyance
  Languor cannot be:
Shadow of annoyance
  Never came near thee:
Thou lovest – but ne'er knew love's sad satiety.

Waking or asleep,
  Thou of death must deem
Things more true and deep
  Than we mortals dream,
Or how could thy notes flow in such a crystal stream?

We look before and after,
  And pine for what is not:
Our sincerest laughter
  With some pain is fraught;
Our sweetest songs are those that tell of saddest thought.

Yet, if we could scorn
    Hate, and pride, and fear;
If we were things born
    Not to shed a tear,
I know not how thy joy we ever should come near.

Better than all measures
    Of delightful sound,
Better than all treasures
    That in books are found,
Thy skill to poet were, thou scorner of the ground!

Teach me half the gladness
    That thy brain must know,
Such harmonious madness
    From my lips would flow,
The world should listen then, as I am listening now.

PERCY BYSSHE SHELLEY

THE SKYLARK

Above the russet clods the corn is seen
Sprouting its spiry points of tender green,
Where squats the hare, to terrors wide awake,
Like some brown clod the harrows failed to break.
Opening their golden caskets to the sun,
The buttercups make schoolboys eager run,
To see who shall be first to pluck the prize –
Up from their hurry see the Skylark flies,
And o'er her half-formed nest, with happy wings,
Winnows the air till in the cloud she sings,
Then hangs a dust spot in the sunny skies,
And drops and drops till in her nest she lies,
Which they unheeded passed – not dreaming then
That birds, which flew so high, would drop again
To nests upon the ground, which anything
May come at to destroy. Had they the wing
Like such a bird, themselves would be too proud
And build on nothing but a passing cloud!
As free from danger as the heavens are free
From pain and toil, there would they build and be,
And sail about the world to scenes unheard
Of and unseen, – O were they but a bird!
So think they, while they listen to its song,
And smile and fancy and so pass along;
While its low nest, moist with the dews of morn,
Lies safely, with the leveret, in the corn.

JOHN CLARE

From THE SKYLARK

How the blithe lark runs up the golden stair
That leans thro' cloudy gates from heaven to earth,
And all alone in the empyreal air
Fills it with jubilant sweet songs of mirth;
How far he seems, how far
With the light upon his wings,
Is it a bird, or star
That shines, and sings?

What matter if the days be dark and frore,
That sunbeam tells of other days to be,
And singing in the light that floods him o'er
In joy he overtakes Futurity;
Under cloud-arches vast
He peeps, and sees behind
Great Summer coming fast
Adown the wind!

And now he dives into a rainbow's rivers,
In streams of gold and purple he is drown'd,
Shrilly the arrows of his song he shivers,
As tho' the stormy drops were turn'd to sound;
And now he issues thro',
He scales a cloudy tower,
Faintly, like falling dew,
His fast notes shower.

Let every wind be hush'd, that I may hear
The wondrous things he tells the World below,
Things that we dream of he is watching near,
Hopes, that we never dream'd, he would bestow;
Alas! the storm hath roll'd
Back the gold gates again,
Or surely he had told
All Heaven to men!

FREDERICK TENNYSON

THE LARK ASCENDING

He rises and begins to round,
He drops the silver chain of sound,
Of many links without a break,
In chirrup, whistle, slur and shake,
All intervolved and spreading wide,
Like water-dimples down a tide
Where ripple ripple overcurls
And eddy into eddy whirls;
A press of hurried notes that run
So fleet they scarce are more than one,
Yet changeingly the trills repeat
And linger ringing while they fleet,
Sweet to the quick o' the ear, and dear
To her beyond the handmaid ear,
Who sits beside our inner springs,
Too often dry for this he brings,
Which seems the very jet of earth
At sight of sun, her music's mirth,
As up he winds the spiral stair,
A song of light, and pierces air
With fountain ardour, fountain play,
To reach the shining tops of day,
And drink in everything discerned
An ecstasy to music turned,
Impelled by what his happy bill
Disperses; drinking, showering still,
Unthinking save that he may give
His voice the outlet, there to live
Renewed in endless notes of glee,
So thirsty of his voice is he,
For all to hear and all to know
That he is joy, awake, aglow,
The tumult of the heart to hear
Through pureness filtered crystal-clear,

And know the pleasure sprinkled bright
By simple singing of delight,
Shrill, irreflective, unrestrained,
Rapt, ringing, on the jet sustained,
Without a break, without a fall,
Sweet silvery, sheer lyrical,
Perennial, quavering up the chord
Like myriad dews of sunny sward
That trembling into fulness shine,
And sparkle dropping argentine;
Such wooing as the ear receives
From zephyr caught in choric leaves
Of aspens when their chattering net
Is flushed to white with shivers wet;
And such the water-spirit's chime
On mountain's height in morning's prime,
Too freshly sweet to seem excess,
Too animate to need a stress;
But wider over many heads
The starry voice ascending spreads,
Awakening, as it waxes thin,
The best in us to him akin;
And every face to watch him raised
Puts on the light of children praised,
So rich our human pleasure ripes
When sweetness or sincereness pipes,
Though nought be promised from the seas,
But only a soft-ruffling breeze
Sweep glittering on a still content,
Serenity in ravishment.

For singing till his heaven fills,
'Tis love of earth that he instils,
And ever winging up and up,
Our valley is his golden cup,
And he the wine which overflows
To lift us with him as he goes:

The woods and brooks, the sheep and kine,
He is, the hills, the human line,
The meadows green, the fallows brown,
The dreams of labour in the town;
He sings the sap, the quickened veins;
The wedding song of sun and rains
He is, the dance of children, thanks
Of sowers, shout of primrose-banks,
And eye of violets while they breathe;
All these the circling song will wreathe,
And you shall hear the herb and tree,
The better heart of men shall see,
Shall feel celestially, as long
As you crave nothing save the song.

Was never voice of ours could say
Our inmost in the sweetest way,
Like yonder voice aloft, and link
All hearers in the song they drink.
Our wisdom speaks from failing blood,
Our passion is too full in flood,
We want the key of his wild note
Of truthful in a tuneful throat,
The song seraphically free
Of taint of personality,
So pure that it salutes the suns,
The voice of one for millions,
In whom the millions rejoice
For giving their one spirit voice.

Yet men have we, whom we revere,
Now names, and men still housing here,
Whose lives, by many a battle-dint
Defaced, and grinding wheels on flint,
Yield substance, though they sing not, sweet
For song our highest heaven to greet:

Whom heavenly singing gives us new,
Enspheres them brilliant in our blue,
From firmest base to farthest leap,
Because their love of Earth is deep,
And they are warriors in accord
With life to serve, and pass reward,
So touching purest and so heard
In the brain's reflex of yon bird:
Wherefore their soul in me, or mine,
Through self-forgetfulness divine,
In them, that song aloft maintains,
To fill the sky and thrill the plains,
With showerings drawn from human stores,
As he to silence nearer soars,
Extends the world at wings and dome,
More spacious making more our home,
Till lost on his aërial rings
In light, and then the fancy sings.

GEORGE MEREDITH

DAY'S BLACK STAR

Is it that small black star,
   Twinkling in broad daylight,
Upon the bosom of
   Yon cloud so white –
Is it that small black thing
   Makes earth and all Heaven ring!

Sing, you black star; and soar
   Until, alas! too soon
You fall to earth in one
   Long singing swoon;
But you will rise again
   To Heaven, from this green plain.

Sing, sing, sweet star; though black,
   Your company's more bright
Than any star that shines
   With a white light;
Sing, Skylark, sing; and give
   To me thy joy to live.

W. H. DAVIES

THE GARDEN

How vainly men themselves amaze
To win the Palm, the Oke, or Bayes;
And their uncessant Labours see
Crown'd from some single Herb or Tree,
Whose short and narrow verged Shade
Does prudently their Toyles upbraid;
While all Flow'rs and all Trees do close
To weave the Garlands of repose.

Fair quiet, have I found thee here,
and Innocence thy Sister dear!
Mistaken long, I sought you then
In busie Companies of Men.
Your sacred Plants, if here below,
Only among the Plants will grow.
Society is all but rude,
To this delicious Solitude.

No white or red was ever seen
So am'rous as this lovely green.
Fond Lovers, cruel as their Flame,
Cut in these Trees their Mistress name.
Little, Alas, they know, or heed,
How far these Beauties Hers exceed!
Fair Trees! where s'eer you barkes I wound,
No Name shall but your own be found.

When we have run our Passions heat,
Love hither makes his best retreat.
The Gods, that mortal Beauty chase,
Still in a Tree did end their race.
Apollo hunted Daphne so,
Only that She might Laurel grow.
And Pan did after Syrinx speed,
Not as a Nymph, but for a Reed.

What wond'rous Life in this I lead!
Ripe Apples drop about my head;
The Luscious clusters of the Vine
Upon my Mouth do crush their Wine;
The Nectaren, and curious Peach,
Into my hands themselves do reach;
Stumbling on Melons, as I pass,
Insnar'd with Flow'rs, I fall on Grass.

Mean while the Mind, from pleasure less,
Withdraws into its happiness:
The Mind, that Ocean where each kind
Does streight its own resemblance find;
Yet it creates, transcending these,
Far other Worlds, and other Seas;
Annihilating all that's made
To a green Thought in a green Shade.

Here at the Fountains sliding foot,
Or at some Fruit-trees mossy root,
Casting the Bodies Vest aside,
My Soul into the boughs does glide:
There like a Bird it sits, and sings,
Then whets, and combs its silver Wings;
And, till prepar'd for longer flight,
Waves in its Plumes the various Light.

Such was that happy Garden-state,
Wile Man there walk'd without a Mate:
After a Place so pure, and sweet,
What other Help could yet be meet!
But 'twas beyond a Mortal's share
To wander solitary there:
Two Paradises 'twere in one,
To live in Paradise alone.

How well the skilful Gardner drew
Of flow'rs and Herbes this Dial new;
Where from above the milder Sun
Does through a fragrant Zodiack run;
And, as it works, th'industrious Bee
Computes its time as well as we.
How could such sweet and wholsome Hours
Be reckon'd but with herbs and flow'rs!

ANDREW MARVELL

TO MARYGOLDS

Give way, and be ye ravisht by the Sun,
(And hang the head when as the Act is done)
Spread as He spreads; wax lesse as He do's wane;
And as He shuts, close up to Maids again.

ROBERT HERRICK

A ROSE

Blowne in the Morning, thou shalt fade ere Noone:
What bootes a Life which in such hast forsakes thee?
Th'art wondrous frolick being to dye so soone:
And passing proud a little colour makes thee.

If thee thy brittle beauty so deceives,
Know then the thing that swells thee is thy bane;
For the same beauty doth, in bloody leaves,
The sentence of thy early death containe.

Some Clownes course Lungs will poyson thy sweet flow'r,
If by the careless Plough thou shalt be torne:
And many *Herods* lye in waite each how'r
To murther thee as soone as thou art borne;

Nay, force thy Bud to blow; – Their Tyrant breath
Anticipating Life, to hasten death.

SIR RICHARD FANSHAWE

THE SICK ROSE

O Rose, thou art sick!
The invisible worm,
That flies in the night,
In the howling storm,

Has found out thy bed
Of crimson joy;
And his dark secret love
Does thy life destroy.

WILLIAM BLAKE

AH! SUN-FLOWER

Ah, Sun-flower! weary of time,
Who countest the steps of the Sun;
Seeking after that sweet golden clime,
Where the traveller's journey is done;

Where the Youth pined away with desire,
And the pale Virgin shrouded in snow,
Arise from their graves, and aspire
Where my Sun-flower wishes to go.

WILLIAM BLAKE

SPEAR THISTLE

Where the broad sheepwalk bare and brown
   [Yields] scant grass pining after showers,
And winds go fanning up and down
   The little strawy bents and nodding flowers,
There the huge thistle, spurred with many thorns,
The suncrackt upland's russet swells adorns.

Not undevoid of beauty there they come,
   Armed warrriors, waiting neither suns nor showers,
Guarding the little clover plots to bloom
   While sheep nor oxen dare not crop their flowers
Unsheathing their own knobs of tawny flowers
When summer cometh in her hottest hours.

The pewit, swopping up and down
   And screaming round the passer bye,
Or running oer the herbage brown
   With copple crown uplifted high,
Loves in its clumps to make a home
Where danger seldom cares to come.

The yellowhammer, often prest
   For spot to build and be unseen,
Will in its shelter trust her nest
   When fields and meadows glow with green;
And larks, though paths go closely bye,
Will in its shade securely lie.

The partridge too, that scarce can trust
   The open downs to be at rest,
Will in its clumps lie down, and dust
   And prune its horseshoe-circled breast,
And oft in shining fields of green
Will lay and raise its brood unseen.

The sheep when hunger presses sore
    May nip the clover round its nest;
But soon the thistle wounding sore
    Relieves it from each brushing guest,
That leaves a bit of wool behind,
The yellowhammer loves to find.

The horse will set his foot and bite
    Close to the ground lark's guarded nest
And snort to meet the prickly sight;
    He fans the feathers of her breast —
Yet thistles prick so deep that he
Turns back and leaves her dwelling free.

Its prickly knobs the dews of morn
    Doth bead with dressing rich to see,
When threads doth hang from thorn to thorn
    Like the small spinner's tapestry;
And from the flowers a sultry smell
Comes that agrees with summer well.

The bee will make its bloom a bed,
    The humble bee in tawny brown;
And one in jacket fringed with red
    Will rest upon its velvet down
When overtaken in the rain,
And wait till sunshine comes again.

And there are times when travel goes
    Along the sheep tracks' beaten ways,
Then pleasure many a praise bestows
    Upon its blossoms' pointed rays,
When other things are parched beside
And hot day leaves it in its pride.

JOHN CLARE

From THE RETIREMENT

STANZES IRREGULIERS
TO MR. ISAAK WALTON

Farewell thou busie World, and may
    We never meet again:
Here I can eat, and sleep, and pray,
And doe more good in one short day,
Than he who his whole Age out-wears
Upon thy most conspicuous Theatres
Where nought but Vice and Vanity do reign.

Good God! how sweet are all things here!
How beautifull the fields appear!
How cleanly do we feed and lie!
Lord! what good hours do we keep!
    How quietly we sleep!
What Peace! what Unanimity!
How innocent from the leud Fashion,
Is all our bus'ness, all our Conversation!

Oh how happy here's our leisure!
Oh how innocent our pleasure!
Oh ye Vallies, oh ye Mountains,
Oh ye Groves and Chrystall Fountains,
    How I love at liberty,
By turn to come and visit ye!

O Solitude, the Soul's best Friend,
That man acquainted with himself dost make,
And all his Maker's Wonders to intend;
    With thee I here converse at will,
    And would be glad to do so still;
For it is thou alone that keep'st the Soul awake.

How calm and quiet a delight
        It is alone
To read, and meditate, and write,
By none offended, nor offending none;
To walk, ride, sit or sleep at one's own ease,
And pleasing a man's self, none other to displease!

Oh my beloved Nymph! fair Dove,
Princess of Rivers, how I love
    Upon thy flow'ry Banks to lie,
        And view thy Silver stream,
When gilded by a Summer's Beam,
And in it all thy wanton Fry
            Playing at liberty
And with my Angle upon them,
        The All of Treachery
I ever learn'd to practise and to try! . . .

Oh my beloved Caves! from Dog-star heats,
And hotter Persecution safe Retreats,
What safety, privacy, what true delight
            In the artificial Night
            Your gloomy entrails make,
            Have I taken, do I take!
How oft, when grief has made me fly
To hide me from Society,
Even of my dearest Friends, have I
    In your recesses friendly shade
    All my sorrows open laid,
And my most secret woes entrusted to your privacy.

Lord! would men let me alone,
What an over-happy one
Should I think my self to be,
Might I in this desart place,
Which most men by their voice disgrace,
    Live but undisturb'd and free!

Here in this despis'd recess
Would I maugre Winter's cold,
And the Summer's worst excess,
Try to live out to sixty full years old,
And all the while
Without an envious eye
On any thriving under Fortune's smile,
Contented live, and then contented die.

CHARLES COTTON

DAY

In the barn the tenant cock,
  Close to Partlet perch'd on high,
Brisky crows (the shepherd's clock!)
  Jocund that the morning's nigh.

Swiftly from the mountain's brow,
  Shadows, nurs'd by night, retire:
And the peeping sun-beam, now,
  Paints with gold the village spire.

Philomel forsakes the thorn,
  Plaintive where she prates at night;
And the lark, to meet the morn,
  Soars beyond the shepherd's sight.

From the low-roof'd cottage ridge,
  See the chatt'ring swallow spring;
Darting through the one-arch'd bridge,
  Quick she dips her dappled wing.

Now the pine-tree's waving top
  Gently greets the morning gale:
Kidlings, now, begin to crop
  Daisies, in the dewy dale.

From the balmy sweets, uncloy'd,
  (Restless till her task be done)
Now the busy bee's employ'd
  Sipping dew before the Sun.

Trickling through the crevic'd rock,
  Where the limpid stream distills,
Sweet refreshment waits the flock
  When 'tis sun-drove from the hills.

Colin, for the promis'd corn
  (Ere the harvest hopes are ripe)
Anxious, hears the huntsman's horn,
  Boldly sounding, drown his pipe.

Sweet, – O sweet, the warbling throng,
  On the white emblossom'd spray!
Nature's universal song
  Echoes to the rising day.

NOON

Fervid on the glitt'ring flood,
  Now the noon-tide radiance glows!
Dropping o'er its infant bud,
  Not a dew-drop's left the rose.

By the brook the shepherd dines;
  From the fierce meridian heat
Shelter'd, by the branching pines,
  Pendant o'er his grassy seat.

Now the flock forsakes the glade,
  Where, uncheck'd, the sun-beams fall;
Sure to find a pleasing shade
  By the ivy'd abbey wall.

Echo in her airy round,
  O'er the river, rock, and hill,
Cannot catch a single sound,
  Save the clack of yonder mill.

Cattle court the zephyrs bland,
  Where the streamlet wanders cool;
Or with languid silence stand
  Midway in the marshy pool.

But from mountain, dell, or stream,
   Not a flutt'ring zephyr springs:
Fearful lest the noon-tide beam
   Scorch its soft, its silken wings.

Not a leaf has leave to stir,
   Nature's lull'd — serene — and still!
Quiet e'en the shepherd's cur,
   Sleeping on the heath-clad hill.

Languid is the landscape round,
   Till the fresh descending shower,
Grateful to the thirsty ground,
   Raises ev'ry fainting flower.

Now the hill — the hedge — is green,
   Now the warblers' throats in tune!
Blithesome is the verdant scene,
   Brighten'd by the beams of noon!

EVENING

O'er the heath the heifer strays
   Free; — (the furrowed task is done)
Now the village windows blaze,
   Burnish'd by the setting Sun.

Now he hides behind the hill,
   Sinking from a golden sky:
Can the pencil's mimic skill
   Copy the refulgent dye?

Trudging as the ploughmen go,
   (To the smoking hamlet bound)
Giant-like their shadows grow,
   Lengthen'd o'er the level ground.

Where the rising forest spreads,
  Shelter for the lordly dome!
To their high-built airy beds,
  See the rooks returning home!

As the lark, with vary'd tune,
  Carols to the evening loud;
Mark the mild resplendent Moon,
  Breaking through a parted cloud!

Now the hermit Howlet peeps
  From the barn, or twisted brake:
And the blue mist slowly creeps,
  Curling on the silver lake.

As the trout in speckled pride,
  Playful from its bosom springs;
To the banks, a ruffled tide
  Verges in successive rings.

Tripping through the silken grass,
  O'er the path divided dale,
Mark the rose-complexion'd lass,
  With her well-pois'd milking pail.

Linnets, with unnumber'd notes,
  And the cuckoo bird with two,
Tuning sweet their mellow throats,
  Bid the setting Sun adieu.

JOHN CUNNINGHAM

From A MIDSOMMER NIGHT'S DREAME

TITANIA TO OBERON

And never, since the middle Sommer's spring,
Met we on hill, in dale, forrest, or mead,
By paved fountaine or by rushy brooke,
Or in the beached margent of the Sea,
To dance our ringlets to the whistling Winde,
But with thy brawles thou hast disturb'd our sport.
Therefore the Windes, piping to us in vaine,
As in revenge, have suck'd up from the Sea
Contagious fogs; which, falling in the Land,
Have every pelting River made so proud,
That they have overborne their Continents.
The Oxe hath therefore stretch'd his yoke in vain,
The Ploughman lost his sweat, and the green Corne
Hath rotted, ere his youth attain'd a beard:
The fold stands empty in the drowned field,
And Crows are fatted with the murrion flocke,
The nine men's Morris is fild up with mud,
And the queint Mazes in the wanton greene,
For lacke of tread, are undistinguishable.
The humane mortals want their winter heere,
No night is now with hymne or caroll blest;
Therefore the Moone (the governesse of floods)
Pale in her anger, washes all the aire;
That Rheumaticke diseases do abound.
And through this distemperature, we see
The seasons alter: hoary headed frosts
Fall in the fresh lap of the Crimson Rose,
And on old Hiems thinne and Icy crowne,
An odorous Chaplet of sweet Sommer buds
Is, as in mockery, set. The spring, the Sommer,
The childing Autumn, angry Winter change
Their wonted Liveries: and the mazed world,

By their increase, now knowes not which is which;
And this same progeny of evils, comes
From our debate, from our dissention:
We are their Parents and originall.

WILLIAM SHAKESPEARE

JULY FUGITIVE

Can you tell me where has hid her
   Pretty Maid July?
I would swear one day ago
   She passed by,
I would swear that I do know
   The blue bliss of her eye:
'Tarry, maid, maid,' I bid her;
   But she hastened by.
Do you know where she has hid her,
   Maid July?

Yet in truth it needs must be
   The flight of her is old;
Yet in truth it needs must be,
   For her nest, the earth, is cold.
No more in the poolèd Even
   Wade her rosy feet,
Dawn-flakes no more plash from them
   To poppies 'mid the wheat.
She has muddied the day's oozes
   With her petulant feet;
Scared the clouds that floated,
   As sea-birds they were,
Slow on the cœrule
   Lulls of the air,
Lulled on the luminous
   Levels of air:
She has chidden in a pet
   All her stars from her;
Now they wander loose and sigh
   Through the turbid blue,
Now they wander, weep, and cry –
   Yea, and I too –
'Where are you, sweet July,
   Where are you?'

Who hath beheld her footprints,
  Or the pathway she goes?
Tell me, wind, tell me, wheat,
  Which of you knows?
Sleeps she swathed in the flushed Arctic
  Night of the Rose?
Or lie her limbs like Alp-glow
  On the lily's snows?
Gales, that are all-visitant,
  Find the runaway;
And for him who findeth her
  (I do charge you say)
I will throw largesse of broom
  Of this summer's mintage,
I will broach a honey-bag
  Of the bee's best vintage.

Breezes, wheat, flowers sweet,
  None of them knows!
How then shall we lure her back
  From the way she goes?
For it were a shameful thing,
  Saw we not this comer
Ere Autumn camp upon the fields
  Red with rout of Summer.

When the bird quits the cage,
  We set the cage outside,
With seed and with water,
  And the door wide,
Haply we may win it so
  Back to abide.
Hang her cage of Earth out
  O'er Heaven's sunward wall,
Its four gates open, winds in watch
  By reinèd cars at all;
Relume in hanging hedgerows

The rain-quenched blossom,
And roses sob their tears out
    On the gale's warm heaving bosom;
Shake the lilies till their scent
    Over-drip their rims
That our runaway may see
    We do know her whims;
Sleek the tumbled waters out
    For her travelled limbs;
Strew and smooth blue night thereon:
    There will – O not doubt her! –
The lovely sleepy lady lie,
    With all her stars about her!

FRANCIS THOMPSON

THE RAINY SUMMER

There's much afoot in heaven and earth this year;
  The winds hunt up the sun, hunt up the moon,
Trouble the dubious dawn, hasten the drear
  Height of a threatening noon.

No breath of boughs, no breath of leaves, of fronds
  May linger or grow warm; the trees are loud;
The forest, rooted, tosses in his bonds,
  And strains against the cloud.

No scents may pause within the garden-fold;
  The rifled flowers are cold as ocean-shells;
Bees, humming in the storm, carry their cold
  Wild honey to cold cells.

ALICE MEYNELL

THE VILLAIN

While joy gave clouds the light of stars,
    That beamed where'er they looked;
And calves and lambs had tottering knees,
    Excited, while they sucked;
While every bird enjoyed his song,
Without one thought of harm or wrong —
I turned my head and saw the wind,
    Not far from where I stood,
Dragging the corn by her golden hair,
    Into a dark and lonely wood.

W. H. DAVIES

STONE TREES

Last night a sword-light in the sky
Flashed a swift terror on the dark.
In that sharp light the fields did lie
Naked and stone-like; each tree stood
Like a tranced woman, bound and stark.
  Far off the wood
With darkness ridged the riven dark.

And cows astonished stared with fear,
And sheep crept to the knees of cows,
And conies to their burrows slid,
And rooks were still in rigid boughs,
And all things else were still or hid.
  From all the wood
Came but the owl's hoot, ghostly, clear.

In that cold trance the earth was held
It seemed an age, or time was nought.
Sure never from that stone-like field
Sprang golden corn, nor from those chill
Gray granite trees was music wrought.
  In all the wood
Even the tall poplar hung stone-still.

It seemed an age, or time was none . . .
Slowly the earth heaved out of sleep
And shivered, and the trees of stone
Bent and sighed in the gusty wind,
And rain swept as birds flocking sweep,
  Far off the wood
Rolled the slow thunders on the wind.

From all the wood came no brave bird,
No song broke through the close-fall'n night,
Nor any sound from cowering herd:
Only a dog's long lonely howl
When from the window poured pale light.
    And from the wood
The hoot came ghostly of the owl.

JOHN FREEMAN

THUNDER-STORM

       A boding Silence reigns,
Dread thro the dun Expanse; save the dull Sound
That from the Mountain, previous to the Storm,
Rolls o'er the muttering Earth, disturbs the Flood,
And shakes the Forest-Leaf without a Breath.
Prone, to the lowest Vale, the aërial Tribes
Descend; the Tempest-loving Raven scarce
Dares wing the dubious Dusk. In rueful Gaze
The Cattle stand, and on the scouling Heavens
Cast a deploring Eye; by Man forsook,
Who to the crouded Cottage hies him fast,
Or seeks the Shelter of the downward Cave.

 'Tis listening Fear, and dumb Amazement all:
When to the startled Eye the sudden Glance
Appears far South, eruptive thro the Cloud;
And following slower, in Explosion vast,
The Thunder raises his tremendous voice.
At first, heard solemn o'er the Verge of Heaven,
The Tempest growls; but as it nearer comes,
And rolls its awful Burden on the Wind,
The Lightnings flash a larger Curve, and more
The Noise astounds: till over Head a Sheet
Of livid Flame, discloses wide, then shuts
And opens wider, shuts and opens still
Expansive, wrapping Ether in a Blaze.
Follows the loosen'd aggravated Roar,
Enlarging, deepening, mingling, Peal on Peal
Crush'd horrible, convulsing Heaven and Earth.

 Down comes a Deluge of sonorous Hail,
Or prone-descending Rain. Wide-rent, the Clouds
Pour a whole Flood; and yet, its Flame unquench'd,
Th' unconquerable Lightning struggles thro,

Ragged and fierce, or in red whirling Balls,
And fires the Mountains with redoubled Rage.
Black from the Stroke, above, the smould'ring Pine
Stands a sad shatter'd Trunk; and, stretch'd below,
A lifeless Groupe the blasted Cattle lie:
Here the soft Flocks, with that same harmless Look
They wore alive, and ruminating still
In Fancy's Eye; and there the frowning Bull,
And Ox half-rais'd. Struck on the castled Cliff,
The venerable Tower and spiry Fane
Resign their aged Pride. The gloomy Woods
Start at the Flash, and from their deep Recess,
Wide-flaming out, their trembling Inmates shake.
Amid *Carnarvon's* Mountains rages loud
The repercussive Roar: with mighty Crush,
Into the flashing Deep, from the rude Rocks
Of *Penmaen Maur* heap'd hideous to the sky,
Tumble the smitten Cliffs; and *Snowdon's* Peak,
Dissolving, instant yields his wintry Load.
Far-seen, the Heights of heathy *Cheviot* blaze,
And Thulè bellows thro her utmost Isles.

    As from the Face of Heaven the shatter'd Clouds
Tumultuous rove, th' interminable Sky
Sublimer swells, and o'er the World expands
A purer Azure. Nature, from the Storm,
Shines out afresh; and thro the lighten'd Air
A higher Luster and a clearer calm,
Diffusive, tremble, while as if in sign
Of Danger past, a glittering Robe of Joy,
Set off abundant by the yellow Ray,
Invests the fields, yet dropping from Distress.

JAMES THOMSON

MY HEART LEAPS UP WHEN I BEHOLD

My heart leaps up when I behold
    A rainbow in the sky:
So was it when my life began;
So is it now I am a man;
So be it when I shall grow old,
    Or let me die!
The Child is father of the Man;
And I could wish my days to be
Bound each to each by natural piety.

WILLIAM WORDSWORTH

A THUNDER SHOWER

And now a cloud, bright, huge and calm,
Rose, doubtful if for bale or balm;
O'ertoppling crags, portentous towers
Appear'd, at beck of viewless powers,
Along a rifted mountain range.
Untraceable and swift in change,
Those glittering peaks, disrupted, spread
To solemn bulks, seen overhead;
The sunshine quench'd, from one dark form
Fumed the appalling light of storm.
Straight to the zenith, black with bale,
The Gipsies' smoke rose deadly pale;
And one wide night of hopeless hue
Hid from the heart the recent blue.
And soon, with thunder crackling loud,
A flash within the formless cloud
Show'd vague recess, projection dim,
Lone sailing rack, and shadowy rim,
Against the whirl of leaves and dust
Kine dropp'd their heads; the tortured gust
Jagg'd and convuls'd the ascending smoke
To mockery of the lightning's stroke.
The blood prick'd, and a blinding flash
And close co-instantaneous crash
Humbled the soul, and the rain all round
Resilient dimm'd the whistling ground,
Nor flagged in force from first to last,
Till, sudden as it came, 'twas past,
Leaving a trouble in the copse
Of brawling birds and tinkling drops.
  Change beyond hope! Far thunder faint
Mutter'd its vast and vain complaint,
And gaps and fractures, fringed with light,
Show'd the sweet skies, with squadrons bright
Of cloudlets, glittering calm and fair
Through gulfs of calm and glittering air.

GO BACK!

But now
From the brow
Of old Skiddaw, high-perched
On the last of the cairns,
Myself and my bairns,
We searched for our sweetest of sweet little Hesperides;
And our lids
Were stung
By the 'saut'
Sharp slung
From the wall
Of a squall,
That wrought,
And blurred,
And slurred
The air
Out there,
So that naught
Of Our Isle,
The while,
Could we see,
But a film of the faintest ivory.
Just half-way down the slope we sit, —
When, suddenly, the sky is lit —
Look, look! as through a sliding panel
Of pearl, our Mona! Has she crossed the Channel
For us? that there she lies almost
A portion of the Cumbrian coast?
Dark purple peaks against the sun,
A gorgeous thing to look upon?
Nay, darling of my soul! I fear
To see your beauty come so near —
I would not have it! This is not your rest —
Go back, go back, into your golden West!

T. E. BROWN

INSCRIPTION FOR A FOUNTAIN

This Sycamore, oft musical with bees, –
Such tents the Patriarchs loved! O long unharmed
May all its aged boughs o'er-canopy
The small round basin, which this jutting stone
Keeps pure from falling leaves! Long may the Spring,
Quietly as a sleeping infant's breath,
Send up cold waters to the traveller
With soft and even pulse! Nor ever cease
Yon tiny cone of sand its soundless dance,
Which at the bottom, like a Fairy's Page,
As merry and no taller, dances still,
Nor wrinkles the smooth surface of the Fount.
Here twilight is and coolness: here is moss,
A soft seat, and a deep and ample shade.
Thou may'st toil far and find no second tree.
Drink, Pilgrim, here! Here rest! and if thy heart
Be innocent, here too shalt thou refresh
Thy spirit, listening to some gentle sound,
Or passing gale or hum of murmuring bees!

SAMUEL TAYLOR COLERIDGE

THE EAGLE

He clasps the crag with crooked hands;
Close to the sun in lonely lands,
Ring'd with the azure world, he stands.

The wrinkled sea beneath him crawls;
He watches from his mountain walls,
And like a thunderbolt he falls.

LORD TENNYSON

DAY-DREAMS

Broad August burns in milky skies,
   The world is blanched with hazy heat;
The vast green pasture, even, lies
   Too hot and bright for eyes and feet.

Amid the grassy levels rears
   The sycamore against the sun
The dark boughs of a hundred years,
   The emerald foliage of one.

Lulled in a dream of shade and sheen,
   With the clement twilight thrown
By that great cloud of floating green,
   A horse is standing, still as stone.

He stirs nor head nor hoof, although
   The grass is fresh beneath the branch;
His tail alone swings to and fro
   In graceful curves from haunch to haunch.

He stands quite lost, indifferent
   To rock or pasture, trace or rein;
He feels the vaguely sweet content
   Of perfect sloth in limb and brain.

WILLIAM CANTON

Come, Sons of Summer, by whose toile
We are the Lords of Wine and Oile:
By whose tough labours, and rough hands,
We rip up first, then reap our lands.
Crown'd with the eares of corne, now come,
And, to the Pipe, sing Harvest-home.
Come forth, my Lord, and see the Cart
Drest up with all the Country Art.
See, here a *Mankin*, there a sheet,
As spotlesse pure, as it is sweet:
The Horses, Mares, and frisking Fillies,
(Clad, all, in Linnen, white as Lillies.)
The Harvest Swaines, and Wenches bound
For joy, to see the *Hock-cart* crown'd.
About the Cart, heare, how the Rout
Of Rurall Younglings raise the shout;
Pressing before, some coming after,
Those with a shout, and these with laughter.
Some blesse the Cart, some kisse the sheaves;
Some prank them up with Oaken leaves:
Some crosse the Fill-horse; some with great
Devotion, stroak the home-borne wheat:
While other Rusticks, lesse attent
To prayers, then to Merryment,
Run after with their breeches rent.
Well, on, brave boyes, to your Lord's Hearth,
Glittering with fire; where, for your mirth,
Ye shall see first the large and cheefe
Foundation of your Feast, Fat Beefe,
With Upper Stories, Mutton, Veale,
And Bacon, (which makes the full meale);
With sev'rall dishes standing by,
As here a Custard, there a Pie,
And here all tempting Frumentie.

And for to make the merry cheere,
If smirking Wine be wanting here,
There's that, which drowns all care, stout Beere;
Which freely drink to your Lord's health,
Then to the Plough (the Commonwealth),
Next to your Flailes, your Fanes, your Fatts;
Then to the Maids with Wheaten Hats:
To the rough Sickle, and crookt Sythe,
Drink frollick boyes, till all be blythe.
Feed, and grow fat; and as ye eat,
Be mindfull, that the lab'ring Neat
(As you) may have their fill of meat.
And know, besides, ye must revoke
The patient Oxe unto the Yoke,
And all goe back unto the Plough,
And Harrow (though they'r hang'd up now).
And, you must know, your Lords words true,
Feed him ye must, whose food fils you.
And that this pleasure is like raine,
Not sent ye for to drowne your paine,
But for to make it spring againe.

ROBERT HERRICK

THE SOLITARY REAPER

Behold her, single in the field,
Yon solitary Highland Lass!
Reaping and singing by herself;
Stop here, or gently pass!
Alone she cuts, and binds the grain,
And sings a melancholy strain;
O listen! for the Vale profound
Is overflowing with the sound.

No Nightingale did ever chaunt
So sweetly to reposing bands
Of Travellers in some shady haunt,
Among Arabian sands:
A voice so thrilling ne'er was heard
In spring-time from the Cuckoo-bird,
Breaking the silence of the seas
Among the farthest Hebrides.

Will no one tell me what she sings?
Perhaps the plaintive numbers flow
For old, unhappy, far-off things,
And battles long ago:
Or is it some more humble lay,
Familiar matter of to-day?
Some natural sorrow, loss, or pain,
That has been, and may be again!

Whate'er the theme, the Maiden sang
As if her song could have no ending;
I saw her singing at her work,
And o'er the sickle bending; –
I listened till I had my fill,
And when I mounted up the hill,
The music in my heart I bore,
Long after it was heard no more.

WILLIAM WORDSWORTH

POPPIES

We are slumberous poppies,
    Lords of Lethe downs,
Some awake, and some asleep,
    Sleeping in our crowns.
What perchance our dreams may know,
Let our serious beauty show.

Central depth of purple
    Leaves more bright than rose,
Who shall tell what brightest thought
    Out of darkest grows?
Who, through what funereal pain
Souls to love and peace attain?

Visions aye are on us,
    Unto eyes of power,
Pluto's always setting sun,
    And Proserpine's bower:
There, like bees, the pale souls come
For our drink with drowsy hum.

Taste, ye mortals, also;
    Milky-hearted, we;
Taste, but with a reverent care;
    Active-patient be.
Too much gladness brings to gloom
Those who on the gods presume.

LEIGH HUNT

From THE POPPY

The sleep-flower sways in the wheat its head,
Heavy with dreams, as that with bread:
The goodly grain and the sun-flushed sleeper
The reaper reaps, and Time the reaper.

I hang mid men my needless head,
And my fruit is dreams, as theirs is bread:
The goodly men and the sun-hazed sleeper
Time shall reap, but after the reaper
The world shall glean of me, me the sleeper.

FRANCIS THOMPSON

From SUMMER'S LAST WILL AND TESTAMENT

Fayre Summer droops, droope men and beasts therefore:
So fayre a summer looke for never more.
All good things vanish lesse then in a day,
Peace, plenty, pleasure sodainely decay.
    Goe not yet away bright soule of the sad yeare,
    The earth is hell when thou leav'st to appeare.

What, shall those flowres, that deckt thy garland erst,
Upon thy grave be wastfully disperst?
O trees, consume your sap in sorrowes sourse.
Streames, turne to teares your tributary course.
    Go not yet hence, bright soule of the sad yeare.
    The earth is hell, when thou leav'st to appeare.

THOMAS NASH

Autumn

AUTUMN

The Autumn skies are flushed with gold,
And fair and bright the rivers run;
These are but streams of winter cold,
And painted mists that quench the sun.

In secret boughs no sweet birds sing,
In secret boughs no bird can shroud;
These are but leaves that take to wing,
And wintry winds that pipe so loud.

'Tis not trees' shade, but cloudy glooms
That on the cheerless valleys fall,
The flowers are in their grassy tombs,
And tears of dew are on them all.

THOMAS HOOD

NUTTING

                  . . . It seems a day
(I speak of one from many singled out)
One of those heavenly days which cannot die;
When, in the eagerness of boyish hope,
I left our Cottage-threshold, sallying forth
With a huge wallet o'er my shoulders slung,
A nutting-crook in hand, and turned my steps
Toward the distant woods, a Figure quaint,
Tricked out in proud disguise of cast-off weeds
Which for that service had been husbanded,
By exhortation of my frugal Dame;
Motley accoutrement, of power to smile
At thorns, and brakes, and brambles, – and, in truth,
More ragged than need was! Among the woods,
And o'er the pathless rocks, I forced my way
Until, at length, I came to one dear nook
Unvisited, where not a broken bough
Drooped with its withered leaves, ungracious sign
Of devastation, but the hazels rose
Tall and erect, with milk-white clusters hung,
A virgin scene! – A little while I stood,
Breathing with such suppression of the heart
As joy delights in; and, with wise restraint
Voluptuous, fearless of a rival, eyed
The banquet, – or beneath the trees I sate
Among the flowers, and with the flowers I played;
A temper known to those, who, after long
And weary expectation, have been blest
With sudden happiness beyond all hope. –
Perhaps it was a bower beneath whose leaves
The violets of five seasons re-appear
And fade, unseen by any human eye;
Where fairy water-breaks do murmur on
For ever, – and I saw the sparkling foam,
And with my cheek on one of those green stones

That, fleeced with moss, beneath the shady trees,
Lay round me, scattered like a flock of sheep,
I heard the murmur and the murmuring sound,
In that sweet mood when pleasure loves to pay
Tribute to ease; and, of its joy secure,
The heart luxuriates with indifferent things,
Wasting its kindliness on stocks and stones,
And on the vacant air. Then up I rose,
And dragged to earth both branch and bough, with crash
And merciless ravage; and the shady nook
Of hazels, and the green and mossy bower,
Deformed and sullied, patiently gave up
Their quiet being: and, unless I now
Confound my present feelings with the past,
Even then, when from the bower I turned away
Exulting, rich beyond the wealth of kings,
I felt a sense of pain when I beheld
The silent trees and the intruding sky. —
Then, dearest Maiden! move along these shades
In gentleness of heart; with gentle hand
Touch — for there is a spirit in the woods.

WILLIAM WORDSWORTH

HIGH WIND

The clouds before him rushed, as they
Were racing home to end the day;
The flying hair of the beeches flew
Out of the East as he went through.

Only the hills unshaken stood.
The lake was tossed into a flood;
She flung her curling wavelets hoar
In wrath on the distracted shore.

Which of the elements hath sinned?
What hath angered thee, O wind?
Thou in all the earth dost see
Nought but it enrageth thee!

MARY COLERIDGE

WIND ON THE LYRE

That was the chirp of Ariel
You heard, as overhead it flew,
The farther going more to dwell,
And wing our green to wed our blue;
But whether note of joy or knell,
Not his own Father-singer knew;
Nor yet can any mortal tell,
Save only how it shivers through;
The breast of us a sounded shell,
The blood of us a lighted dew.

GEORGE MEREDITH

From THE GRASSHOPPER

Oh thou that swing'st upon the waving eare
  Of some well-filled Oaten Beard,
Drunke ev'ry night with a Delicious teare
  Dropt thee from Heav'n, where now th'art reard.

The Joyes of Earth and Ayre are thine intire,
  That with thy feet and wings dost hop and flye;
And when thy Poppy workes thou dost retire
  To thy Carv'd Acorn-bed to lye.

Up with the Day, the Sun thou welcomst then,
  Sportst in the guilt-plats of his Beames,
And all these merry dayes mak'st merry men,
  Thy selfe, and Melancholy streames.

But ah the Sickle! Golden Eares are Cropt;
  Ceres and *Bacchus* bid goodnight;
Sharpe frosty fingers all your Flowr's have topt,
  And what scithes spar'd, Winds shave off quite.

Poore verdant foole! and now green Ice! thy Joys
  Large and as lasting as thy Porch of Grasse,
Bid us lay in 'gainst Winter, Raine, and poize
  Their flouds, with an o'erflowing glasse . . .

RICHARD LOVELACE

THE STUDY OF A SPIDER

From holy flower to holy flower
Thou weavest thine unhallowed bower.
The harmless dewdrops, beaded thin,
Ripple along thy ropes of sin.
Thy house a grave, a gulf thy throne
Affright the fairies every one.
Thy winding sheets are grey and fell,
Imprisoning with nets of hell
The lovely births that winnow by,
Winged sisters of the rainbow sky:
Elf-darlings, fluffy, bee-bright things,
And owl-white moths with mealy wings,
And tiny flies, as gauzy thin
As e'er were shut electrum in.
These are thy death spoils, insect ghulo,
With their dear life thy fangs are foul.
Thou felon anchorite of pain
Who sittest in a world of slain.
Hermit, who tunest song unsweet
To heaving wing and writhing feet.
A glutton of creation's sighs,
Miser of many miseries.
Toper, whose lonely feasting chair
Sways in inhospitable air.
The board is bare, the bloated host
Drinks to himself toast after toast.
His lip requires no goblet brink,
But like a weasel must he drink.
The vintage is as old as time
And bright as sunset, pressed and prime.

Ah, venom mouth and shaggy thighs
And paunch grown sleek with sacrifice,
Thy dolphin back and shoulders round
Coarse-hairy, as some goblin hound

Whom a hag rides to sabbath on,
While shuddering stars in fear grow wan.
Thou palace priest of treachery,
Thou type of selfish lechery,
I break the toils around thy head
And from their gibbets take thy dead.

LORD DE TABLEY

THISTLEDOWN

This might have been a place for sleep
But, as from that small hollow there
Hosts of bright thistledown begin
Their dazzling journey through the air,
An idle man can only stare.

They grip their withered edge of stalk
In brief excitement for the wind;
They hold a breathless final talk,
And when their filmy cables part
One almost hears a little cry.

Some cling together while they wait
And droop and gaze and hesitate,
But others leap along the sky,
Or circle round and calmly choose
The gust they know they ought to use.

While some in loving pairs will glide,
Or watch the others as they pass,
Or rest on flowers in the grass,
Or circle through the shining day
Like silver butterflies at play.

Some catch themselves to every mound,
Then lingeringly and slowly move
As if they knew the precious ground
Were opening for their fertile love:
They almost try to dig, they need
So much to plant their thistle-seed.

HAROLD MONRO

From THE SEASONS (AUTUMN)

The Western Sun withdraws the shorten'd Day;
And humid Evening, gliding o'er the Sky,
In her chill Progress, to the Ground condens'd
The Vapours throws. Where creeping Waters ooze,
Where Marshes stagnate, and where Rivers wind,
Cluster the rolling Fogs, and swim along
The dusky-mantled Lawn. Meanwhile the Moon,
Full-orb'd, and breaking thro the scatter'd Clouds,
Shews her broad Visage in the crimson'd East.
Turn'd to the Sun direct, her spotted Disk,
Where Mountains rise, umbrageous Dales descend,
And Caverns deep, as optic Tube descries,
A smaller Earth, gives us his Blaze again,
Void of its Flame, and sheds a softer Day.
Now thro the passing Cloud she seems to stoop,
Now up the pure Cerulean rides sublime.
Wide the pale Deluge floats, and streaming mild
O'er the sky'd Mountain to the shadowy Vale,
While Rocks and Floods reflect the quivering Gleam,
The whole Air whitens with a boundless Tide
Of silver Radiance, trembling round the World.

JAMES THOMSON

ODE TO THE WEST WIND

I

O Wild West Wind, thou breath of Autumn's being,
Thou, from whose unseen presence the leaves dead
Are driven, like ghosts from an enchanter fleeing,

Yellow, and black, and pale, and hectic red,
Pestilence-stricken multitudes: O thou
Who chariotest to their dark wintry bed

The wingèd seeds, where they lie cold and low,
Each like a corpse within its grave, until
Thine azure sister of the Spring shall blow

Her clarion o'er the dreaming earth, and fill
(Driving sweet buds like flocks to feed in air)
With living hues and odours plain and hill:

Wild Spirit, which art moving everywhere;
Destroyer and preserver; hear, oh, hear!

II

Thou on whose stream, mid the steep sky's commotion,
Loose clouds like earth's decaying leaves are shed,
Shook from the tangled boughs of Heaven and Ocean,

Angels of rain and lightning: there are spread
On the blue surface of thine aëry surge,
Like the bright hair uplifted from the head

Of some fierce Maenad, even from the dim verge
Of the horizon to the zenith's height,
The locks of the approaching storm. Thou dirge

Of the dying year, to which this closing night
Will be the dome of a vast sepulchre,
Vaulted with all thy congregated might

Of vapours, from whose solid atmosphere
Black rain, and fire, and hail will burst: oh, hear!

III

Thou who didst waken from his summer dreams
The blue Mediterranean, where he lay,
Lulled by the coil of his crystalline streams,

Beside a pumice isle in Baiae's bay,
And saw in sleep old palaces and towers
Quivering within the wave's intenser day,

All overgrown with azure moss and flowers
So sweet, the sense faints picturing them! Thou
For whose path the Atlantic's level powers

Cleave themselves into chasms, while far below
The sea-blooms and the oozy woods which wear
The sapless foliage of the ocean, know

Thy voice, and suddenly grow gray with fear,
And tremble and despoil themselves: oh, hear!

IV

If I were a dead leaf thou mightest bear;
If I were a swift cloud to fly with thee;
A wave to pant beneath thy power, and share

The impulse of thy strength, only less free
Than thou, O uncontrollable! If even
I were as in my boyhood, and could be

The comrade of thy wanderings over Heaven,
As then, when to outstrip thy skiey speed
Scarce seemed a vision; I would ne'er have striven

As thus with thee in prayer in my sore need.
Oh, lift me as a wave, a leaf, a cloud!
I fall upon the thorns of life! I bleed!

A heavy weight of hours has chained and bowed
One too like thee: tameless, and swift, and proud.

<h2 style="text-align:center">V</h2>

Make me thy lyre, even as the forest is:
What if my leaves are falling like its own!
The tumult of thy mighty harmonies

Will take from both a deep, autumnal tone,
Sweet though in sadness. Be thou, Spirit fierce,
My spirit! Be thou me, impetuous one!

Drive my dead thoughts over the universe
Like withered leaves to quicken a new birth!
And, by the incantation of this verse,

Scatter, as from an unextinguished hearth
Ashes and sparks, my words among mankind!
Be through my lips to unawakened earth

The trumpet of a prophecy! O Wind
If Winter comes, can Spring be far behind?

PERCY BYSSHE SHELLEY

TO AUTUMN

Season of mists and mellow fruitfulness,
  Close bosom-friend of the maturing sun;
Conspiring with him how to load and bless
  With fruit the vines that round the thatch-eves run;
To bend with apples the moss'd cottage-trees,
  And fill all fruit with ripeness to the core;
    To swell the gourd, and plump the hazel shells
  With a sweet kernel; to set budding more,
And still more, later flowers for the bees,
Until they think warm days will never cease,
    For Summer has o'er-brimm'd their clammy cells.

Who hath not seen thee oft amid thy store?
  Sometimes whoever seeks abroad may find
Thee sitting careless on a granary floor,
  Thy hair soft-lifted by the winnowing wind;
Or on a half-reap'd furrow sound asleep,
  Drows'd with the fume of poppies, while thy hook
    Spares the next swath and all its twined flowers:
And sometimes like a gleaner thou dost keep
  Steady thy laden head across a brook;
  Or by a cyder-press, with patient look,
    Thou watchest the last oozings hours by hours.

Where are the songs of Spring? Ay, where are they?
  Think not of them, thou hast thy music too, —
While barred clouds bloom the soft-dying day,
  And touch the stubble-plains with rosy hue;
Then in a wailful choir the small gnats mourn
  Among the river sallows, borne aloft
    Or sinking as the light wind lives or dies;
And full-grown lambs loud bleat from hilly bourn;
  Hedge-crickets sing; and now with treble soft
  The red-breast whistles from a garden-croft;
    And gathering swallows twitter in the skies.

JOHN KEATS

ODE—AUTUMN

I saw old Autumn in the misty morn
Stand shadowless like Silence, listening
To silence, for no lonely bird would sing
Into his hollow ear from woods forlorn,
Nor lowly hedge nor solitary thorn;
Shaking his languid locks all dewy bright
With tangled gossamer that fell by night,
    Pearling his coronet of golden corn.

Where are the songs of Summer? — With the sun,
Oping the dusky eyelids of the south,
Till shade and silence waken up as one,
And Morning sings with a warm odorous mouth.
Where are the merry birds? — Away, away,
On panting wings through the inclement skies,
    Lest owls should prey
    Undazzled at noon-day,
And tear with horny beak their lustrous eyes.

Where are the blooms of Summer? — In the west,
Blushing their last to the last sunny hours,
When the mild Eve by sudden Night is prest
Like tearful Proserpine, snatch'd from her flow'rs
    To a most gloomy breast.
Where is the pride of Summer, — the green prime, —
The many, many leaves all twinkling? — Three
On the moss'd elm; three on the naked lime
Trembling, — and one upon the old oak tree!
    Where is the Dryad's immortality? —
Gone into mournful cypress and dark yew,
Or wearing the long gloomy Winter through
    In the smooth holly's green eternity.

The squirrel gloats o'er his accomplish'd hoard,
The ants have brimm'd their garners with ripe grain,
 And honey bees have stored
The sweets of summer in their luscious cells;
The swallows all have wing'd across the main;
But here the Autumn melancholy dwells,
 And sighs her tearful spells
Amongst the sunless shadows of the plain.
  Alone, alone,
   Upon a mossy stone,
She sits and reckons up the dead and gone,
With the last leaves for a love-rosary;
Whilst all the wither'd world looks drearily,
Like a dim picture of the drownèd past
In the hush'd mind's mysterious far-away,
Doubtful what ghostly thing will steal the last
Into that distance, grey upon the grey.

O go and sit with her, and be o'ershaded
Under the languid downfall of her hair;
She wears a coronal of flowers faded
Upon her forehead, and a face of care; —
There is enough of wither'd everywhere
To make her bower, — and enough of gloom;
There is enough of sadness to invite,
If only for the rose that died, whose doom
Is Beauty's, — she that with the living bloom
Of conscious cheeks most beautifies the light;
There is enough of sorrowing, and quite
Enough of bitter fruits the earth doth bear, —
Enough of chilly droppings for her bowl;
Enough of fear and shadowy despair,
To frame her cloudy prison for the soul!

THOMAS HOOD

From C I D E R

Whoe'er expect his lab'ring trees should bend
With fruitage, and a kindly harvest yield,
Be this his first concern, to find a track
Impervious to the winds, begirt with hills
That intercept the Hyperborean blasts
Tempestuous, and cold Eurus' nipping force,
Noxious to feeble buds; but to the west
Let him free entrance grant; let Zephirs bland
Administer their tepid genial airs:
Nought fear he from the west, whose gentle warmth
Discloses well the earth's all-teeming womb,
Invigorating tender seeds, whose breath
Nurtures the orange and the citron groves,
Hesperian fruits, and wafts their odours sweet
Wide thro' the air, and distant shores perfumes.
Nor only do the hills exclude the winds,
But when the black'ning clouds in sprinkling show'rs
Distil from the high summits down the rain
Runs trickling; with the fertile moisture cheer'd
The Orchats smile; joyous the farmers see
Their thriving plants, and bless the heav'nly dew . . .

I nor advise nor reprehend the choice
Of Marcleyhill;[1] the Apple no where finds
A kinder mould: yet it is unsafe to trust
Deceitful ground: who knows but that once more
This mount may journey, and his present site
Forsaking to thy neighbour's bounds transfer

---

[1] February the 7th, 1571, at six o'clock in the evening, this hill roused itself
with a roaring noise, and by seven the next morning had moved forty paces; it
kept moving for three days together, carrying with it sheep in their cots, hedgerows and trees, and in its passage overthrew Kinnaston chapel, and turned two
highways near an hundred yards from their former position. The ground thus
moved was about twenty-six acres, which opened itself and carried the earth
before it for four hundred yards space, leaving that which was pasture in the
place of the tillage, and the tillage overspread with pasture. See Speed's
Account of Herefordshire, page 49, and Camden's *Britannia*.

The goodly plants, affording matter strange
For law debates? if therefore thou incline
To deck this rise with fruits of various tastes,
Fail not by frequent vows t' implore success;
Thus piteous Heav'n may fix the wand'ring glebe . . .

Wouldst thou thy vats with gen'rous juice should froth?
Respect thy Orchats: think not that the trees
Spontaneous will produce an wholesome draught.
Let art correct thy breed: from parent bough
A scion meetly sever, after force
A way into the crabstock's closewrought grain
By wedges, and within the living wound
Enclose the foster twig: nor overnice
Refuse with thy own hands around to spread
The binding clay: erelong their diff'ring veins
Unite, and kindly nourishment convey
To the new pupil: now he shoots his arms
With quickest growth; now shake the teeming trunk.
Down rain th'impurpled balls, ambrosial fruit!
Whether the wilding's fibres are contriv'd
To draw th' earth's purest spirit, and resift
Its seculence, which in more porous stocks
Of Cider plants finds passage free, or else
The native verjuice of the crab, deriv'd
Thro' th' infixed graff, a grateful mixture forms
Of tart and sweet; whatever be the cause,
This doubtful progeny, by nicest tastes
Expected, best acceptance finds, and pays
Largest revenues to the Orchat lord.
    Some think the quince and Apple would combine
In happy union; others fitter deem
The sloestem, bearing sylvan plums austere.
Who knows but both may thrive? howe'er, what loss
To try the pow'rs of both, and search how far
Two diff'rent natures may concur to mix
In close embraces, and strange offspring bear?

Thou'lt find that plants will frequent changes try
Undamag'd, and their marriageable arms
Conjoin with others. So Silurian plants
Admit the peach's odoriferous globe,
And pears of sundry forms: at diff'rent times
Adopted plums will alien branches grace,
And men have gather'd from the hawthorn's branch
Large medlars, imitating regal crowns . . .

When swelling buds their od'rous foliage shed,
And gently harden into fruit, the wise
Spare not the little offsprings if they grow
Redundant, but the thronging clusters thin
By kind avulsion, else the starv'ling brood,
Void of sufficient sustenance, will yield
A slender autumn, which the niggard soul
Too late shall weep, and curse his thrifty hand,
That would not timely ease the pond'rous boughs.

It much conduces all the cares to know
Of gard'ning, how to scare nocturnal thieves,
And how the little race of birds, that hop
From spray to spray scooping the costliest fruit
Insatiate, undisturb'd. Priapus' form
Avails but little; rather guard each row
With the false terrours of a breathless kite.
This done the tim'rous flock with swiftest wing
Scud thro' the air; their fancy represents
His mortal talons and his rav'nous beak
Destructive; glad to shun his hostile gripe
They quit their thefts, and unfrequent the fields.
Besides, the filthy swine will oft' invade
Thy firm enclosure, and with delving snout
The rooted forest undermine: forthwith
Halloo thy furious mastiff; bid him vex
The noxious herd, and print upon their ears
A sad memorial of their past offence.

The flagrant Procyon will not fail to bring
Large shoals of slow housebearing snails that creep
O'er the ripe fruitage, paring slimy tracks
In the sleek rinds, and unprest Cider drink.
No art averts this pest; on thee it lies
With morning and with ev'ning hand to rid
The preying reptiles; nor if wise wilt thou
Decline this labour, which itself rewards
With pleasing gain, whilst the warm limbeck draws
Salubrious waters from the nocent brood.
   Myriads of wasps now also clust'ring hang
And drain a spurious honey from thy groves,
Their winter food; tho' oft' repuls'd again
They rally undismay'd: but fraud with ease
Ensnares the noisome swarms: let ev'ry bough
Bear frequent vials, pregnant with the dregs
Of moyle or mum, or treacle's viscous juice;
They by th'alluring odour drawn in haste
Fly to the dulcet cates, and crowding sip
Their palatable bane. Joyful thou'lt see
The clammy surface all o'erstrown with tribes
Of greedy insects, that with fruitless toil
Flap filmy pennons oft' to extricate
Their feet, in liquid shackles bound, till death
Bereave them of their worthless souls. Such doom
Waits luxury and lawless love of gain! . . .

                                    Now prepare
Materials for thy mill, a sturdy post
Cylindrick, to support the grinder's weight
Excessive, and a flexile sallow entrench'd,
Rounding, capacious of the juicy hord.
Nor must thou not be mindful of thy press
Long ere the vintage, but with timely care
Shave the goat's shaggy beard, lest thou too late
In vain shouldst seek a strainer to dispart
The husky terrene dregs from purer must.

Be cautious next a proper steed to find
Whose prime is past; the vig'rous horse disdains
Such servile labours, or if forc'd forgets
His past achievements and victorious palms:
Blind Bayard rather, worn with work and years,
Shall roll th' unwieldy stone; with sober pace
He'll tread the circling path till dewy eve
From early dayspring, pleas'd to find his age
Declining not unuseful to his lord . . .

                    A frugal man I knew,
Rich in one barren acre, which subdu'd
By endless culture with sufficient must
His casks replenish'd yearly: he no more
Desir'd nor wanted, diligent to learn
The various seasons, and by skill repel
Invading pests, successful in his cares
Till the damp Libyan wind, with tempests arm'd
Outrageous, bluster'd horrible amidst
His Cider grove: o'erturn'd by furious blasts
The sightly ranks fall prostrate, and around
Their fruitage scatter'd, from the genial boughs
Stripp'd immature: yet did he not repine
Nor curse his stars, but prudent his fall'n heaps
Collecting cherish'd with the tepid wreaths
Of tedded grass and the sun's mellowing beams
Rivall'd with artful heats, and thence procur'd
A costly liquor, by improving time
Equall'd with what the happiest vintage bears . . .

  Learn now the promise of the coming year
To know, that by no flatt'ring signs abus'd
Thou wisely may'st provide. The various moon
Prophetick and attendant stars explain
Each rising dawn; ere icy crusts surmount
The current stream the heav'nly orbs serene
Twinkle with trembling rays, and Cynthia glows

With light unsully'd: now the fowler, warn'd
By these good omens, with swift early steps
Treads the crimp earth, ranging thro' fields and glades
Offensive to the birds: sulphureous death
Checks their mid flight, and heedless while they strain
Their tuneful throats the tow'ring heavy lead
O'ertakes their speed: they leave their little lives
Above the clouds, precipitant to earth.
　　The woodcocks' early visit and abode
Of long continuance in our temp'rate clime
Foretell a lib'ral harvest. He, of times
Intelligent, the harsh Hyperborean ice
Shuns for our equal winters: when our suns
Cleave the chill'd soil he backward wings his way
To Scandinavian frozen summers, meet
For his numb'd blood. But nothing profits more
Than frequent snows: O may'st thou often see
Thy furrows whiten'd by the woolly rain
Nutritious! secret nitre lurks within
The porous wet, quick'ning the languid glebe.
　　Sometimes thou shalt with fervent vows implore
A mod'rate wind: the Orchat loves to wave
With winter wind before the gems exert
Their feeble heads: the loosen'd roots then drink
Large increment, earnest of happy years.
　　Nor will it nothing profit to observe
The monthly stars, their pow'rful influence
O'er planted fields, what vegetables reign
Under each sign. On our account has Jove
Indulgent to all moons some succulent plant
Allotted, that poor helpless man might slake
His present thirst, and matter find for toil.
Now will the corinths, now the rasps, supply
Delicious draughts; the quinces now, or plums
Or cherries, or the fair Thisbein fruit,
Are press'd to wines: the Britons squeeze the works
Of sed'lous bees, and mixing odorus herbs

Prepare balsamick cups, to wheezing lungs
Medicinal and short-breath'd ancient fires.
    But if thou'rt indefatigably bent
To toil, and omnifarious drinks wouldst brew,
Besides the Orchat ev'ry hedge and bush
Affords assistance; ev'n afflictive birch,
Curs'd by unletter'd idle youth, distils
A limpid current from her wounded bark
Profuse of nursing sap. When solar beams
Parch thirsty human veins the damask'd meads
Unforc'd display ten thousand painted flow'rs
Useful in potables. Thy little sons
Permit to range the pastures; gladly they
Will mow the cowslip posies faintly sweet,
From whence thou artificial wines shalt drain
Of icy taste, that in mid fervours best
Slake craving thirst and mitigate the day . . .

    There are that a compounded fluid drain
From diff'rent mixtures, woodcock, pippin, moyle,
Rough eleot, sweet pearmain: the blended streams
(Each mutually correcting each) create
A pleasurable medley, of what taste
Hardly distinguish'd; as the show'ry arch
With lifted colours gay, or, azure, gules,
Delights and puzzles the beholder's eye
That views the wat'ry braid with thousand shews
Of painture vary'd, yet is unskill'd to tell
Or where one colour rises or one faints . . .

    Soon as thy liquor from the narrow cells
Of close-prest husks is freed thou must refrain
Thy thirsty soul; let none persuade to broach
Thy thick unwholesome undigested cades;
The hoary frosts and northern blasts take care
Thy muddy bev'rage to serene; and drive
Precipitant the baser ropy lees.

And now thy wine is transpicuous, purg'd from all
Its earthy gross, yet let it feed a while
On the fat refuse, lest too soon disjoin'd
From sprightly it to sharp or vapid change.
When to convenient vigour it attains
Suffice it to provide a brazen tube
Inflext; selftaught and voluntary flies
The defecated liquor, thro' the vent
Ascending, then by downward track convey'd
Spouts into subject vessels lovely clear;
As when a noontide sun with summer beams
Darts thro' a cloud her wat'ry skirts are edg'd
With lucid amber or undrossy gold,
So and so richly the purg'd liquid shines . . .

            The Muses still require
Humid regalement, nor will aught avail
Imploring Phœbus with unmoisten'd lips.
Thus to the gen'rous bottle all incline,
By parching thirst allur'd. With vehement suns
When dusty summer bakes the crumbling clods
How pleasant is it beneath the twisted arch
Of a retreating bow'r in mid-day's reign
To ply the sweet carouse, remote from noise,
Secur'd of fev'rish heats! When th' aged year
Inclines and Boreas' spirit blusters frore
Beware th' inclement heav'ns; now let thy hearth
Crackle with juiceless boughs; thy ling'ring blood
Now instigate with th' Apple's pow'rful streams.

JOHN PHILIPS

From THE LAND

... And gardener, let your spud be sharp to ridge
The loam from spiny hedge to hedge;
Labour within your garden square
Till back be broke and light grow rare,
But never heed the sinews' pain
If you may snatch before the rain
Crisp days when clods will turn up rough;
Gentleman robin brown as snuff
With spindle legs and bright round eye
Shall be your autumn company.
Trench deep; dig in the rotting weeds;
Slash down the thistle's greybeard seeds;
Then make the frost your servant; make
His million fingers pry and break
The clods by glittering midnight stealth
Into the necessary tilth.
Then may you shoulder spade and hoe,
And heavy-booted homeward go,
For no new flowers shall be born
Save hellebore on Christmas morn,
And bare gold jasmine on the wall,
And violets, and soon the small
Blue netted iris, like a cry
Startling the sloth of February.

VICTORIA SACKVILLE-WEST

THE DYING SWAN

The plain was grassy, wild and bare,
Wide, wild, and open to the air,
Which had built up everywhere
  An under-roof of doleful gray.
With an inner voice the river ran,
Adown it floated a dying swan,
    And loudly did lament.
  It was the middle of the day.
Ever the weary wind went on,
    And took the reed-tops as it went.

Some blue peaks in the distance rose,
And white against the cold-white sky,
Shone out their crowning snows.
  One willow over the river wept,
And shook the wave as the wind did sigh;
Above in the wind was the swallow,
    Chasing itself at its own wild will,
    And far thro' the marish green and still
    The tangled water-courses slept,
Shot over with purple, and green, and yellow.

The wild swan's death-hymn took the soul
Of that waste place with joy
Hidden in sorrow: at first to the ear
The warble was low, and full and clear;
And floating about the under-sky,
Prevailing in weakness, the coronach stole
Sometimes afar, and sometimes anear;
But anon her awful jubilant voice,
With a music strange and manifold,
Flow'd forth on a carol free and bold;
As when a mighty people rejoice
With shawms, and with cymbals, and harps of gold,
And the tumult of their acclaim is roll'd

Thro' the open gates of the city afar,
To the shepherd who watcheth the evening star.
And the creeping mosses and clambering weeds,
And the willow-branches hoar and dank,
And the wavy swell of the soughing reeds,
And the wave-worn horns of the echoing bank,
And the silvery marish-flowers that throng
The desolate creeks and pools among,
Were flooded over with eddying song.

LORD TENNYSON

THE DYING SWAN

O silver-throated Swan
Struck, struck! a golden dart
Clean through thy breast has gone
Home to thy heart.
Thrill, thrill, O silver throat!
O silver trumpet, pour
Love for defiance back
On him who smote!
And brim, brim o'er
With love; and ruby-dye thy track
Down thy last living reach
Of river, sail the golden light . . .
Enter the sun's heart . . . even teach,
O wondrous-gifted Pain, teach thou
The god to love, let him learn how.

T. STURGE MOORE

SEED-TIME

Flowers of the willow-herb are wool;
Flowers of the briar berries red;
Speeding their seed as the breeze may rule,
Flowers of the thistle loosen the thread.
Flowers of the clematis drip in beard,
Slack from the fir-tree youngly climbed;
Chaplets in air, flies foliage seared;
Heeled upon earth, lie clusters rimed.

Where were skies of the mantle stained
Orange and scarlet, a coat of frieze
Travels from North till day has waned,
Tattered, soaked in the ditch's dyes;
Tumbles the rook under gray or slate;
Else enfolding us, damps to the bone;
Narrows the world to my neighbour's gate;
Paints me Life as a wheezy crone.

Now seems none but the spider lord;
Star in circle his web waits prey,
Silvering bush-mounds, blue brushing sward;
Slow runs the hour, swift flits the ray.
Now to his thread-shroud is he nigh,
Nigh to the tangle where wings are sealed,
He who frolicked the jewelled fly;
All is adroop on the down and the weald.

Mists more lone for the sheep-bell enwrap
Nights that tardily let slip a morn
Paler than moons, and on noontide's lap
Flame dies cold, like the rose late born.
Rose born late, born withered in bud! —
I, even I, for a zenith of sun
Cry, to fulfil me, nourish my blood:
O for a day of the long light, one!

Master the blood, nor read by chills,
Earth admonishes: Hast thou ploughed,
Sown, reaped, harvested grain for the mills,
Thou hast the light over shadow of cloud.
Steadily eyeing, before that wail
Animal-infant, thy mind began,
Momently nearer me: should sight fail,
Plod in the track of the husbandman.

Verily now is our season of seed,
Now in our Autumn; and Earth discerns
Them that have served her in them that can read,
Glassing, where under the surface she burns,
Quick at her wheel, while the fuel, decay,
Brightens the fire of renewal: and we?
Death is the word of a bovine day,
Know you the breast of the springing To-be.

GEORGE MEREDITH

INVERSNAID

This darksome burn, horseback brown,
His rollrock highroad roaring down,
In coop and in comb the fleece of his foam
Flutes, and low to the lake falls home.

A windpuff-bonnet of fawn-froth
Turns and twindles over the broth
Of a pool so pitchblack, fell-frowning,
It rounds and rounds Despair to drowning.

Degged with dew, dappled with dew
Are the groins of the braes that the brook treads through,
Wiry heathpacks, flitches of fern,
And the beadbonny ash that sits over the burn.

What would the world be, once bereft
Of wet and of wildness? Let them be left,
O let them be left, wildness and wet;
Long live the weeds and the wilderness yet.

GERARD MANLEY HOPKINS

SONG

The feathers of the willow
Are half of them grown yellow
  Above the swelling stream;
And ragged are the bushes,
And rusty now the rushes,
  And wild the clouded gleam.

The thistle now is older,
His stalk begins to moulder,
  His head is white as snow;
The branches all are barer,
The linnet's song is rarer,
  The robin pipeth now.

R. W. DIXON

AUTUMN

Syren of sullen moods and fading hues,
Yet haply not incapable of joy,
   Sweet Autumn! I thee hail
   With welcome all unfeigned;

And oft as morning from her lattice peeps
To beckon up the sun, I seek with thee
   To drink the dewy breath
   Of fields left fragrant then,

In solitudes, where no frequented paths
But what thy own foot makes betray thy home,
   Stealing obtrusive there
   To meditate thy end:

By overshadowed ponds, in woody nooks,
With ramping sallows lined, and crowding sedge,
   Which woo the winds to play,
   And with them dance for joy;

And meadow pools, torn wide by lawless floods,
Where water-lilies spread their oily leaves,
   On which, as wont, the fly
   Oft battens in the sun;

Where leans the mossy willow half way oer,
On which the shepherd crawls astride to throw
   His angle, clear of weeds
   That crowd the water's brim;

Or crispy hills, and hollows scant of sward,
Where step by step the patient lonely boy
   Hath cut rude flights of stairs
   To climb their steepy sides;

Then track along their feet, grown hoarse with noise,
The crawling brook, that ekes its weary speed,
    And struggles through the weeds
    With faint and sullen brawl.

These haunts I long have favoured, more as now
With thee thus wandering, moralizing on,
    Stealing glad thoughts from grief,
    And happy, though I sigh.

Sweet Vision, with the wild dishevelled hair,
And raiment shadowy of each wind's embrace,
    Fain would I win thy harp
    To one accordant theme;

Now not inaptly craved, communing thus,
Beneath the curdled arms of this stunt oak,
    While pillowed on the grass,
    We fondly ruminate

Oer the disordered scenes of woods and fields,
Ploughed lands, thin travelled with half-hungry sheep,
    Pastures tracked deep with cows,
    Where small birds seek for seed:

Marking the cow-boy that so merry trills
His frequent, unpremeditated song,
    Wooing the winds to pause,
    Till echo brawls again;

As on with plashy step, and clouted shoon,
He roves, half indolent and self-employed,
    To rob the little birds
    Of hips and pendent haws,

And sloes, dim covered as with dewy veils,
And rambling bramble-berries, pulp and sweet,
    Arching their prickly trails
    Half oer the narrow lane:

276

Noting the hedger front with stubborn face
The dank blea wind, that whistles thinly by
  His leathern garb, thorn proof,
  And cheek red hot with toil.

While oer the pleachy lands of mellow brown,
The mower's stubbling scythe clogs to his foot
  The ever eking whisp,
  With sharp and sudden jerk,

Till into formal rows the russet shocks
Crowd the blank field to thatch time-weathered barns,
  And hovels rude repair,
  Stript by disturbing winds.

See! from the rustling scythe the haunted hare
Scampers circuitous, with startled ears
  Prickt up, then squat, as bye
  She brushes to the woods,

Where reeded grass, breast-high and undisturbed,
Forms pleasant clumps, through which the soothing winds
  Soften her rigid fears,
  And lull to calm repose.

Wild sorceress! me thy restless mood delights,
More than the stir of summer's crowded scenes,
  Where, jostled in the din,
  Joy palled my ear with song;

Heart-sickening for the silence that is thine,
Not broken inharmoniously, as now
  That lone and vagrant bee
  Booms faint with weary chime.

Now filtering winds thin winnow through the woods
In tremulous noise, that bids, at every breath,
  Some sickly cankered leaf
  Let go its hold, and die.

And now the bickering storm, with sudden start,
In flirting fits of anger carps aloud,
    Thee urging to thine end,
    Sore wept by troubled skies.

And yet, sublime in grief, thy thoughts delight
To show me visions of most gorgeous dyes,
    Haply forgetting now
    They but prepare thy shroud;

Thy pencil dashing its excess of shades,
Improvident of waste, till every bough
    Burns with thy mellow touch
    Disorderly divine.

Soon must I view thee as a pleasant dream
Droop faintly, and so sicken for thine end,
    As sad the winds sink low
    In dirges for their queen;

While in the moment of their weary pause,
To cheer thy bankrupt pomp, the willing lark
    Starts from his shielding clod,
    Snatching sweet scraps of song.

Thy life is waning now, and silence tries
To mourn, but meets no sympathy in sounds,
    As stooping low she bends,
    Forming with leaves thy grave;

To sleep inglorious there mid tangled woods,
Till parch-lipped summer pines in drought away,
    Then from thine ivied trance
    Awake to glories new.

JOHN CLARE

TO AUTUMN

O Autumn, laden with fruit, and stained
With the blood of the grape, pass not, but sit
Beneath my shady roof; there thou may'st rest,
And tune thy jolly voice to my fresh pipe,
And all the daughters of the year shall dance!
Sing now the lusty song of fruits and flowers.

'The narrow bud opens her beauties to
The sun, and love runs in her thrilling veins;
Blossoms hang round the brows of morning, and
Flourish down the bright cheek of modest eve,
Till clust'ring Summer breaks forth into singing,
And feather'd clouds strew flowers round her head.

'The spirits of the air live on the smells
Of fruit; and joy, with pinions light, roves round
The gardens, or sits singing in the trees.'
Thus sang the jolly Autumn as he sat;
Then rose, girded himself, and o'er the bleak
Hills fled from our sight; but left his golden load.

WILLIAM BLAKE

From A JOURNEY INTO THE PEAK

To SIR ASTON COCKAIN

Sir, Coming home into this *Frozen Clime*,
Grown cold, and almost senceless, as my Rhyme,
I found that Winters bold impetuous rage
Prevented *Time*, and antidated *Age*,
For in my Veins, did nought but Crystal dwell,
Each Hair was frozen to an Icicle.
My flesh was Marble, so, that as I went,
I did appear a walking *Monument*:
'T might have been judg'd, rather than Marble, Flint,
Had there been any spark of fire in't.
    My Mistress looking back, to bid *good Night*,
    Was Metamorphos'd like the *Sodomite*.

Like *Sinon's* horse, our horses were become,
And since they could not go, they slided home;
The hills were hard, to such a quality,
So beyond *Reason* in *Philosophie*,
If Pegasus had kick'd at one of those,
Homer's Odysseus had been writ in Prose.

    These are strange stories, Sir, to you, who sweat
Under the warm *Sun's* comfortable heat;
Whose happy Seat of *Pooley* far out-vies
The fabled Pleasures of blest *Paradise*:
Whose *Canaan* fills your House with Wine and Oyl,
Till't crack with burdens of a fruitful Soil:
Which House, if it were plac'd above the *Sphere*
Would be a Palace fit for *Jupiter*.

CHARLES COTTON

Evening

SUNSET (FRAGMENT)

It will not shine again,
Its sad course is done;
I have seen the last ray wane
Of the cold, bright sun.

None but me beheld him dying,
Parting with the parting day;
Wind of evening, sadly sighing,
Bore his soul from earth away.

Coldly, bleakly, dreamily
Evening died on Elbe's shore;
Winds were in the cloudy sky,
Sighing, mourning ever more.

EMILY BRONTË

EVENING QUATRAINS

I

The Day's grown old, the fainting Sun
Has but a little way to run,
And yet his Steeds, with all his skill.
Scarce lug the Chariot down the Hill.

II

With Labour spent, and Thirst opprest,
Whilst they strain hard to gain the West,
From Fetlocks hot drops melted light,
Which turn to Meteors in the Night.

III

The Shadows now so long do grow,
That Brambles like tall Cedars show,
Mole-hills seem Mountains, and the Ant
Appears a monstrous Elephant.

IV

A very little little Flock
Shades thrice the ground that it would stock;
Whilst the small Stripling following them,
Appears a mighty *Polypheme*.

V

These being brought into the Fold,
And by the thrifty Master told,
He thinks his Wages are well paid,
Since none are either lost, or stray'd.

VI

Now lowing Herds are each-where heard,
Chains rattle in the Villain's Yard,[1]
The Cart's on Tayl set down to rest,
Bearing on high the Cuckold's Crest.

[1] Farmyard.

VII

The hedge is stript, the Clothes brought in,
Nought's left without should be within,
The Bees are hiv'd, and hum their Charm,
Whilst every Houəs does seem a Swarm.

VIII

The Cock now to the Roost is prest;
For he must call up all the rest;
The Sow's fast pegg'd within the Sty,
To still her squeaking Progeny.

IX

Each one has had his Supping Mess,
The Cheese is put into the Press,
The Pans and Bowls clean scalded all,
Rear'd up against the Milk-house Wall.

X

And now on Benches all are sat
In the cool Air to sit and chat,
Till *Phœbus*, dipping in the West,
Shall lead the World the way to Rest.

CHARLES COTTON

ODE TO EVENING

If aught of oaten stop, or pastoral song,
May hope, chaste Eve, to soothe thy modest ear,
    Like thy own solemn springs,
    Thy springs and dying gales;

O nymph reserved, while now the bright-hair'd sun
Sits in yon western tent, whose cloudy skirts,
    With brede etherial wove,
    O'er hang his wavy bed:

Now air is hush'd, save where the weak-eyed bat
With short shrill shriek flits by on leathern wing,
    Or where the beetle winds
    His small but sullen horn,

As oft he rises, 'midst the twilight path
Against the pilgrim borne in heedless hum:
    Now teach me, maid composed,
    To breathe some soften'd strain,

Whose numbers, stealing through thy darkening vale,
May not unseemly with its stillness suit,
    As, musing slow, I hail
    Thy genial loved return!

For when thy folding-star arising shows
His paly circlet, at his warning lamp
    The fragrant hours, and elves
    Who slept in buds the day,

And many a nymph who wreathes her brows with sedge,
And sheds the freshening dew, and, lovelier still,
    The pensive pleasures sweet,
    Prepare thy shadowy car:

Then lead, calm votaress, where some sheety lake
Cheers the lone heath, or some time-hallow'd pile,
      Or upland fallows grey
      Reflect its last cool gleam.

Or if chill blustering winds, or driving rain,
Prevent my willing feet, be mine the hut
      That from the mountain's side
      Views wilds and swelling floods,

And hamlets brown, and dim-discover'd spires,
And hears their simple bell, and marks o'er all
      Thy dewy fingers draw
      The gradual dusky veil.

While Spring shall pour his show'rs, as oft he wont,
And bathe thy breathing tresses, meekest Eve!
      While Summer loves to sport
      Beneath thy lingering light;

While sallow Autumn fills thy lap with leaves,
Or Winter, yelling through the troublous air,
      Affrights thy shrinking train,
      And rudely rends thy robes:

So long, regardful of thy quiet rule,
Shall Fancy, Friendship, Science, rose-lipp'd Health
      Thy gentlest influence own,
      And hymn thy favourite name!

WILLIAM COLLINS

IT IS A BEAUTEOUS EVENING, CALM AND FREE

It is a beauteous evening, calm and free,
The holy time is quiet as a Nun
Breathless with adoration; the broad sun
Is sinking down in its tranquillity;
The gentleness of heaven broods o'er the Sea:
Listen! the mighty Being is awake,
And doth with his eternal motion make
A sound like thunder – everlastingly.
Dear Child! dear Girl! that walkest with me here,
If thou appear untouched by solemn thought,
Thy nature is not therefore less divine:
Thou liest in Abraham's bosom all the year;
And worship'st at the Temple's inner shrine,
God being with thee when we know it not.

WILLIAM WORDSWORTH

ON WESTWELL DOWNES

When Westwell Downes I gan to tread,
Where cleanely wynds the greene did sweepe,
Methought a landskipp there was spread,
Here a bush and there a sheepe:
    The pleated wrinkles of the face
    Of wave-swolne earth did lend such grace,
    As shadowings in Imag'ry
    Which both deceive and please the eye.

The sheep sometymes did tread the maze
By often wynding in and in,
And sometymes round about they trace
Which milkmayds call a Fairie ring:
    Such semicircles have they runne,
    Such lynes acrosse so trymly spunne
    That sheppeards learne whenere they please
    A new Geometry with ease.

The slender food upon the downe
Is allwayes even, allwayes bare,
Which neither spring nor winter's frowne
Can ought improve or ought impayre:
    Such is the barren Eunuches chynne,
    Which thus doth evermore begynne
    With tender downe to be orecast
    Which never comes to haire at last.

Here and there twoe hilly crests
Amiddst them hugg a pleasant greene,
And these are like two swelling breasts
That close a tender fall betweene.
    Here would I sleepe, or read, or pray
    From early morne till flight of day:
    But harke! a sheepe-bell calls mee upp,
    Like Oxford colledge bells, to supp.

WILLIAM STRODE

T

THE BUZZARDS

When evening came and the warm glow grew deeper
And every tree that bordered the green meadows
And in the yellow cornfields every reaper
And every corn-shock stood above their shadows
Flung eastward from their feet in longer measure,
Serenely far there swam in the sunny height
A buzzard and his mate who took their pleasure
Swirling and poising idly in golden light.
On great pied motionless moth-wings borne along.
   So effortless and so strong,
Cutting each other's paths, together they glided,
Then wheeled asunder till they soared divided
Two valleys' width (as though it were delight
To part like this, being sure they could unite
So swiftly in their empty, free dominion),
Curved headlong downward, towered up the sunny steep,
Then, with a sudden lift of the one great pinion,
Swung proudly to curve and from its height
Took half a mile of sunlight in one long sweep.
And we, so small on the swift immense hillside,
Stood tranced, until our souls arose uplifted
   On those far-sweeping, wide,
Strong curves of flight, – swayed up and hugely drifted,
Were washed, made strong and beautiful in the tide
Of sun-bathed air. But far beneath, beholden
Through shining deeps of air, the fields were golden
And rosy burned the heather where cornfields ended.
And still those buzzards wheeled, while light withdrew
Out of the vales and to surging slopes ascended,
Till the loftiest-flaming summit died to blue.

MARTIN ARMSTRONG

MARGARITAE SORORI

A late lark twitters from the quiet skies;
And from the west,
Where the sun, his day's work ended,
Lingers as in content,
There falls on the old grey city
An influence luminous and serene,
A shining peace.

The smoke ascends
In a rosy-and-golden haze. The spires
Shine, and are changed. In the valley
Shadows rise. The lark sings on. The sun,
Closing his benediction,
Sinks, and the darkening air
Thrills with a sense of the triumphing night —
Night with her train of stars
And her great gift of sleep.

So be my passing!
My task accomplished and the long day done,
My wages taken, and in my heart
Some late lark singing,
Let me be gathered to the quiet west,
The sundown splendid and serene,
Death.

W. E. HENLEY

A SUMMER'S EVENING

Clere had the day bin from the dawne,
  All chequer'd was the Skye,
Thin Clouds, like Scarfs of Cobweb Lawne,
  Vayl'd Heaven's most glorious eye.

The Winde had no more strength then this,
  That leisurely it blew,
To make one leafe the next to kisse
  That closly by it grew.

The Rils that on the Pebbles playd
  Might now be heard at will;
This world they onely Musick made,
  Else everything was still.

The Flowers like brave imbroydered Gerles,
  Lookt as they most desired
To see whose head with orient Pearles
  Most curiously was tyred;

And to itself the subtil Ayre
  Such soverainty assumes,
That it receiv'd too large a share
  From Nature's rich perfumes.

MICHAEL DRAYTON

DAYS TOO SHORT

When Primroses are out in Spring,
 And small, blue violets come between;
 When merry birds sing on boughs green,
And rills, as soon as born, must sing;

When butterflies will make side-leaps,
 As though escaped from Nature's hand
 Ere perfect quite; and bees will stand
Upon their heads in fragrant deeps;

When small clouds are so silvery white
 Each seems a broken rimmèd moon —
 When such things are, this world too soon,
For me, doth wear the veil of Night.

W. H. DAVIES

TO DAISIES, NOT TO SHUT SO SOONE

Shut not so soon; the dull-ey'd night
  Has not as yet begunne
To make a seizure on the light,
  Or to seale up the Sun.

No Marigolds yet closèd are;
  No shadowes great appeare;
Nor doth the early Shepheards Starre
  Shine like a spangle here.

Stay but till my *Julia* close
  Her life-begetting eye;
And let the whole world then dispose
  It selfe to live or dye.

ROBERT HERRICK

SPEAK OF THE NORTH

Speak of the North! A lonely moor
Silent and dark and trackless swells,
The waves of some wild streamlet pour
Hurriedly through its ferny dells.

Profoundly still the twilight air,
Lifeless the landscape; so we deem
Till like a phantom gliding near
A stag bends down to drink the stream.

And far away a mountain zone,
A cold, white waste of snow-drifts lies,
And one star, large and soft and lone,
Silently lights the unclouded skies.

CHARLOTTE BRONTË

From ODE TO THE SETTING SUN

THE PRELUDE

The wailful sweetness of the violin[1]
  Floats down the hushèd waters of the wind,
The heart-strings of the throbbing harp begin
  To long in aching music. Spirit-pined,

In wafts that poignant sweetness drifts, until
  The wounded soul ooze sadness. The red sun,
A bubble of fire, drops slowly toward the hill,
  While one bird prattles that the day is done.

O setting Sun, that as in reverent days
  Sinkest in music to thy smoothèd sleep,
Discrowned of homage, though yet crowned with rays,
  Hymned not at harvest more, though reapers reap:

For thee this music wakes not. O deceived,
  If thou hear in these thoughtless harmonies
A pious phantom of adorings reaved,
  And echo of fair ancient flatteries!

Yet, in this field where the Cross planted reigns,
  I know not what strange passion bows my head
To thee, whose great command upon my veins
  Proves thee a god for me not dead, not dead!

For worship it is too incredulous,
  For doubt – oh, too believing-passionate!
What wild divinity makes my heart thus
  A fount of most baptismal tears? – Thy straight

Long beam lies steady on the Cross. Ah me!
  What secret would thy radiant finger show?
Of thy bright mastership is this the key?
  Is *this* thy secret, then? And is it woe?

[1] From itinerant musicians, near a monastery-field.

Fling from thine ear the burning curls, and hark
    A song thou hast not heard in Northern day;
For Rome too daring, and for Greece too dark,
    Sweet with wild wings that pass, that pass away!

FRANCIS THOMPSON

STEPPING WESTWARD

While my Fellow-Traveller and I were walking by the side
of Loch Katrine, one fine evening after sunset, in our road to
a Hut where in the course of our Tour we had been hospitably
entertained some weeks before, we met, in one of the loneliest
parts of that solitary region, two well-dressed Women, one
of whom said to us, by way of greeting, 'What, you are
stepping westward?'

'What, you are stepping westward?' —*'Yea.'*
— 'Twould be a *wildish* destiny,
If we, who thus together roam
In a strange land, and far from home,
Were in this place the guests of Chance:
Yet who would stop, or fear to advance,
Though home or shelter he had none,
With such a Sky to lead him on?

The dewy ground was dark and cold;
Behind, all gloomy to behold;
And stepping westward seemed to be
A kind of *heavenly* destiny:
I liked the greeting; 'twas a sound
Of something without place or bound;
And seemed to give me spiritual right
To travel through that region bright.

The voice was soft, and she who spake
Was walking by her native Lake:
The salutation had to me
The very sound of courtesy:
Its power was felt; and while my eye
Was fixed upon the glowing sky,
The echo of the voice enwrought
A human sweetness with the thought
Of travelling through the world that lay
Before me in my endless way.

WILLIAM WORDSWORTH

IN ROMNEY MARSH

As I went down to Dymchurch Wall,
　I heard the South sing o'er the land;
I saw the yellow sunlight fall
　On knolls where Norman churches stand.

And ringing shrilly, taut and lithe,
　Within the wind a core of sound,
The wire from Romney town to Hythe
　Alone its airy journey wound.

A veil of purple vapour flowed
　And trailed its fringe along the Straits;
The upper air like sapphire glowed;
　And roses filled Heaven's central gates.

Masts in the offing wagged their tops;
　The swinging waves pealed on the shore;
The saffron beach, all diamond drops
　And beads of surge, prolonged the roar.

As I came up from Dymchurch Wall,
　I saw above the Down's low crest
The crimson brands of sunset fall,
　Flicker and fade from out the west.

Night sank: like flakes of silver fire
　The stars in one great shower came down;
Shrill blew the wind; and shrill the wire
　Rang out from Hythe to Romney town.

The darkly shining salt sea drops
　Streamed as the waves clashed on the shore;
The beach, with all its organ stops
　Pealing again, prolonged the roar.

JOHN DAVIDSON

THE EVENING STAR

See how her body pants and glows,
    See how she shakes her silver wings!
Ten thousand stars, and more, are mute,
    And she, and she alone, that sings.

Ten thousand stars, and more, are mute,
    All listening in the quiet sky,
While that bright star sings wildly there,
    And happy they hear more than I.

Bring me my strange invention now,
    That I may sit at home in ease
And have fresh music brought by air
    From towns beyond the curly seas.

In vain, in vain; the power to hear
    The music of those heavenly spheres
Is but a wild, fantastic dream –
    But who can read the unborn years?

W. H. DAVIES

TO THE EVENING STAR

Thou fair-hair'd angel of the evening,
Now, whilst the sun rests on the mountains, light
Thy bright torch of love; thy radiant crown
Put on, and smile upon our evening bed!
Smile on our loves, and while thou drawest the
Blue curtains of the sky, scatter thy silver dew
On every flower that shuts its sweet eyes
In timely sleep. Let thy west wind sleep on
The lake; speak silence with thy glimmering eyes,
And wash the dusk with silver. Soon, full soon,
Dost thou withdraw; then the wolf rages wild,
And the lion glares thro' the dun forest:
The fleeces of our flocks are cover'd with
Thy sacred dew; protect them with thine influence.

WILLIAM BLAKE

THE SHOWER

Waters above! eternal springs!
The dew that silvers the Dove's wings!
Oh welcom, welcom, to the sad;
Give dry dust drink, drink that makes glad.
Many fair ev'nings, many flow'rs
Sweetened with rich and gentle showers
Have I enjoyed, and down have run
Many a fine and shining sun;
But never, till this happy hour,
Was blest with such an evening-shower!

HENRY VAUGHAN

Winter

I, singularly moved
To love the lovely that are not beloved,
Of all the Seasons, most
Love Winter, and to trace
The sense of the Trophonian pallor on her face.
It is not death, but plenitude of peace;
And the dim cloud that does the world enfold
Hath less the characters of dark and cold
Than warmth and light asleep;
And correspondent breathing seems to keep
With the infant harvest, breathing soft below
Its eider coverlet of snow.
Nor is in field or garden anything
But, duly look'd into, contains serene
The substance of things hoped for, in the Spring,
And evidence of Summer not yet seen.
On every chance-mild day
That visits the moist shaw,
The honeysuckle, 'sdaining to be crost
In urgence of sweet life by sleet or frost.
'Voids the time's law
With still increase
Of leaflet new, and little, wandering spray;
Often, in sheltering brakes,
As one from rest disturb'd in the first hour,
Primrose or violet bewilder'd wakes,
And deems 'tis time to flower;
Though not a whisper of her voice he hear,
The buried bulb does know
The signals of the year,
And hails far Summer with his lifted spear;
The gorse-field dark, by sudden, gold caprice,
Turns, here and there, into a Jason's fleece;
Lilies that, soon in Autumn, slipp'd their gowns of green

And vanish'd into earth,
And came again, ere Autumn died, to birth,
Stand full-array'd amidst the wavering shower,
And perfect for the Summer, less the flower;
In nook of pale or crevice of crude bark,
Thou canst not miss,
If close thou spy, to mark
The ghostly chrysalis,
That, if thou touch it, stirs in its dream dark;
And the flush'd Robin, in the evenings hoar,
Does of Love's Day, as if he saw it, sing.
But sweeter yet than dream or song of Summer or Spring
Are Winter's sometime smiles, that seem to well
From infancy ineffable;
Her wandering, languorous gaze
So unfamiliar, so without amaze,
On the elemental, chill adversity,
The uncomprehended rudeness; and her sigh
And solemn, gathering tear,
And look of exile from some great repose, the sphere
Of ether, moved by ether only, or
By something still more tranquil.

COVENTRY PATMORE

WINTER

I

Hark, hark, I hear the *North* Wind roar,
See how he riots on the shoar;
And with expanded Wings at stretch,
Ruffles the Billows on the Beach.

II

Hark, how the routed Waves complain,
And call for Succor to the Main,
Flying the Storm as if they meant
To creep into the Continent.

III

Surely all Æoll's huffing Brood
Are met to War against the Flood,
Which seem surpriz'd, and have not yet
Had time his Levies to compleat.

IV

The beaten Bark, her Rudder lost,
Is on the rowling Billows tost;
Her Keel now plows the Ouse, and soon
Her Top-Mast tilts against the Moon.

V

'Tis strange! the Pilot keeps his seat;
His bounding Ship does so curvet,
Whilst the poor Passengers are found,
In their own fears already drown'd.

VI

Now Fins do serve for Wings, and bear
Their Scaly Squadrons through the Air;
Whilst the Air's Inhabitants do stain
Their gaudy Plumage in the Main.

VII

Now Stars concealed in Clouds do peep
Into the secrets of the deep;
And Lobsters spued up from the brine,
With *Cancer's* constellations shine.

VIII

Sure *Neptune's* Watery Kingdoms yet
Since first their corral Graves were wet,
Were ne'er disturbed with such alarms,
Nor had such trial of their Arms.

IX

See where a Liquid Mountain rides,
Made of innumerable Tides,
And tumbles headlong to the Strand,
As if the Sea would come to Land.

X

A Sail, a Sail, I plainly spy,
Betwixt the Ocean and the Sky,
An *Argosy*, a tall built Ship,
With all her Pregnant Sails a-trip.

XI

Nearer, and nearer, she makes way,
With Canvis Wings into the Bay;
And now upon the Deck appears
A crowd of busy Mariners.

XII

Methinks I hear the Cordage crack,
With furrowing *Neptune's* foaming Back,
Who wounded, and revengeful roars
His Fury to the neighb'ring Shoars.

XIII

With massy trident high, he heaves
Her sliding Keel above the Waves,
Opening his Liquid Arms to take
The bold invader in his wrack.

XIV

See how she dives into his Chest,
Whilst raising up his floating Brest
To clasp her in, he makes her rise
Out of the reach of his surprise.

XV

Nearer she comes, and still doth sweep
The Azure Surface of the deep,
And now at last the Waves have thrown
Their Rider on our *Albion*.

XVI

Under the Black cliff's spumy base,
The Sea-sick Hulk her fraight displays,
And as she walloweth on the Sand,
Vomits her burthen to the Land.

XVII

With Heads erect, and plying Oar,
The Ship-wrack'd Mates make to the shoar;
And dreadless of their danger, climb
The floating Mountains of the brine.

XVIII

Hark, hark, the noise, their Ecchoes make
The Island's Silver Waves to shake;
Sure with these throes, the lab'ring Main
'S delivered of a Hurricane.

XIX

And see the Seas becalm'd behind,
Not crispt with any breeze of Wind;
The Tempest has forsook the Waves,
And on the Land begins his braves.

XX

Hark, hark, their Voices higher rise,
They tear the Welkin with their Cries;
The very Rocks their fury feel,
And like Sick Drunkards nod, and reel.

XXI

Louder, and louder, still they come,
Nile's Cataracts to these are dumb;
The *Cyclops* to these Blades are still,
Whose Anvils shake the burning Hill.

XXII

Were all the Star-enlightened Skies,
As full of Ears as sparkling Eyes;
This rattle in the Christal Hall,
Would be enough to deaf them all.

XXIII

What monstrous Race is hither tost,
Thus to Alarm our *British* Coast;
With Outcries, such as never yet
War, or Confusion could beget.

XXIV

Oh! now I know them! Let us home
Our Mortal Enemy is come,
Winter and all his blust'ring train,
Have made a voyage o're the Main.

Banisht the Countrys of the Sun,
The Fugitive is hither run,
To ravish from our fruitful Fields
All that the teeming Season yields.

Like an Invader, not a Guest,
He comes to Riot, not to Feast;
And in wild fury overthrows,
Whatever does his march oppose.

With bleak and with congealing Winds,
The Earth in shining Chains he binds;
And still as he doth farther pass,
Quarries his way with Liquid Glass.

Hark, how the blusterors of the Bear,
Their Gibbouse[1] Cheeks in triumph tear,
And with continued Shouts do ring
The entry of their Palsy'd King.

The Squadron nearest to your Eye,
Is his Forlorn[2] of Infantry,
Bow-men of unrelenting Minds,
Whose Shafts are Feathered with the Winds.

Now you may see his Vanguard rise
Above the Earthy Precipice,
Bold Horse on bleakest Mountains bred,
With Hail instead of Provend fed.

[1] Swelling, puffed out.   [2] A front-line vanguard.

Their Launces are the pointed Locks,
Torn from the Brows of Frozen Rocks,
Their Shields are Chrystals and their Swords,
The Steel the crusted Rock affords.

XXXII

See the main Body now appears,
And hark the *Æolian* trumpetters,
By their Hoarse Levets[1] do declare,
That the bold General Rides there.

XXXIII

And look where Mantled up in White,
He sleds it like the *Muscovite*;
I know him by the Port he bears,
And his Life-guard of Mountaineers.

XXXIV

Their Caps are Fur'd with Hoary Frosts,
The Bravery their cold Kingdom boasts;
Their spungy Plaids are Milk White Frieze,
Spun from the Snowy Mountains Fleece.

XXXV

Their Partizans are fine carved Glass,
Fringed with the Morning's spangled Grass;
And Pendant by their brawny Thighs,
Hang Cimetars of burnisht Ice.

XXXVI

See, see, the Reer-ward now has won
The *Promontory's* trembling Crown,
Whilst at their numerous Spurs, the Ground
Groans out a hollow murmering sound.

[1] Trumpet-calls.

XXXVII

The Forlorn now halts for the Van;
The Reer-guard draws up to the Main;
And now they altogether croud
Their Troops into a threatening Cloud.

XXXVIII

Fly, fly; the Foe advances fast;
Into our Fortress, let us hast
Where all the Roarers of the *North*
Can neither Storm, nor Starve us forth.

XXXIX

There under Ground a Magazine
Of Sovereign juice is cellar'd in,
Liquor that will the Siege maintain,
Should *Phœbus* ne're return again.

XL

'Tis that, that gives the Poet rage,
And thaws the gelly'd Blood of Age;
Matures the Young, restores the Old,
And makes the fainting Coward bold.

XLI

It lays the careful Head to rest,
Calms Palpitations in the Breast,
Renders our Lives' misfortune Sweet,
And *Venus* frolick in the Sheet.

XLII

Then let the chill Sciorocco blow,
And gird us round with Hills of Snow;
Or else go whistle to the shoar,
And make the hollow Mountains roar.

XLIII

Whilst we together jovial sit
Careless, and Crown'd with Mirth and Wit;
Where though bleak Winds confine us home,
Our Fancies round the World shall roam.

XLIV

We'll think of all the Friends we know,
And Drink to all worth Drinking to:
When having Drunk all thine and mine,
We rather shall want Healths than Wine.

XLV

But where Friends fail us, we'll supply
Our friendships with our Charity;
Men that remote in Sorrows live,
Shall by our lusty Brimmers thrive.

XLVI

We'll Drink the Wanting into Wealth,
And those that Languish into Health,
The Afflicted into Joy, th' Opprest
Into Security and Rest.

XLVII

The Worthy in Disgrace shall find
Favour return again more kind,
And in restraint who stifled lye,
Shall taste the Air of Liberty.

XLVIII

The Brave shall triumph in Success,
The Lovers shall have Mistresses,
Poor unregarded Virtue Praise,
And the Neglected Poet Baies.

XLIX

Thus shall our Healths do others good,
Whilst we ourselves do all we wou'd;
For freed from Envy and from Care,
What would we be, but what we are?

L

'Tis the plump Grape's Immortal Juice
That does this happiness produce,
And will preserve us free together,
Maugre mischance, or Wind and Weather.

LI

Then let Old Winter take his course,
And roar abroad till he be hoarse,
And his Lungs crack with Ruthless Ire,
It shall but serve to blow our fire.

LII

Let him our little Castle ply,
With all his loud Artillery,
Whilst Sack and Claret Man the Fort
His Fury shall become our Sport.

LIII

Or, let him *Scotland* take, and there
Confine the plotting Presbyter;
His Zeal may Freeze, whilst we kept warm
With Love and Wine, can know no harm.

CHARLES COTTON

TO WINTER

'O Winter! bar thine adamantine doors:
The north is thine; there hast thou built thy dark
Deep-founded habitation. Shake not thy roofs,
Nor bend thy pillars with thine iron car.'

He hears me not, but o'er the yawning deep
Rides heavy; his storms are unchain'd, sheathèd
In ribbèd steel; I dare not lift mine eyes,
For he hath rear'd his sceptre o'er the world.

Lo! now the direful monster, whose skin clings
To his strong bones, strides o'er the groaning rocks:
He withers all in silence, and in his hand
Unclothes the earth, and freezes up frail life.

He takes his seat upon the cliffs, — the mariner
Cries in vain. Poor little wretch, that deal'st
With storms! — till heaven smiles, and the monster
Is driv'n yelling to his caves beneath mount Hecla.

WILLIAM BLAKE

All Nature feels the renovating Force
Of Winter, only to the thoughtless Eye
Is Ruin seen. The Frost-concocted Glebe
Draws in abundant vegetable Soul,
And gathers Vigour for the coming year.
A stronger Glow sits on the lively Cheek
Of ruddy Fire: and luculent along
The purer Rivers flow: their sullen Deeps,
Transparent, open to the Shepherd's Gaze,
And murmur hoarser at the fixing Frost.
    What art thou, Frost? and whence are thy keen Stores
Deriv'd, thou secret all-invading Power,
Whom even th' illusive Fluid cannot fly?
Is not thy potent Energy, unseen,
Myriads of little Salts, or hook'd, or shap'd
Like double Wedges, and diffus'd immense
Thro Water, Earth, and Ether? Hence at Eve,
Steam'd eager from the red Horizon round,
With the fierce Rage of Winter deep suffused,
An icy Gale, oft shifting, o'er the Pool
Breathes a blue Film, and in its mid Career
Arrests the bickering Stream. The loosen'd Ice
Let down the Flood, and half dissolved by Day,
Rustles no more; but to the sedgy Bank
Fast grows, or gathers round the pointed Stone
A crystal Pavement, by the Breath of Heaven
Cemented firm; till, seized from Shore to Shore,
The whole imprison'd River growls below.
Loud rings the frozen Earth, and hard reflects
A double Noise; while, at his evening Watch,
The village Dog deters the nightly Thief;
The Heifer lows; the distant Waterfall
Swells in the Breeze; and, with the hasty Tread
Of Traveller, the hollow-sounding Plain
Shakes from afar. The full ethereal Round,

Infinite Worlds disclosing to the View,
Shines out intensely keen; and, all one Cope
Of starry Glitter, glows from Pole to Pole.
From Pole to Pole the rigid Influence falls,
Thro the still Night, incessant, heavy, strong,
And seizes Nature fast. It freezes on;
Till Morn, late-rising o'er the drooping World,
Lifts her pale Eye unjoyous. Then appears
The various Labour of the silent Night:
Prone from the dripping Eave, and dumb Cascade,
Whose idle Torrents only seem to roar,
The pendant Icicle: the Frost-Work fair,
Where transient Hues, and fancy'd Figures rise;
Wide-spouted o'er the Hill, the frozen Brook,
A livid Tract, cold-gleaming on the Morn;
The Forest bent beneath the plumy wave;
And by the Frost refined the whiter Snow,
Incrusted hard, and sounding to the Tread
Of early Shepherd, as he pensive seeks
His pining Flock, or from the Mountain-top,
Pleased with the slippery Surface, swift descends.

Pure, quick, and sportful, is the wholesome Day;
But soon elapsed. The horizontal Sun,
Broad o'er the South, hangs at his utmost Noon;
And, ineffectual, strikes the gelid Cliff.
His azure Gloss the Mountain still maintains,
Nor feels the feeble Touch. Perhaps the Vale
Relents a while to the reflected Ray;
Or from the Forest falls the cluster'd Snow,
Myriads of Gems, that in the waving Gleam
Gay-twinkle as they scatter. Thick around
Thunders the Sport of those, who with the Gun,
And Dog impatient bounding at the Shot,
Worse than the Season, desolate the Fields;
And, adding to the Ruins of the Year,
Distress the footed or the feather'd Game.

JAMES THOMSON

THE SOUTH WIND

The south wind rose at dusk of the winter day,
The warm breath of the western sea
Circling wrapp'd the isle with his cloke of cloud,
And it now reach'd even to me, at dusk of the day,
And moan'd in the branches aloud:
While here and there, in patches of dark space,
A star shone forth from its heavenly place,
As a spark that is borne in the smoky chase;
And, looking up, there fell on my face —
Could it be drops of rain
Soft as the wind, that fell on my face?
Gossamers light as threads of the summer dawn,
Suck'd by the sun from midmost calms of the main,
From groves of coral islands secretly drawn,
O'er half the round of earth to be driven,
Now to fall on my face
In silky skeins spun from the mists of heaven.

Who art thou, in wind and darkness and soft rain
Thyself that robest, that bendest in sighing pines
To whisper thy truth? that usest for signs
A hurried glimpse of the moon, the glance of a star
In the rifted sky?
Who art thou, that with thee I
Woo and am wooed?
That robing thyself in darkness and soft rain
Choosest my chosen solitude,
Coming so far
To tell thy secret again,
As a mother her child, in her folding arm
Of a winter night by a flickering fire,
Telleth the same tale o'er and o'er
With gentle voice, and I never tire,
So imperceptibly changeth the charm,

As Love on buried ecstasy buildeth his tower,
– Like as the stem that beareth the flower
By trembling is knit to power; -
Ah! long ago
In thy first rapture I renounced my lot,
The vanity, the despondency and the woe,
And seeking thee to know
Well was't for me, and evermore
I am thine, I know not what.

For me thou seekest ever, me wondering a day
In the eternal alternations, me
Free for a stolen moment of chance
To dream a beautiful dream
In the everlasting dance
Of speechless worlds, the unsearchable scheme,
To me thou findest the way,
Me and whomsoe'er
I have found my dream to share
Still with thy charm encircling; even to-night
To me and my love in darkness and soft rain
Under the sighing pines thou comest again,
And staying our speech with mystery of delight,
Of the kiss that I give a wonder thou makest,
And the kiss that I take thou takest.

ROBERT BRIDGES

THE WINTER MORNING WALK

'Tis morning; and the sun with ruddy orb
Ascending fires the horizon: while the clouds
That crowd away before the driving wind,
More ardent as the disk emerges more,
Resemble most some city in a blaze,
Seen through the leafless wood. His slanting ray
Slides ineffectual down the snowy vale,
And tinging all with his own rosy hue,
From every herb and every spiry blade
Stretches a length of shadow o'er the field.
Mine, spindling into longitude immense,
In spite of gravity, and sage remark
That I myself am but a fleeting shade,
Provokes me to a smile. With eye askance
I view the muscular proportion'd limb
Transform'd to a lean shank. The shapeless pair,
As they design'd to mock me, at my side
Take step for step; and as I near approach
The cottage, walk along the plaster'd wall,
Preposterous sight! the legs without the man.
The verdure of the plain lies buried deep
Beneath the dazzling deluge; and the bents,
And coarser grass upspearing o'er the rest,
Of late unsightly and unseen now shine
Conspicuous, and in bright apparel clad,
And fledged with icy feathers, nod superb.
The cattle mourn in corners where the fence
Screens them, and seem half-petrified to sleep
In unrecumbent sadness. There they wait
Their wonted fodder, not like hungering man
Fretful if unsupplied, but silent, meek,
And patient of the slow-paced swain's delay.
He from the stack carves out the accustom'd load,
Deep plunging, and again deep plunging oft,

His broad keen knife into the solid mass;
Smooth as a wall the upright remnant stands,
With such undeviating and even force
He severs it away; no needless care
Lest storms should overset the leaning pile
Deciduous, or its own unbalanced weight.
Forth goes the woodman, leaving unconcern'd
The cheerful haunts of man, to wield the axe
And drive the wedge in yonder forest drear,
From morn to eve his solitary task.
Shaggy, and lean, and shrewd, with pointed ears
And tail cropp'd short, half lurcher, and half cur,
His dog attends him. Close behind his heel
Now creeps he slow; and now with many a frisk
Wide scampering, snatches up the drifted snow
With ivory teeth, or ploughs it with his snout;
Then shakes his powder'd coat, and barks for joy.
Heedless of all his pranks, the sturdy churl
Moves right toward the mark; nor stops for aught,
But now and then with pressure of his thumb
To adjust the fragrant charge of a short tube
That fumes beneath his nose: the trailing cloud
Streams far behind him, scenting all the air,
Now from the roost, or from the neighbouring pale,
Where, diligent to catch the first faint gleam
Of smiling day, they gossip'd side by side,
Come trooping at the housewife's well-known call
The feather'd tribes domestic. Half on wing,
And half on foot, they brush the fleecy flood,
Conscious, and fearful of too deep a plunge.
The sparrows peep, and quit the sheltering eaves
To seize the fair occasion. Well they eye
The scatter'd grain, and thievishly resolved
To escape the impending famine, often scared
As oft return, a pert voracious kind.
Clean riddance quickly made, one only care
Remains to each, the search of sunny nook,

Or shed impervious to the blast. Resign'd
To sad necessity, the cock forgoes
His wonted strut, and wading at their head
With well-considered steps, seems to resent
His alter'd gait and stateliness retrench'd.
How find the myriads that in summer cheer
The hills and valleys with their ceaseless songs,
Due sustenance, or where subsist they now?
Earth yields them nought: the imprison'd worm is safe
Beneath the frozen clod; all seeds of herbs
Lie cover'd close, and berry-bearing thorns
That feed the thrush (whatever some suppose,)
Afford the smaller minstrels no supply.
The long protracted rigour of the year
Thins all their numerous flocks. In chinks and holes
Ten thousand seek an unmolested end,
As instinct prompts, self-buried ere they die.
The very rooks and daws forsake the fields,
Where neither grub nor root nor earth-nut now
Repays their labour more; and perch'd aloft
By the way-side, or stalking in the path,
Lean pensioners upon the traveller's track,
Pick up their nauseous dole, though sweet to them,
Of voided pulse or half-digested grain.
The streams are lost amid the splendid blank,
O'erwhelming all distinction. On the flood,
Indurated and fix'd, the snowy weight
Lies undissolved; while silently beneath
And unperceived, the current steals away.
Not so, where scornful of a check it leaps
The mill-dam, dashes on the restless wheel,
And wantons in the pebbly gulf below:
No frost can bind it there; its utmost force
Can but arrest the light and smoky mist
That in its fall the liquid sheet throws wide.
And see where it has hung the embroider'd banks
With forms so various, that no powers of art,

The pencil or the pen, may trace the scene!
Here glittering turrets rise, upbearing high
(Fantastic misarrangement!) on the roof
Large growth of what may seem the sparkling trees
And shrubs of fairy land. The crystal drops
That trickle down the branches, fast congeal'd,
Shoot into pillars of pellucid length,
And prop the pile they but adorn'd before.
Here grotto within grotto safe defies
The sunbeam: there emboss'd and fretted wild,
The growing wonder takes a thousand shapes
Capricious, in which fancy seeks in vain
The likeness of some object seen before.
Thus nature works as if to mock at art,
And in defiance of her rival powers:
By these fortuitous and random strokes
Performing such inimitable feats,
As she with all her rules can never reach.
Less worthy of applause, though more admired,
Because a novelty, the work of man,
Imperial mistress[1] of the fur-clad Russ!
Thy most magnificent and mighty freak,
The wonder of the north. No forest fell
When thou wouldst build; no quarry sent its stores
To enrich thy walls; but thou didst hew the floods,
And make thy marble of the glassy wave.
In such a palace Aristæus found
Cyrene, when he bore the plaintive tale
Of his lost bees to her maternal ear:
In such a palace poetry might place
The armoury of winter; where his troops,
The gloomy clouds, find weapons, arrowy sleet,
Skin-piercing volley, blossom-bruising hail,
And snow that often blinds the traveller's course,
And wraps him in an unexpected tomb.

[1] Anna. This Empress constructed a palace of ice on the bank of the Neva
in 1740. It lasted from January to March.

Silently as a dream the fabric rose;
No sound of hammer or of saw was there.
Ice upon ice, the well-adjusted parts
Were soon conjoin'd, nor other cement ask'd
Than water interfused to make them one.
Lamps gracefully disposed, and of all hues,
Illumined every side; a watery light
Gleam'd through the clear transparency, that seem'd
Another moon new risen, or meteor fallen
From heaven to earth, of lambent flame serene.
So stood the brittle prodigy; though smooth
And slippery the materials, yet frostbound
Firm as a rock. Nor wanted aught within,
That royal residence might well befit,
For grandeur or for use. Long wavy wreaths
Of flowers, that fear'd no enemy but warmth,
Blush'd on the panels. Mirror needed none
Where all was vitreous; but in order due
Convivial table and commodious seat
(What seem'd at least commodious seat) was there,
Sofa and couch and high-built throne august.
The same lubricity was found in all,
And all was moist to the warm touch; a scene
Of evanescent glory, once a stream,
And soon to slide into a stream again.
Alas! 'twas but a mortifying stroke
Of undesigned severity, that glanced
(Made by a monarch) on her own estate,
On human grandeur and the courts of kings.
'Twas transient in its nature, as in show
'Twas durable; as worthless, as it seem'd
Intrinsically precious; to the foot
Treacherous and false; it smiled, and it was cold.

WILLIAM COWPER

NOVEMBER

Sybil of months, and worshipper of winds,
   I love thee, rude and boisterous as thou art;
And scraps of joy my wandering ever finds
   Mid thy uproarious madness – when the start
Of sudden tempests stirs the forest leaves
   Into hoarse fury, till the shower set free
Stills the huge swells. Then ebb the mighty heaves,
   That sway the forest like a troubled sea.
I love thy wizard noise, and rave in turn
   Half-vacant thoughts and rhymes of careless form;
Then hide me from the shower, a short sojourn,
   Neath ivied oak; and mutter to the storm,
Wishing its melody belonged to me,
That I might breathe a living song to thee.

JOHN CLARE

NOVEMBER

The mellow year is hastening to its close;
The little birds have almost sung their last,
Their small notes twitter in the dreary blast –
That shrill-piped harbinger of early snows;
The patient beauty of the scentless rose,
Oft with the Morn's hoar crystal quaintly glassed,
Hangs, a pale mourner for the summer past,
And makes a little summer where it grows:
In the chill sunbeam of the faint brief day
The dusky waters shudder as they shine,
The russet leaves obstruct the straggling way
Of oozy brooks, which no deep banks define,
And the gaunt woods, in ragged, scant array,
Wrap their old limbs with sombre ivy twine.

HARTLEY COLERIDGE

SNOW

The keener Tempests come: and fuming dun
From all the livid East, or piercing North,
Thick Clouds ascend – in whose capacious Womb
A vapoury Deluge lies, to Snow congeal'd.
Heavy they roll their fleecy World along;
And the Sky saddens with the gather'd Storm.
Through the hush'd Air the whit'ning Shower descends,
At first thin-wavering; till at last the Flakes
Fall broad, and wide, and fast, dimming the Day
With a continual Flow. The cherish'd Fields
Put on their Winter-Robe of purest White.
'Tis Brightness all; save where the new Snow melts,
Along the mazy Current. Low, the Woods
Bow their hoar Head; and, ere the languid Sun
Faint from the West emits his Evening Ray,
Earth's universal Face, deep-hid and chill,
Is one wild dazzling Waste, that buries wide
The Works of Man. Drooping, the Labourer-Ox
Stands covered o'er with Snow, and then demands
The Fruit of all his Toil. The Fowls of Heaven,
Tamed by the cruel Season, croud around
The winnowing Store, and claim the little Boon
Which Providence assigns them. One alone,
The Red-Breast, sacred to the household Gods,
Wisely regardful of th' embroiling Sky,
In joyless Fields and thorny Thickets, leaves
His shivering Mates, and pays to trusted Man
His annual Visit. Half-afraid, he first
Against the Window beats; then, brisk, alights
On the warm Hearth; then, hopping o'er the Floor,
Eyes all the smiling Family askance,
And pecks, and starts, and wonders where he is:
Till, more familiar grown, the Table-Crumbs
Attract his slender Feet. The foodless Wilds

Pour forth their brown Inhabitants. The Hare,
Though timorous of Heart, and hard beset
By Death in various Forms, dark Snares, and Dogs,
And more unpitying Men, the Garden seeks,
Urged on by fearless Want. The bleating Kind
Eye the black Heaven, and next the glistening Earth,
With Looks of dumb Despair; then, sad-dispersed,
Dig for the wither'd Herb thro Heaps of Snow.

    Now, Shepherds, to your helpless Charge be kind;
Baffle the raging Year, and fill their Pens
With Food at Will; lodge them below the Storm,
And watch them strict: for from the bellowing East,
In this dire Season, oft the Whirlwind's Wing
Sweeps up the Burthen of whole wintry Plains
In one wide Waft, and o'er the hapless Flocks,
Hid in the Hollow of two neighbouring Hills,
The billowy Tempest whelms; till, upward urged,
The Valley to a shining Mountain swells,
Tipt with a Wreath, high-curling in the Sky.
JAMES THOMSON

WINTER AT THE FARM

When now, unsparing as the scourge of war,
Blasts follow blasts, and groves dismantled roar,
Around their home the storm-pinch'd cattle lows,
No nourishment in frozen pastures grows:
Yet frozen pastures every morn resound
With fair abundance thundering to the ground.
For though on hoary twigs no buds peep out,
And e'en the hardy bramble cease to sprout,
Beneath dread Winter's level sheets of snow
The sweet nutritious turnip deigns to grow.
Till now imperious want and wide-spread dearth
Bid labour claim her treasures from the earth.
On Giles, and such as Giles, the labour falls,
To strew the frequent load where hunger calls.
On driving gales sharp hail indignant flies,
And sleet, more irksome still, assails his eyes;
Snow clogs his feet; or if no snow is seen,
The field with all its juicy store to screen,
Deep goes the frost, till every root is found
A rolling mass of ice upon the ground.
No tender ewe can break her nightly fast,
Nor heifer strong begin the cold repast,
Till Giles with ponderous beetle foremost go,
And scattering splinters fly at every blow:
When pressing round him eager for the prize,
From their mix'd breath warm exhalations rise.

If now in beaded rows drops deck the spray,
While Phœbus grants a momentary ray,
Let but a cloud's broad shadow intervene,
And stiffen'd into gems the drops are seen;
And down the furrow'd oak's broad southern side
Streams of dissolving rime no longer glide.

Though night approaching bids for rest prepare,
Still the flail echoes through the frosty air;
Nor stops till deepest shades of darkness come,
Sending at length the weary labourer home.
From him, with bed and nightly food supplied,
Throughout the yard, housed round on every side,
Deep-plunging cows, their rustling feast enjoy,
And snatch sweet mouthfuls from the passing boy,
Who moves unseen beneath his trailing load,
Fills the tall racks, and leaves a scatter'd road;
Where oft the swine from ambush warm and dry,
Bolt out, and scamper headlong to their sty,
When Giles, with well-known voice, already there,
Deigns them a portion of his evening care.

Him, though the cold may pierce, and storms molest,
Succeeding hours shall cheer with warmth and rest:
Gladness to spread, and raise the grateful smile,
He hurls the faggot bursting from the pile,
And many a log and rifted trunk conveys,
To heap the fire and to extend the blaze
That quivering strong through every opening flies,
Whilst smoky columns unobstructed rise.
For the rude architect, unknown to fame
(Nor symmetry nor elegance his aim),
Who spreads his floors of solid oak on high,
On beams rough-hewn, from age to age that lie,
Bade his wide fabric unimpair'd sustain
Pomona's store, and cheese, and golden grain;
Bade from its central base, capacious laid,
The well-wrought chimney rear its lofty head;
Where since hath many a savoury ham been stored,
And tempests howl'd, and Christmas gambols roar'd.

ROBERT BLOOMFIELD

IN DECEMBER

The heavy dung-cart stumbles by
   Leading the harvest to the fields,
That from cow-byre and stall and sty
   The farmstead in the winter yields.

Like shocks in a reaped field of rye
   The small black heaps of lively dung
Sprinkled in the grass-meadow lie
   Licking the air with smoky tongue.

This is Earth's food that man piles up
   And with his fork will thrust on her,
And Earth will lie and slowly sup
   With her moist mouth through half the year.

ANDREW YOUNG

SWEDES

They have taken the gable from the roof of clay
On the long swede pile. They have let in the sun
To the white and gold and purple of curled fronds
Unsunned. It is a sight more tender-gorgeous
At the wood-corner where Winter moans and drips
Than when, in the Valley of the Tombs of Kings,
A boy crawls down into a Pharaoh's tomb
And, first of Christian men, beholds the mummy,
God and monkey, chariot and throne and vase,
Blue pottery, alabaster, and gold.

But dreamless long-dead Amen-hotep lies.
This is a dream of Winter, sweet as Spring.

EDWARD THOMAS

A FROSTY DAY

Grass afield wears silver thatch;
  Palings all are edged with rime;
Frost-flowers pattern round the latch;
  Cloud nor breeze dissolve the clime;

When the waves are solid floor,
  And the clods are iron-bound,
And the boughs are crystall'd hoar,
  And the red leaf nailed a-ground.

When the fieldfare's flight is slow,
  And a rosy vapour rim,
Now the sun is small and low,
  Belts along the region dim.

When the ice-crack flies and flaws,
  Shore to shore, with thunder shock,
Deeper than the evening daws,
  Clearer than the village clock.

When the rusty blackbird strips
  Bunch by bunch, the coral thorn;
And the pale day-crescent dips,
  New to heaven, a slender horn.

LORD DE TABLEY

A WINTER SKETCH

When the snow begins to feather,
  And the woods begin to roar,
Clashing angry boughs together,
  As the breakers grind the shore.
Nature then a bankrupt goes,
Full of wreck and full of woes.

When the swan for warmer forelands
  Leaves the sea-firth's icebound edge:
When the gray geese from the moorlands
  Cleave the cloud in noisy wedge.
Woodlands stand in frozen chains,
Hung with ropes of solid rains.

Shepherds creep to byre and haven,
  Sheep in drifts are nipped and numb:
Some belated rook or raven
  Rocks upon a sign-post dumb.
Mere-waves solid as a clod
Roar with skaters thunder-shod.

All the roofs and chimneys rumble,
  Roads are ridged with slush and sleet;
Down the orchard apples tumble,
  Ploughboys stamp their frosty feet.
Millers, jolted down the lanes,
Hardly feel for cold their reins.

Snipes are calling from the trenches,
  Frozen half and half at flow,
In the porches servant wenches
  Work with shovels at the snow.
Rusty blackbirds, weak of wing,
Clean forget they once could sing.

Dogs and boys fetch down the cattle,
   Deep in mire and powdered pale:
Spinning wheels commence to rattle,
   Landlords spice the smoking ale.
Hail, white winter, lady fine,
In a cup of elder wine.

LORD DE TABLEY

From THE BOROUGH

The ocean too has winter-views serene,
When all you see through densest fog is seen;
When you can hear the fishers near at hand
Distinctly speak, yet see not where they stand;
Or sometimes them and not their boat discern,
Or half-conceal'd some figure at the stern;
The view's all bounded, and from side to side
Your utmost prospect but a few ells wide;
Boys who, on shore, to sea the pebble cast,
Will hear it strike against the viewless mast;
While the stern boatman growls his fierce disdain,
At whom he knows not, whom he threats in vain.
    'Tis pleasant then to view the nets float past,
Net after net till you have seen the last;
And as you wait till all beyond you slip,
A boat comes gliding from an anchor'd ship,
Breaking the silence with the dipping oar,
And their own tones, as labouring for the shore;
Those measured tones which with the scene agree,
And give a sadness to serenity.

GEORGE CRABBE

SNOW STORM

What a night! The wind howls, hisses, and but stops
To howl more loud, while the snow volley keeps
Incessant batter at the window pane,
Making our comfort feel as sweet again;
And in the morning, when the tempest drops,
At every cottage door mountainous heaps
Of snow lie drifted, that all entrance stops
Until the beesom and the shovel gain
The path, and leave a wall on either side.
The shepherd rambling valleys white and wide
With new sensations his old memory fills,
When hedges left at night, no more descried,
Are turned to one white sweep of curving hills,
And trees turned bushes half their bodies hide.

The boy that goes to fodder with surprise
Walks oer the gate he opened yesternight.
The hedges all have vanished from his eyes;
Een some tree tops the sheep could reach to bite.
The novel scene emboldens new delight,
And, though with cautious steps his sports begin,
He bolder shuffles the huge hills of snow,
Till down he drops and plunges to the chin,
And struggles much and oft escape to win –
Then turns and laughs but dare not further go;
For deep the grass and bushes lie below,
Where little birds that soon at eve went in
With heads tucked in their wings now pine for day
And little feel boys oer their heads can stray.

JOHN CLARE

THE PINES

The eye might fancy that those pines,
Where a light falls in pallid lines,
Were struck by the sunlight at noon,
Or shadow-broken gleam of the moon;
But snowflakes rustle down the air,
Circling and rising here and there
As though uncertain where to fall,
Filling the wood with a deep pall,
The wood that hastens darkness to hide all.

The hurricane of snow last night
Felled one; its roots, surprised by light,
Clutch at the air in wild embrace;
Peace like an echo fills the place
Save for the quiet labour of snow,
That, falling flake on flake below,
The torn limbs and the red wounds stanches,
And with a sheet the dead trunk blanches,
And lays white delicate wreaths among the branches.

ANDREW YOUNG

THE ROBIN

Poore bird! I doe not envie thee;
Pleas'd in the gentle Melodie
   Of thy owne Song.
Let crabbed winter Silence all
The winged Quire; he never shall
   Chaine up thy Tongue:
      Poore Innocent!
When I would please my selfe, I looke on thee;
And guess some sparkes of that Felicitie,
     That Selfe-Content.

When the bleake Face of winter Spreads
The Earth, and violates the Meads
   Of all their Pride;
When Sapless Trees and Flowere are fled,
Back to their Causes, and lye dead
   To all beside:
      I see thee Set,
Bidding defiance to the bitter Ayre,
Upon a wither'd Spray; by cold made bare.
     And drooping yet.

There, full in notes, to ravish all
My Earth, I wonder what to call
   My dullness; when
I heare thee, prettie Creature, bring
Thy better odes of Praise, and Sing,
   To puzzle men:
      Poore pious Elfe!
I am instructed by thy harmonie,
To sing the Time's uncertaintie,
     Safe in my Selfe.

Poore Redbreast, caroll out thy Laye,
And teach us mortalls what to saye.
   Here cease the Quire
Of ayerie Choristers; noe more
Mingle your notes; but catch a Store
   From her Sweet Lire;
      You are but weake,
Mere summer Chanters; you have neither wing
Nor voice, in winter. Prettie Redbreast, Sing,
      What I would speake.

GEORGE DANIEL

ROBIN REDBREAST

Robin on a leafless bough,
    Lord in Heaven, how he sings!
Now cold Winter's cruel wind
    Makes playmates of poor, dead things.

How he sings for joy this morn!
    How his breast doth pant and glow!
Look you how he stands and sings,
    Half-way up his legs in snow!

If these crumbs of bread were pearls,
    And I had no bread at home,
He should have them for that song;
    Pretty Robin Redbreast, Come.

W. H. DAVIES

DESOLATE

From the sad eaves the drip-drop of the rain!
The water washing at the latchel door;
A slow step plashing by upon the moor!
A single bleat far from the famished fold:
The clicking of an embered hearth and cold;
The rainy Robin tic-tac at the pane.

'So as it is with thee
Is it with me,
So as it is and it used not to be,
With thee used not to be,
Nor me.'
So singeth Robin on the willow-tree,
The rainy Robin tic-tac at the pane.

Here in this breast all day
The fire is dim and low,
Within I care not to stay,
Without I care not to go.
A sadness ever sings
Of unforgotten things,
And the bird of love is patting at the pane;
But the wintry water deepens at the door,
And a step is plashing by upon the moor
Into the dark upon the darkening moor,
And alas, alas, the drip-drop of the rain!

SYDNEY DOBELL

343

ROBIN'S CROSS

A little cross,
To tell my loss;
A little bed
To rest my head;
A little tear is all I crave
Under my very little grave.

I strew thy bed
Who loved thy lays;
The tear I shed,
The cross I raise,
With nothing more upon it than
Here lies the Little Friend of Man!

GEORGE DARLEY

SONNET

How large that thrush looks on the bare thorn-tree!
   A swarm of such, three little months ago,
   Had hidden in the leaves and let none know
Save by the outburst of their minstrelsy.
A white flake here and there – a snow-lily
   Of last night's frost – our naked flower-beds hold;
   And for a rose-flower on the darkling mould
The hungry redbreast gleams. No bloom, no bee.
The current shudders to its ice-bound sedge:
   Nipped in their bath, the stark reeds one by one
   Flash each its clinging diamond in the sun:
'Neath winds which for this Winter's sovereign pledge
Shall curb great king-masts to the ocean's edge
   And leave memorial forest-kings o'erthrown.

DANTE GABRIEL ROSSETTI

A WIDOW BIRD SATE MOURNING

A widow bird sate mourning for her love
   Upon a wintry bough;
The frozen wind crept on above,
   The freezing stream below.

There was no leaf upon the forest bare,
   No flower upon the ground,
And little motion in the air
   Except the mill-wheel's sound.

PERCY BYSSHE SHELLEY

ALONE

The abode of the nightingale is bare,
Flowered frost congeals in the gelid air,
The fox howls from his frozen lair:
      Alas, my loved one is gone,
      I am alone:
      It is winter.

Once the pink cast a winy smell,
The wild bee hung in the hyacinth bell,
Light in effulgence of beauty fell:
      Alas, my loved one is gone,
      I am alone:
      It is winter.

My candle a silent fire doth shed,
Starry Orion hunts o'erhead;
Come moth, come shadow, the world is dead:
      Alas, my loved one is gone,
      I am alone:
      It is winter.

WALTER DE LA MARE

The boughs, the boughs are bare enough
But earth has never felt the snow.
Frost-furred our ivies are, and rough

With bills of rime the brambles shew.
The hoarse leaves crawl on hissing ground
Because the sighing wind is low.

But if the rain-blasts be unbound
And from dank feathers wring the drops
The clogged brook runs with choking sound

Kneading the mounded mire that stops
His channel under damming coats
Of foliage fallen in the copse.

A simple passage of weak notes
Is all the winter bird dare try
The bugle moon by daylight floats

So glassy white about the sky,
So like a berg of hyaline,
And pencilled blue so daintily,

I never saw her so divine
But through black branches, rarely drest
In scarves of silky shot and shine.

The webbèd and the watery west
Where yonder crimson fireball sits
Looks laid for feasting and for rest.

I see long reefs of violets
In beryl-covered fens so dim,
A gold-water Pactolus frets

Its brindled wharves and yellow brim,
The waxen colours weep and run
And slendering to his burning rim

Into the flat blue mist the sun
Drops out and all our day is done.

GERARD MANLEY HOPKINS

WINTER RAIN

Every valley drinks,
   Every dell and hollow;
Where the kind rain sinks and sinks,
   Green of Spring will follow.

Yet a lapse of weeks –
   Buds will burst their edges,
Strip their wool-coats, glue-coats, streaks,
   In the woods and hedges;

Weave a bower of love
   For birds to meet each other,
Weave a canopy above
   Nest and egg and mother.

But for fattening rain
   We should have no flowers,
Never a bud or leaf again
   But for soaking showers;

Never a mated bird
   In the rocking tree-tops,
Never indeed a flock or herd
   To graze upon the lea-crops.

Lambs so woolly white,
   Sheep the sun-bright leas on,
They could have no grass to bite
   But for rain in season.

We should find no moss
   In the shadiest places,
Find no waving meadow grass
   Pied with broad-eyed daisies.

But miles of barren sand,
　　With never a son or daughter;
Not a lily on the land,
　　Or lily on the water.

CHRISTINA ROSSETTI

It seemed corrival of the world's great prime,
  Made to un-edge the scythe of Time,
    And last with stateliest rhyme.

No tender Dryad ever did indue
  That rigid chiton of rough yew,
    To fret her white flesh through:

But some god like to those grim Asgard lords,
  Who walk the fables of the hordes
    From Scandinavian fjords,

Upheaved its stubborn girth, and raised unriven,
  Against the whirl-blast and the levin,
    Defiant arms to Heaven.

When doom puffed out the stars, we might have said,
  It would decline its heavy head,
    And see the world to bed.

For this firm yew did from the vassal leas,
  And rain and air, its tributaries,
    Its revenues increase,

And levy impost on the golden sun,
  Take the blind years as they might run,
    And no fate seek or shun.

But now our yew is strook, is fallen – yea,
  Hacked like dull wood of every day
    To this and that, men say.

Never! – To Hades' shadowy shipyards gone,
  Dim barge of Dis, down Acheron
    It drops, or Lethe wan.

Stirred by its fall — poor destined bark of Dis! —
   Along my soul a bruit there is
      Of echoing images,

Reverberations of mortality:
   Spelt backward from its death, to me
      Its life reads saddenedly.

Its breast was hollowed as the tooth of eld:
   And boys, there creeping unbeheld,
      A laughing moment dwelled.

Yet they, within its very heart so crept,
   Reached not the heart that courage kept
      With winds and years beswept.

And in its boughs did close and kindly nest
   The birds, as they within its breast,
      By all its leaves caressed.

But bird nor child might touch by any art
   Each other's or the tree's hid heart,
      A whole God's breadth apart . . .

FRANCIS THOMPSON

THE DARKLING THRUSH

I leant upon a coppice gate
  When Frost was spectre-gray
And Winter's dregs made desolate
  The weakening eye of day.
The tangled bine-stems scored the sky
  Like strings of broken lyres,
And all mankind that haunted nigh
  Had sought their household fires.

The land's sharp features seemed to be
  The Century's corpse outleant,
His crypt the cloudy canopy,
  The wind his death-lament.
The ancient pulse of germ and birth
  Was shrunken hard and dry,
And every spirit upon earth
  Seemed fervourless as I.

At once a voice arose among
  The bleak twigs overhead
In a full-hearted evensong
  Of joy illimited;
An aged thrush, frail, gaunt, and small,
  In blast-beruffled plume,
Had chosen thus to fling his soul
  Upon the growing gloom.

So little cause for carolings
  Of such ecstatic sound
Was written on terrestial things
  Afar or nigh around,
That I could think there trembled through
  His happy good-night air
Some blessed Hope, whereof he knew
  And I was unaware.

THOMAS HARDY

Night

From THE NIGHT

Dear Night, this world's defeat;
The stop to busie fools; Care's check and curb;
The Day of Spirits; my Soul's calm retreat
    Which none disturb;
  Christs progress, and his prayer time;
  The hours to which high Heaven doth chime;

Gods silent searching flight,
When my Lords head is fill'd with dew, and all
His locks are wet with the clear drops of night;
    His still, soft call;
  His knocking time; The Souls dumb watch,
  When Spirits their fair kindred catch:

Were all my loud, evil days
Calm and unhaunted as is thy dark Tent,
Whose peace but by some Angels wing or voice
    Is seldom rent;
  Then I in Heaven all the long year
  Would keep, and never wander here.

But living where the Sun
Doth all things wake, and where all mix and tyre
Themselves and others, I consent and run
    To ev'ry myre,
  And by this worlds ill-guiding light,
  Erre more then I can do by night.

There is in God (some say)
A deep, but dazzling darkness; As men here
Say it is late and dusky, because they
    See not all clear;
  O for that Night! where I in him
  Might live invisible and dim!

HENRY VAUGHAN

TO NIGHT

Swiftly walk o'er the western wave,
          Spirit of Night,
Out of the misty eastern cave
Where, all the long and lone daylight,
Thou wovest dreams of joy and fear
Which make thee terrible and dear —
          Swift be thy flight!

Wrap thy form in a mantle gray,
          Star in-wrought;
Blind with thine hair the eyes of Day;
Kiss her until she be wearied out;
Then wander o'er city and sea and land,
Touching all with thine opiate wand —
          Come, long-sought!

When I arose and saw the dawn,
          I sigh'd for thee;
When light rode high, and the dew was gone,
And noon lay heavy on flower and tree,
And the weary Day turn'd to his rest,
Lingering like an unlov'd guest,
          I sigh'd for thee.

Thy brother Death came, and cried:
          Wouldst thou me?
Thy sweet child Sleep, the filmy-eyed,
Murmur'd like a noontide bee:
Shall I nestle near thy side?
Wouldst thou me? — And I replied
          No, not thee!

Death will come when thou art dead,
    Soon, too soon!
Sleep will come when thou art fled.
Of neither would I ask the boon
I ask of thee, belovèd Night —
Swift be thine approaching flight,
    Come soon, soon!

PERCY BYSSHE SHELLEY

NIGHT

The sun descending in the west,
The evening star does shine;
The birds are silent in their nest,
And I must seek for mine.
The moon, like a flower,
In heaven's high bower,
With silent delight
Sits and smiles on the night.

Farewell, green fields and happy groves,
Where flocks have took delight.
Where lambs have nibbled, silent moves
The feet of angels bright:
Unseen they pour blessing,
And joy without ceasing,
On each bud and blossom,
And each sleeping bosom.

They look in every thoughtless nest,
Where birds are cover'd warm;
They visit caves of every beast,
To keep them all from harm.
If they see any weeping
That should have been sleeping,
They pour sleep on their head,
And sit down by their bed.

When wolves and tygers howl for prey,
They pitying stand and weep;
Seeking to drive their thirst away,
And keep them from the sheep.
But if they rush dreadful,
The angels, most heedful,
Receive each mild spirit,
New worlds to inherit.

And there the lion's ruddy eyes
Shall flow with tears of gold,
And pitying the tender cries,
And walking round the fold,
Saying 'wrath, by his meekness,
And, by his health, sickness
Is driven away
From our immortal day.

'And now beside thee, bleating lamb,
I can lie down and sleep;
Or think on him who bore thy name,
Graze after thee and weep.
For, wash'd in life's river,
My bright mane for ever
Shall shine like the gold
As I guard o'er the fold.'

WILLIAM BLAKE

From C O M U S

The Star that bids the Shepherd fold,
Now the top of Heav'n doth hold,
And the gilded Car of Day,
His glowing Axle doth allay
In the steep *Atlantick* stream,
And the slope Sun his upward beam
Shoots against the dusky Pole,
Pacing toward the other gole
Of his Chamber in the East.
Mean while welcom Joy, and Feast,
Midnight shout and revelry,
Tipsie dance, and Jollity . . .
We that are of purer fire
Imitate the Starry Quire,
Who in their nightly watchful Sphears,
Lead in swift round the Months and Years.
The Sounds, and Seas with all their finny drove
Now to the Moon in wavering Morrice move,
And on the Tawny Sands and Shelves,
Trip the pert Fairies and the dapper Elves;
By dimpled Brook and Fountain brim,
The Wood-Nymphs deckt with Daisies trim,
Their merry wakes and pastimes keep:
What hath night to do with sleep?

JOHN MILTON

HYMNUS

Queene and Huntresse, chaste, and fayre,
  Now the Sunne is layde to sleepe,
Seated, in thy silver Chayre,
  State in wonted manner keepe:
    Hesperus intreats thy light,
    Goddesse excellently bright.

Earth, let not thy envious shade
  Dare it self to interpose;
Cynthias shining orbe was made
  Heaven to cleare, when day did close:
    Bless us then with wishèd sight,
    Goddess excellently bright.

Lay thy Bowe of Pearle apart
  And thy Christall-shining Quiver;
Give unto the flying Hart,
  Space to breath, how short soever.
    Thou, that mak'st a day of night,
    Goddesse excellently Bright.

BEN JONSON

MOONRISE (*Fragment*)

I awoke in the Midsummer not to call night, in the white and
    the walk of the morning:
The moon, dwindled and thinned to the fringe of a finger-nail
    held to the candle,
Or paring of paradisaical fruit, lovely in waning but lustreless,
Stepped from the stool, drew back from the barrow, of dark
    Maenefa the mountain;
A cusp still clasped him, a fluke yet fanged him, entangled
    him, not quit utterly.
This was the prized, the desirable sight, unsought, presented
    so easily,
Parted me leaf and leaf, divided me eyelid and eyelid of
    slumber.

GERARD MANLEY HOPKINS

From THE MERCHANT OF VENICE

Lorenzo. How sweet the Moonlight sleepes upon this banke!
  Heere will we sit, and let the sounds of musicke
  Creepe in our eares: soft stilnesse and the night
  Become the tutches of sweet harmony:
  Sit, Jessica, looke how the floore of heaven
  Is thick inlayed with pattens of bright gold,
  There's not the smallest orbe which thou beholdst
  But in his motion like an Angell sings,
  Still quiring to the young-eyed Cherubins;
  Such harmony is in immortall soules;
  But whilst this muddy vesture of decay
  Doth grossely close it in, we cannot hear it.
  WILLIAM SHAKESPEARE

SONNET

With how sad steps, O Moone, thou clim'st the skies!
How silently, and with how wan a face!
What, may it be that even in heav'nly place
That busie archer his sharpe arrowes tries!
Sure, if that long-with-love-acquainted eyes
Can judge of love, thou feel'st a lover's case,
I reade it in thy lookes; thy languisht grace,
To me, that feele the like, thy state discries.
Then, ev'n of fellowship, O Moone, tell me,
Is constant love deem'd there but want of wit?
Are beauties there as proud as here they be?
Do they above love to be lov'd, and yet
Those lovers scorne whom that love doth possesse?
Do they call virtue there ungratefulnesse?[1]

SIR PHILIP SIDNEY

[1] 'He (Sidney) means, Do they call ungratefulness there a virtue?'—*Essays of Elia.*

TO THE MOON

Art thou pale for weariness
  Of climbing heaven and gazing on the earth,
  Wandering companionless
Among the stars that have a different birth, —
And ever changing, like a joyless eye
That finds no object worth its constancy?

PERCY BYSSHE SHELLEY

From THE FARMER'S BOY

MOONLIGHT WALK

In part these nightly terrors to dispel,
Giles, ere he sleep, his little flock must tell.
From the fire-side with many a shrug he hies,
Glad if the full-orb'd moon salute his eyes,
And through the unbroken stillness of the night
Shed on his path her beams of cheering light.
With sauntering step he climbs the distant stile,
Whilst all around him wears a placid smile:
There views the white-robed clouds in clusters **driven**,
And all the glorious pageantry of heaven.
Low, on the utmost boundary of the sight,
The rising vapours catch the silvery light;
Thence fancy measures, as they parting fly,
Which first will throw its shadow on the eye,
Passing the source of light; and thence away,
Succeeded quick by brighter still than they.
For yet above these wafted clouds are seen
(In a remoter sky, still more serene)
Others, detach'd in ranges through the air,
Spotless as snow, and countless as they're fair;
Scatter'd immensely wide from east to west,
The beauteous semblance of a flock at rest.
These, to the raptured mind, aloud proclaim
Their mighty Shepherd's everlasting name.

ROBERT BLOOMFIELD

AT A LUNAR ECLIPSE

Thy shadow, Earth, from Pole to Central Sea,
Now steals along upon the Moon's meek shine
In even monochrome and curving line
Of imperturbable serenity.

How shall I link such sun-cast symmetry
With the torn troubled form I know as thine,
That profile, placid as a brow divine,
With continents of moil and misery?

And can immense Mortality but throw
So small a shade, and Heaven's high human scheme
Be hemmed within the coasts yon arc implies?

Is such the stellar gauge of earthly show,
Nation at war with nation, brains that teem,
Heroes, and women fairer than the skies?

THOMAS HARDY

ON AN ECLIPSE OF THE MOON

Struggling, and faint, and fainter didst thou wane,
O Moon! and round thee all thy starry train
Came forth to help thee, with half-open eyes,
And trembled every one with still surprise,
That the black Spectre should have dared assail
Their beauteous queen and seize her sacred veil.

WALTER SAVAGE LANDOR

VENUS

Is that star dumb, or am I deaf?
  Hour after hour I listen here
To catch the lovely music played
  By Venus down the evening air.

Before the other stars come out,
  Before the Moon is in her place –
I sit and watch those fingers move,
  And mark the twitching of her face.

Hour after hour I strain my ears
  For lovely notes that will not come:
Is it my mortal flesh that's deaf,
  Or that long-fingered star that's dumb?

W. H. DAVIES

THE STARRE

Bright spark, shot from a brighter place,
  Where beams surround my Saviours face,
    Canst thou be any where
      So well as there?

Yet, if thou wilt from thence depart,
  Take a bad lodging in my heart;
    For thou canst make a debter,
      And make it better.

First with thy fire-work burn to dust
  Folly, and worse than folly, lust:
    Then with thy light refine,
      And make it shine:

So disengag'd from sinne and sicknesse,
  Touch it with thy celestiall quicknesse,
    That it may hang and move
      After thy love.

Then with our trinitie of light,
  Motion, and heat, let's take our flight
    Unto the place where thou
      Before didst bow.

Get me a standing there, and place
  Among the beams, which crown the face
    Of him, who dy'd to part
      Sinne and my heart:

That so among the rest I may
  Glitter, and curle, and wind as they:
    That winding is their fashion
      Of adoration.

Sure thou wilt joy, by gaining me
To flie home like a laden bee
Unto that hive of beams
And garland-streams.

GEORGE HERBERT

MY STAR

All that I know
　Of a certain star
Is, it can throw
　(Like the angled spar)
Now a dart of red,
　Now a dart of blue;
Till my friends have said
　They would fain see, too,
My star that dartles the red and the blue!
Then it stops like a bird; like a flower, hangs furled:
　They must solace themselves with the Saturn above it.
What matter to me if their star is a world?
　Mine has opened its soul to me; therefore I love it.

ROBERT BROWNING

THE STARLIGHT NIGHT

Look at the stars! look, look up at the skies!
  O look at all the fire-folk sitting in the air!
  The bright boroughs, the circle-citadels there!
Down in dim woods the diamond delves! the elves' eyes!
The grey lawns cold where gold, where quickgold lies!
  Wind-beat whitebeam! airy abeles set on a flare!
  Flake-doves sent floating forth at a farmyard scare! –
Ah well! it is all a purchase, all is a prize.
Buy then! bid then! – What? – Prayer, patience, alms, vows
Look, look: a May-mess, like on orchard boughs!
  Look! March-bloom, like on mealed-with-yellow sallows!
These are indeed the barn; withindoors house
The shocks. This piece-bright paling shuts the spouse
  Christ home, Christ and his mother and all his hallows.

GERARD MANLEY HOPKINS

THE NIGHT-PIECE, TO JULIA

Her Eyes the Glow-worms lend thee,
The Shooting Starres attend thee
   And the Elves also,
    Whose little eyes glow,
Like the sparks of fire, befriend thee.

No *Will-o'-th'-Wispe* mis-light thee;
Nor Snake, or Slow-worme bite thee:
     But on, on thy way
     Not making a stay,
Since Ghost ther's none to affright thee.

Let not the darke thee cumber;
What though the Moon do's slumber?
     The Starres of the night
     Will lend thee their light,
Like Tapers cleare without number.

Then *Julia* let me wooe thee,
Thus, thus to come unto me:
     And when I shall meet
     Thy silv'ry feet,
My soule Ile poure into thee.

ROBERT HERRICK

THE MOWER TO THE GLO-WORMS

Ye living Lamps, by whose dear light
The Nightingale does sit so late,
And studying all the Summer-night,
Her matchless Songs does meditate;

Ye Country Comets, that portend
No War, nor Prince's funeral,
Shining unto no higher end
Than to presage the Grasses fall;

Ye Glo-worms, whose officious Flame
To wandering Mowers shows the way,
That in the Night have lost their aim,
And after foolish Fires do stray;

Your courteous Lights in vain you wast,
Since *Juliana* here is come,
For She my Mind hath so displac'd
That I shall never find my home.

ANDREW MARVELL

THE GLOWORME

Stay, fairest Chariessa, stay and mark
This animated Gem, whose fainter spark
Of fading light, its birth had from the dark:

A Star thought by the erring Passenger,
Which falling from its native Orb dropt here,
And makes the Earth (its Centre,) now its Sphere.

Should many of these sparks together be,
He that the unknown light far off should see,
Would think it a terrestrial Galaxie.

Take't up, fair Saint; see how it mocks thy fright,
The paler flame doth not yield heat, though light,
Which thus deceives thy Reason, through thy sight.

But see how quickly it (ta'ne up) doth fade,
To shine in darkness onely being made,
By th' brightness of thy light turn'd to a shade;

And burnt to ashes by thy flaming eyes
On the chaste Altar of thy hand it dies,
As to thy greater light a sacrifice.

THOMAS STANLEY

THE NIGHTINGALE

The Nightingale as soon as *April* bringeth
Unto her rested sens a perfect waking,
While late bare earth, proud of new clothing springeth
Sings out her woes, a thorn her song-book making:
    And mournfully bewayling,
    Her throat in Tunes expresseth
    What grief her breast oppresseth
    For Tereus' force on her chaste will prevailing.
        O *Philomela* fair! O take som gladness,
        That here is juster caus of plaintfull sadness:
        Thine earth now springs, mine fadeth,
        Thy thorn without, my thorn my heart invadeth.

Alas, shee hath no other caus of anguish
But Tereus' love, on her by strong hand worken,
Wherein she suffering all her spirits languish,
Full woman-like complains her will was broken.
    But I who daily craving,
    Cannot have to content mee,
    Have more caus to lament mee,
    Since wanting is more wo than too much having.
        O *Philomela* fair, O take som gladness,
        That here is juster caus of plaintfull sadness:
        Thine earth now springs, mine fadeth,
        Thy thorn without, my thorn my heart invadeth.

SIR PHILIP SIDNEY

AN ODE

As it fell upon a Day,
In the merrie Month of May,
Sitting in a pleasant shade,
Which a grove of Myrtles made,
Beastes did leape, and Birds did sing,
Trees did grow, and Plants did spring:
Every thing did banish mone,
Save the Nightingale alone.
Shee (poore Bird) as all forlorne,
Leand her Breast up-till a Thorne,
And there sung the dolefulst Ditty,
That to heare it was great Pitty.
Fie, fie, fie, now would she cry
Teru Teru, by and by:
That to heare her so complaine,
Scarce I could from Teares refraine:
For her griefes so lively showne,
Made me thinke upon mine owne.
Ah (thought I) thou mournst in vaine;
None takes Pitty on thy paine:
Senslesse Trees, they cannot heere thee;
Ruthless Beares, they wil not cheer thee.
King *Pandion,* hee is dead:
All thy friends are lapt in Lead.
All thy fellow Birds doe singe,
Carelesse of thy sorrowing.
Whilst as fickle Fortune smilde,
Thou and I, were both beguilde.
Everie one that flatters thee,
Is no friend in miserie:
Words are easie, like the winds;
Faithfull friends are hard to finde:
Everie man will bee thy friend,
Whilst thou hast wherewith to spend:
But if store of Crownes be scant,

No man will supply thy want.
If that one be prodigall,
Bountifull, they will him call.
And with such-like flattering,
Pitty but he were a King.
If hee bee adict to vice,
Quickly him, they will intice.
If to Woemen hee be bent,
They have at Commaundement.
But if Fortune once doe frowne,
Then farewell his great renowne:
They that fawnd on him before,
Use his company no more.
Hee that is thy friend indeed,
He will helpe thee in thy neede:
If thou sorrow, hee will weepe:
If thou wake, hee cannot sleepe:
Thus of everie griefe, in hart,
Hee, with thee, doeth beare a Part.
These are certaine Signes, to knowe
Faithfull friend, from flatt'ring foe.

RICHARD BARNFIELD

SONNET

O Nightingale, that on yon bloomy Spray
  Warb'lst at eeve, when all the Woods are still,
  Thou with fresh hope the Lovers heart dost fill,
  While the jolly hours lead on propitious *May*,
Thy liquid notes that close the eye of Day,
  First heard before the shallow Cuccoo's bill
  Portend success in love; O if *Jove's* will
  Have linkt that amorous power to thy soft lay,
Now timely sing, ere the rude Bird of Hate
  Foretell my hopeless doom in som Grove ny:
  As thou from yeer to yeer hast sung too late
For my relief; yet hadst no reason why,
  Whether the Muse, or Love call thee his mate,
  Both them I serve, and of their train am I.

JOHN MILTON

DEAR QUIRISTER...

Dear Quirister, who from those Shadowes sends
(Ere that the blushing Dawne dare show her Light)
Such sad lamenting Straines, that Night attends,
Become all Eare, Starres stay to heare thy Plight.
If one whose Griefe even Reach of Thought transcends,
Who ne're (not in a Dreame) did taste Delight,
May thee importune who like Case pretends,
And seemes to joy in Woe, in Woes Despight?
Tell me (so may thou Fortune milder trie,
And long long sing) for what thou thus complaines?
Sith (Winter gone) the Sunne in dapled Skie
Now smiles on Meadowes, Mountaines, Woods and Plaines:
    The Bird, as if my questions did her move,
    With trembling Wings sobb'd foorth *I love, I love.*

WILLIAM DRUMMOND OF HAWTHORNDEN

From MUSICKS DUELL

Now Westward *Sol* had spent the richest Beames
Of Noons high Glory, when hard by the streams
Of *Tiber*, on the sceane of a greene plat,
Under protection of an Oake; there sate
A sweet Lutes-master; in whose gentle aires
Hee lost the Dayes heat, and his owne hot cares.
    Close in the covert of the leaves there stood
A Nightingale, come from the neighbouring wood:
(The sweet inhabitant of each glad Tree,
Their Muse, their *Syren*, harmlesse *Syren* shee)
There stood she listning, and did entertaine
The Musicks soft report: and mould the same
In her owne murmures, that what ever mood
His curious fingers lent, her voyce made good:
The man perceiv'd his Rivall, and her Art;
Dispos'd to give the light-foot Lady sport,
Awakes his Lute, and 'gainst the fight to come
Informes it, in a sweet *Praeludium*
Of closer straines, and ere the warre begin,
Hee lightly skirmishes on every string
Charg'd with a flying touch: and straightway shee
Carves out her dainty voyce as readily,
Into a thousand sweet distinguish'd Tones,
And reckons up in soft divisions,
Quicke volumes of wild Notes; to let him know
By that shrill taste, she could doe something too.
    His nimble hands instinct then taught each string
A cap'ring cheerefullnesse; and made them sing
To their owne dance; now negligently rash
Hee throwes his Arme, and with a long drawne dash
Blends all together; then distinctly trips
From this to that; then quicke returning skips
And snatches this againe, and pauses there.
Shee measures every measure, every where

Meets art with art; sometimes as if in doubt
Not perfect yet, and fearing to bee out
Trailes her plaine Ditty in one long-spun note,
Through the sleeke passage of her open throat:
A cleare unwrinkled song, then doth shee point it
With tender accents, and severely joynt it
By short diminutives, that being rear'd
In controverting warbles evenly shar'd,
With her sweet selfe shee wrangles; Hee amazed
That from so small a channell should be rais'd
The torrent of a voyce, whose melody
Could melt into such sweet variety
Straines higher yet; that tickled with rare art
The tattling strings (each breathing in his part)
Most kindly doe fall out; the grumbling Base
In surly groanes disdaines the Trebles Grace.
The high-perch't treble chirps at this, and chides,
Untill his finger (Moderatour) hides
And closes the sweet quarrell, rousing all
Hoarse, shrill, at once; as when the Trumpets call
Hot Mars to th' Harvest of Deaths field, and woo
Mens hearts into their hands; this lesson too
Shee gives him backe; her supple Brest thrills out
Sharpe Aires, and staggers in a warbling doubt
Of dallying sweetnesse, hovers o'er her skill,
And folds in wav'd notes with a trembling bill,
The plyant Series of her slippery song.
Then starts shee suddenly into a Throng
Of short thicke sobs, whose thundring volleys float,
And roll themselves over her lubricke throat
In panting murmurs still'd out of her Breast
That ever-bubbling spring; the sugred Nest
Of her delicious soule, that there does lye
Bathing in streames of liquid Melodie;
Musicks best seed-plot, where in ripen'd Aires
A Golden-headed Harvest fairely reares

His Honey-dropping tops, plow'd by her breath
Which their reciprocally laboureth
In that sweet soyle. It seemes a holy quire
Founded to th' Name of great *Apollo's* lyre.
Whose sylver-roofe rings with the sprightly notes
Of sweet-lipp'd Angell-Imps, that swill their throats
In creame of Morning Helicon, and then
Prefer soft Anthems to the Eares of men,
To woo them from their Beds, still murmuring
That men can sleepe while they their Mattens sing:
(Most divine service) whose so early lay,
Prevents the Eye-lidds of the blushing day.
There might you heare her kindle her soft voyce,
In the close murmur of a sparkling noyse.
And lay the ground-worke of her hopefull song,
Still keeping in the foreward streame, so long
Till a sweet whirle-wind (striving to get out)
Heaves her soft Bosome, wanders round about,
And makes a pretty Earthquake in her breast,
Till the fledg'd Notes at length forsake their Nest;
Fluttering in wanton shoales, and to the Sky
Wing'd with their owne wild Eccho's prattling fly.
Shee opes the floodgate, and lets loose a Tide
Of streaming sweetnesse, which in state doth ride
On the wav'd backe of every swelling straine,
Rising and falling in a pompous traine.
And while shee thus discharges a shrill peale
Of flashing Aires; she qualifies their zeale
With the coole Epode of a graver Note,
Thus high, thus low, as if her silver throat
Would reach the brazen voyce of war's hoarse Bird;
Her little soule is ravisht: and so pour'd
Into loose extasies, that shee is plac't
Above her selfe, Musicks *Enthusiast* . . .

RICHARD CRASHAW

ON THE DEATH OF A NIGHTINGALE

Goe solitary wood, and henceforth be
Acquainted with no other Harmonie,
Then the Pyes chattering, or the shreeking note
Of bodeing Owles, and fatall Ravens throate.
Thy sweetest Chanters dead, that warbled forth
Layes, that might tempests calme, and still the North;
And call downe Angels from their glorious Spheare
To heare her Songs, and learn new Anthems there.
That soule is fled, and to *Elisium* gone;
Thou a poore desert left; goe then and runne,
Beg there to stand a grove, and if shee please
To sing againe beneath thy shadowy Trees;
The soules of happy Lovers crown'd with blisses
Shall flock about thee, and keepe time with kisses.

THOMAS RANDOLPH

TO THE NIGHTINGALE

Exert thy voice, sweet harbinger of spring!
  This moment is thy time to sing,
  This moment I attend thy praise
And set my numbers to thy lays.
  Free as thine shall be the song,
  As thy music, short or long.
Poets, wild as thou were born,
  Pleasing best when unconfin'd,
  When to please is least design'd,
Soothing but their cares to rest.
  Cares do still their thoughts molest,
  And still th'unhappy poet's breast,
Like thine, when best he sings, is plac'd against a thorn.

She begins. Let all be still!
  Muse, thy promise now fulfil!
Sweet, oh sweet! still sweeter yet
Can thy words such accents fit?
Canst thou syllables refine,
Melt a sense that shall retain
Still some spirit of the brain,
Till with sounds like these it join?
  'Twill not be! Then change thy note,
  Let division shake thy throat.
Hark! division now she tries,
Yet as far the Muse outflies.
  Cease then, prithee, cease thy tune:
  Trifler, wilt thou sing till June?
Till thy bus'ness all lies waste,
And the time of building's past!
  Thus we poets that have speech,
  Unlike what thy forests teach,
  If a fluent vein be shown
  That's transcendent to our own,
Criticise, reform, or preach,
Or censure what we cannot teach.

 LADY WINCHILSEA

From THE NIGHTINGALE

No cloud, no relique of the sunken day
Distinguishes the West, no long thin slip
Of Sullen light, no obscure trembling hues.
Come, we will rest on this old mossy bridge!
You see the glimmer of the stream beneath,
But hear no murmuring: it flows silently,
O'er its soft bed of verdure. All is still,
A balmy night! and though the stars be dim,
Yet let us think upon the vernal showers
That gladden the green earth, and we shall find
A pleasure in the dimness of the stars.
And Hark! the nightingale begins its song,
'Most musical, most melancholy' bird!
A melancholy bird? Oh! idle thought!
In Nature there is nothing melancholy.
But some night-wandering man whose heart was pierced
With the remembrance of a grievous wrong,
Or slow distemper, or neglected love,
(And so, poor wretch! fill'd all things with himself,
And made all gentle sounds tell back the tale
Of his own sorrow) he, and such as he,
First named these notes a melancholy strain.

                    . . . And I know a grove
Of large extent, hard by a castle huge,
Which the great lord inhabits not; and so
This grove is wild with tangling underwood,
And the trim walks are broken up, and grass,
Thin grass and king-cups grow within the paths.
But never elsewhere in one place I knew
So many nightingales: and far and near,
In wood and thicket, over the wide grove,
They answer and provoke each other's songs.
With skirmish and capricious passagings,
And murmurs musical and swift jug jug,

And one low piping sound more sweet than all –
Stirring the air with such an harmony,
That should you close your eyes, you might almost
Forget it was not day! On moonlight bushes,
Whose dewy leaflets are but half disclosed,
You may perchance behold them on the twigs,
Their bright, bright eyes, their eyes both bright and full,
Glistening, while many a glow-worm in the shade
Lights up her love-torch.

SAMUEL TAYLOR COLERIDGE

ODE TO A NIGHTINGALE

My heart aches, and a drowsy numbness pains
    My sense, as though of hemlock I had drunk.
Or emptied some dull opiate to the drains
    One minute past, and Lethe-wards had sunk:
'Tis not through envy of thy happy lot,
    But being too happy in thine happiness,
        That thou, light-wingèd Dryad of the trees,
            In some melodious plot
    Of beechen green, and shadows numberless,
    Singest of summer in full-throated ease.

O, for a draught of vintage! that hath been
    Cool'd a long age in the deep-delvèd earth,
Tasting of Flora and the country green,
    Dance, and Provençal song, and sunburnt mirth!
O for a beaker full of the warm South,
    Full of the true, the blushful Hippocrene,
        With beaded bubbles winking at the brim,
            And purple-stained mouth;
    That I might drink, and leave the world unseen,
    And with thee fade away into the forest dim:

Fade far away, dissolve, and quite forget
    What thou among the leaves hast never known,
The weariness, the fever, and the fret
    Here, when men sit and hear each other groan;
Where palsy shakes a few, sad, last grey hairs,
    Where youth grows pale, and spectre-thin, and dies;
        Where but to think is to be full of sorrow
            And leaden-eyed despairs,
    Where Beauty cannot keep her lustrous eyes,
    Or new Love pine at them beyond to-morrow.

Away! away! for I will fly to thee,
    Not charioted by Bacchus and his pards,
But on the viewless wings of Poesy,
    Though the dull brain perplexes and retards:
Already with thee! tender is the night,
    And haply the Queen-Moon is on her throne,
        Cluster'd around by all her starry Fays;
            But here there is no light,
    Save what from heaven is with the breezes blown
        Through verdurous glooms and winding mossy ways.

I cannot see what flowers are at my feet,
    Nor what soft incense hangs upon the boughs,
But, in embalmèd darkness, guess each sweet
    Wherewith the seasonable month endows
The grass, the thicket, and the fruit-tree wild;
    White hawthorn, and the pastoral eglantine;
        Fast fading violets cover'd up in leaves;
            And mid-May's eldest child,
    The coming musk-rose, full of dewy wine,
        The murmurous haunt of flies on summer eves.

Darkling I listen; and, for many a time
    I have been half in love with easeful Death,
Call'd him soft names in many a musèd rhyme,
    To take into the air my quiet breath;
Now more than ever seems it rich to die,
    To cease upon the midnight with no pain,
        While thou art pouring forth thy soul abroad
            In such an ecstasy!
Still wouldst thou sing, and I have ears in vain —
    To thy high requiem become a sod.

Thou wast not born for death, immortal Bird!
    No hungry generations tread thee down;
The voice I hear this passing night was heard
    In ancient days by emperor and clown:

Perhaps the self-same song that found a path
　　Through the sad heart of Ruth, when, sick for home,
　　　She stood in tears amid the alien corn;
　　　　The same that oft-times hath
　　Charm'd magic casements, opening on the foam
Of perilous seas, in faery lands forlorn.

Forlorn! the very word is like a bell
　　To toll me back from thee to my sole self!
Adieu! the fancy cannot cheat so well
　　As she is fam'd to do, deceiving elf.
Adieu! adieu! thy plaintive anthem fades
　　Past the near meadows, over the still stream,
　　　Up the hill-side; and now 'tis buried deep
　　　　In the next valley-glades:
　　Was it a vision, or a waking dream?
　　Fled is that music: – Do I wake or sleep?

JOHN KEATS

PHILOMELA

Hark! ah, the nightingale –
The tawny-throated!
Hark, from that moonlit cedar what a burst!
What triumph! hark! – what pain!

O wanderer from a Grecian shore,
Still, after many years, in distant lands,
Still nourishing in thy bewilder'd brain
That wild, unquench'd, deep-sunken, old-world pain –
Say, will it never heal?
And can this fragrant lawn
With its cool trees, and night,
And the sweet, tranquil Thames,
And moonshine, and the dew,
To thy rack'd heart and brain
Afford no balm?

Dost thou to-night behold,
Here, through the moonlight on this English grass,
The unfriendly palace in the Thracian wild?
Dost thou again peruse
With hot cheeks and sear'd eyes
The too clear web, and thy dumb sister's shame?
Dost thou once more assay
Thy flight, and feel come over thee,
Poor fugitive, the feathery change
Once more, and once more seem to make resound
With love and hate, triumph and agony,
Lone Daulis, and the high Cephissian vale?
Listen, Eugenia –
How thick the bursts come crowding through the leaves!
Again – thou hearest?
Eternal passion!
Eternal pain!

MATTHEW ARNOLD

THE VOICE

The nightingale I had not heard,
Though charmed by many another bird;
If no one tells me it is her,
How shall I know whose voice is near?
She sings, I'm told, in some dark wood,
Ten yards of moonlight from the road.

This night, as I go forth alone,
Before the month of June has gone,
What voice is this among the trees,
So startling sweet? The matchless ease,
The passion, power that will not fail —
The nightingale! The nightingale!

I ask no man what bird is this,
The singer of such pain and bliss;
All other birds sing from their throats,
But from her heart come this bird's notes:
To them I give my common cheers,
But you, my love, I thank with tears.

W. H. DAVIES

SWEET SUFFOLKE OWLE

Sweet Suffolke Owle, so trimly dight,
With feathers like a Lady bright,
Thou sing'st alone, sitting, by night,
    Te whit, te whoo,
Thy note that forth so freely roules,
With shrill command the Mouse controules,
And sings a dirge for dying soules,
    Te whit, te whoo.

ANON.

TO THE OWL

Grave Bird, that shelter'd in thy lonely bower,
  On some tall oak with ivy overspread,
  Or in some silent barn's deserted shed,
  Or mid the fragments of some ruin'd tower,
Still, as of old, at this sad solemn hour,
  When now the toiling Sons of Care are fled,
  And the freed Ghost slips from his wormy bed,
  Complaineth loud of Man's ungentle power,
That drives thee from the cheerful face of day
  To tell thy sorrows to the pale-eyed Night,
  Like thee, escaping from the sunny ray,
I woo this gloom, to hide me from the sight
  Of that fell Tribe whose persecuting sway
  On Me and Thee alike is bent to light.

THOMAS RUSSELL

A NOCTURNAL REVERIE

In such a night when every louder wind
Is to its distant cavern safe confin'd;
And only gentle Zephyr fans its wings,
And lonely Philomel, still waking, sings;
Or from some tree, fam'd for the owl's delight,
She, hollowing clear, directs the wand'rer right;
In such a night, when passing clouds give place,
Or thinly veil the heaven's mysterious face;
When in some river overhung with green,
The waving moon and trembling leaves are seen;
When fresh'ned grass now bears itself upright,
And makes cool banks to pleasing rest invite,
Whence springs the woodbine and the bramble-rose,
And where the sleepy cowslip shelter'd grows;
Whilst now a paler hue the foxglove takes,
Yet chequers still with red the dusky brakes,
When scatter'd glow-worms, but in twilight fine,
Show trivial beauties, watch their hour to shine;
Whilst Salisbury stands the test of every light,
In perfect charm and perfect virtue bright:
When odours, which declin'd repelling day,
Thro' temp'rate air uninterrupted stray;
When darken'd groves their softest shadows wear,
And falling waters we distinctly hear;
When thro' the gloom more venerable shows
Some ancient fabric, awful in repose,
While sunburnt hills their swarthy looks conceal,
And swelling haycocks thicken up the vale;
When the loos'd horse now, as his pasture leads,
Comes slowly grazing thro' th' adjoining meads,
Whose stealing pace, and lengthened shade we fear,
Till torn up forage in his teeth we hear:
When nibbling sheep at large pursue their food,
And unmolested kine rechew the cud;

When curlews cry beneath the village walls,
And to her straggling brood the partridge calls;
Their short-lived jubilee the creatures keep,
Which but endures whilst tyrant man does sleep;
When a sedate content the spirit feels,
And no fierce light disturbs, whilst it reveals,
But silent musings urge the mind to seek
Something too high for syllables to speak;
Till the free soul to a compos'dness charm'd,
Finding the elements of rage disarm'd,
O'er all below, a solemn quiet grown,
Joys in th' inferior world and thinks it like her own:
In such a night let me abroad remain,
Till morning breaks, and all's confus'd again:
Our cares, our toils, our clamours are renew'd,
Or pleasures, seldom reach'd, again pursued.

LADY WINCHILSEA

THE MIDNIGHT SKATERS

The hop-poles stand in cones,
   The icy pond lurks under,
The pole-tops steeple to the thrones
   Of stars, sound gulfs of wonder;
But not the tallest there, 'tis said,
Could fathom to this pond's black bed.

Then is not death at watch
   Within those secret waters?
What wants he but to catch
   Earth's heedless sons and daughters?
With but a crystal parapet
Between, he has his engines set.

Then on, blood shouts, on, on,
   Twirl, wheel and whip above him,
Dance on this ball-floor thin and wan,
   Use him as though you love him;
Court him, elude him, reel and pass,
And let him hate you through the glass.

EDMUND BLUNDEN

OUT IN THE DARK

Out in the dark over the snow
The fallow fawns invisible go
With the fallow doe;
And the winds blow
Fast as the stars are slow.

Stealthily the dark haunts round
And, when the lamp goes, without sound
At a swifter bound
Than the swiftest hound,
Arrives, and all else is drowned:

And I and star and wind and deer
Are in the dark together – near,
Yet far, – and fear
Drums in my ear
In that sage company drear.

How weak and little is the light,
All the universe of sight,
Love and delight,
Before the might,
If you love it not, of night.

EDWARD THOMAS

HYMN TO DARKNESS

Hail thou most sacred Venerable thing!
  What Muse is worthy thee to sing?
Thee, from whose pregnant universal womb
All things, even Light thy Rival, first did Come.
What dares he not attempt that sings of thee
  Thou First and greatest Mystery?
Who can the Secrets of thy essence tell?
Thou like the light of God art inaccessible.

Before Great Love this Monument did raise
  This ample Theater of Praise.
Before the folding Circles of the Skie
Were tun'd by Him who is all Harmony.
Before the Morning Stars their Hymn began,
  Before the Councel held for Man.
Before the birth of either Time or Place,
Thou reign'st unquestion'd Monarch in the empty Space.

Thy native lot thou didst to light resign,
  But still half of the Globe is thine.
Here with a quiet but yet awefull hand
Like the best Emperours thou dost command.
To thee the Stars above their brightness owe
  And mortals their repose below.
To thy protection Fear and Sorrow flee,
And those that weary are of light, find rest in thee.

The Light and Glory be th' Almighty's Throne,
  Darkness is His pavilion.
From that His radiant Beauty, but from thee
He has His Terrour and His Majesty.
Thus when He first proclaim'd His sacred Law,
  And would His Rebel subjects awe,
Like Princes on some great solemnity
H' appear'd in's Robes of State, and Clad Himself with thee.

402

The Blest above do thy sweet umbrage prize,
  When Cloy'd with light, they veil their eyes.
The Vision of the Deity is made
More sweet and Beatific by thy Shade.
But we poor Tenants of this Orb below
  Don't here thy excellency know,
Till Death our understandings does improve,
And then our Wiser ghosts thy silent night-walks love.

But thee I now admire, thee would I chuse
  For my Religion, or my Muse.
'Tis hard to tell whether thy reverend shade
Has more good Votarys or Poets made.
From thy dark Caves were Inspirations given
  And from thick groves went vows to Heaven.
Hail then thou Muse's and Devotion's Spring,
'Tis just we should adore, 'tis just we should thee sing.
JOHN NORRIS

When I survay the bright
 Coelestiall spheare:
So rich with jewels hung, that night
Doth like an Aethiop bride appeare.

My soule her wings doth spread
 And heaven-ward flies,
Th' Almighty's Mysteries to read
In the large volumes of the skies.

For the bright firmament
 Shootes forth no flame
So silent, but is eloquent
In speaking the Creators name.

No unregarded star
 Contracts its light
Into so small a Charactar,
Remov'd far from our humane sight:

But if we stedfast looke,
 We shall discerne
In it as in some holy booke,
How man may heavenly knowledge learne.

It tells the Conqueror,
 That farre-stretcht powre
Which his proud dangers traffique for,
Is but the triumph of an houre.

That from the farthest North;
 Some Nation may
Yet undiscovered issue forth,
And ore his new got conquest sway.

Some Nation yet shut in
　　With hils of ice
May be let out to scourge his sinne
'Till they shall equall him in vice.

And then they likewise shall
　　Their ruine have,
For as your selves your Empires fall,
And every Kingdome hath a grave.

Thus those Coelestiall fires,
　　Though seeming mute
The fallacie of our desires
And all the pride of life confute.

For they have watcht since first
　　The World had birth:
And found sinne in it self accurst,
And nothing permanent on earth.

WILLIAM HABINGTON

NIGHT AND DEATH

Mysterious night! when our first parent knew
Thee from report divine, and heard thy name,
Did he not tremble for this lovely frame,
This glorious canopy of light and blue?
Yet 'neath a curtain of translucent dew,
Bathed in the rays of the great setting flame,
Hesperus with the host of heaven came,
And lo! creation widened in man's view.
Who could have thought such darkness lay concealed
Within they beams, O Sun! or who could find,
Whilst flow'r and leaf and insect stood revealed,
That to such countless orbs thou mad'st us blind?
    Why do we then shun Death with anxious strife?
    If Light can thus deceive, wherefore not Life?

JOSEPH BLANCO WHITE

SONG OF THE NIGHT AT DAYBREAK

All my stars forsake me,
And the dawn-winds shake me.
Where shall I betake me?

Whither shall I run
Till the set of sun,
Till the day be done?

To the mountain-mine,
To the boughs o' the pine,
To the blind man's eyne,

To a brow that is
Bowed upon the knees,
Sick with memories.

ALICE MEYNELL

Nature
and Man
(2)

LEISURE

What is this life if, full of care,
We have no time to stand and stare.

No time to stand beneath the boughs
And stare as long as sheep or cows.

No time to see, when woods we pass,
Where squirrels hide their nuts in grass.

No time to see, in broad daylight,
Streams full of stars, like stars at night.

No time to turn at Beauty's glance,
And watch her feet, how they can dance.

No time to wait till her mouth can
Enrich that smile her eyes began.

A poor life this if, full of care,
We have no time to stand and stare.

W. H. DAVIES

THE TYGER

Tyger! Tyger! burning bright
In the forests of the night,
What immortal hand or eye
Could frame thy fearful symmetry?

In what distant deeps or skies
Burnt the fire of thine eyes?
On what wings dare he aspire?
What the hand dare seize the fire?

And what shoulder, and what art,
Could twist the sinews of thy heart?
And when thy heart began to beat,
What dread hand? and what dread feet?

What the hammer? what the chain?
In what furnace was thy brain?
What the anvil? what dread grasp
Dare its deadly terrors clasp?

When the stars threw down their spears,
And water'd heaven with their tears,
Did he smile his work to see?
Did he who made the Lamb make thee?

Tyger! Tyger! burning bright
In the forests of the night,
What immortal hand or eye,
Dare frame thy fearful symmetry?

WILLIAM BLAKE

TO A SNOWFLAKE

What heart could have thought you? –
Past our devisal
(O filigree petal!)
Fashioned so purely,
Fragilely, surely,
From what Paradisal
Imagineless metal,
Too costly for cost?
Who hammered you, wrought you,
From argentine vapour? –
'God was my shaper.
Passing surmisal,
He hammered, He wrought me,
From curled silver vapour,
To lust of his mind: –
Thou could'st not have thought me!
So purely, so palely,
Tinily surely,
Mightily, frailly,
Insculped and embossed,
With His hammer of wind,
And His graver of frost.'

FRANCIS THOMPSON

TO A DAISY

Slight as thou art, thou art enough to hide,
  Like all created things, secrets from me,
  And stand a barrier to eternity.
And I, how can I praise thee well and wide

From where I dwell – upon the hither side?
  Thou little veil for so great mystery,
  When shall I penetrate all things and thee,
And then look back? For this I must abide,

Till thou shalt grow and fold and be unfurled
Literally between me and the world.
  Then I shall drink from in beneath a spring,

And from a poet's side shall read his book.
  O daisy mine, what will it be to look
    From God's side even of such a simple thing?

ALICE MEYNELL

FLOWER IN THE CRANNIED WALL

Flower in the crannied wall,
I pluck you out of the crannies,
I hold you here, root and all, in my hand,
Little flower – but *if* I could understand
What you are, root and all, and all in all,
I should know what God and man is.

LORD TENNYSON

Survivor sole, and hardly such, of all
That once lived here, thy brethren! at my birth,
(Since which I number threescore winters past),
A shatter'd veteran, hollow-trunk'd perhaps,
As now, and with excoriate forks deform.
Relic of ages! could a mind, imbued
With truth from heaven, created thing adore,
I might with reverence kneel, and worship thee.
    It seems idolatry, with some excuse,
When our forefather Druids in their oaks
Imagined sanctity. The conscience, yet
Unpurified by an authentic act
Of amnesty, the meed of blood divine,
Loved not the light, but, gloomy, into gloom
Of thickest shades, like Adam after taste
Of fruit proscribed, as to a refuge, fled.
    Thou wast a bauble once; a cup and ball
Which babes might play with; and the thievish jay,
Seeking her food, with ease might have purloin'd
The auburn nut that held thee, swallowing down
Thy yet close-folded latitude of boughs
And all thy embryo vastness at a gulp.
But Fate thy growth decreed; autumnal rains
Beneath thy parent tree mellow'd the soil
Design'd thy cradle; and a skipping deer,
With pointed hoof dibbling the glebe, prepared
The soft receptacle, in which, secure,
Thy rudiments should sleep the winter through.
    So Fancy dreams. Disprove it, if ye can,
Ye reasoners broad awake, whose busy search
Of argument, employed too oft amiss,
Sifts half the pleasures of short life away!
    Thou fell'st mature; and, in the loamy clod
Swelling with vegetative force instinct
Didst burst thine egg, as theirs the fabled Twins,

Now stars; two lobes protruding, pair'd exact;
A leaf succeeded, and another leaf,
And, all the elements thy puny growth
Fostering propitious, thou becamest a twig.
    Who lived when thou wast such? Oh, couldst thou speak
As in Dodona once thy kindred trees
Oracular, I would not curious ask
The future, best unknown, but at thy mouth
Inquisitive, the less ambiguous past.
    By thee I might correct, erroneous oft,
The clock of history, facts and events
Timing more punctual, unrecorded facts
Recovering, and misstated setting right –
Desperate attempt, till trees shall speak again!
    Time made thee what thou wast, king of the woods;
And time hath made thee what thou art – a cave
For owls to roost in. Once thy spreading boughs
O'erhung the champaign; and the numerous flocks
That grazed it, stood beneath that ample cope
Uncrowded, yet safe shelter'd from the storm.
No flock frequents thee now. Thou hast outlived
Thy popularity, and art become
(Unless verse rescues thee awhile) a thing
Forgotten, as the foliage of thy youth.
    While thus through all the stages thou hast push'd
Of treeship – first a seedling hid in grass:
Then twig; then sapling; and, as century roll'd
Slow after century, a giant bulk
Of girth enormous, with moss-cushion'd root
Upheaved above the soil, and sides emboss'd
With prominent wens globose, – till at the last
The rottenness, which Time is charged to inflict
On other mighty ones, found also thee.
    What exhibitions various hath the world
Witness'd of mutability in all
That we account most durable below!
Change is the diet, on which all subsist,

Created changeable, and change at last
Destroys them. Skies uncertain, now the heat
Transmitting cloudless, and the solar beam
Now quenching in a boundless sea of clouds, –
Calm and alternate storm, moisture and drought,
Invigorate by turns the springs of life
In all that live, plant, animal, and man,
And in conclusion mar them. Nature's threads,
Fine passing thought, e'en in her coarsest works,
Delight in agitation, yet sustain
The force, that agitates not unimpair'd;
But, worn by frequent impulse, to the cause
Of their best tone their dissolution owe.
    Thought cannot spend itself, comparing still
The great and little of thy lot, thy growth
From almost nullity into a state
Of matchless grandeur, and declension thence,
Slow, into such magnificent decay.
Time was when, settling on thy leaf, a fly
Could shake thee to the root – and time has been
When tempests could not. At thy firmest age
Thou hadst within thy bole solid contents,
That might have ribb'd the sides and plank'd the deck
Of some flagg'd admiral; and tortuous arms,
The shipwright's darling treasure, didst present
To the four-quarter'd winds, robust and bold,
Warped into tough knee-timber,[1] many a load!
But the axe spared thee. In those thriftier days
Oaks fell not, hewn by thousands, to supply
The bottomless demands of contest, waged
For senatorial honours. Thus to Time
The task was left to whittle thee away
With his sly scythe, whose ever-nibbling edge,
Noiseless, an atom and an atom more,

---

[1] Knee-timber is found in the crooked arms of oak, which, by reason of their distortion, are easily adjusted to the angle formed where the deck and the ship's sides meet.—C.

Disjoining from the rest, has, unobserved,
Achieved a labour, which had, far and wide,
By man perform'd, made all the forest ring.
  Embowell'd now, and of thy ancient self
Possessing nought but the scoop'd rind, that seems
A huge throat calling to the clouds for drink,
Which it would give in rivulets to thy root,
Thou temptest none, but rather much forbid'st
The feller's toil, which thou couldst ill requite.
Yet is thy root sincere, sound as the rock,
A quarry of stout spurs, and knotted fangs,
Which, crook'd into a thousand whimsies, clasp
The stubborn soil, and hold thee still erect.
  So stands a kingdom, whose foundation yet
Fails not in virtue, and in wisdom laid,
Though all the superstructure, by the tooth
Pulverised of venality, a shell
Stands now, and semblance only of itself!
  Thine arms have left thee. Winds have rent them off
Long since, and rovers of the forest wild
With bow and shaft have burnt them. Some have left
A splinter'd stump bleach'd to a snowy white;
And some memorial none where once they grew.
Yet life still lingers in thee, and puts forth
Proof not contemptible of what she can,
Even where death predominates. The spring
Finds thee not less alive to her sweet force
Than yonder upstarts of the neighbouring wood,
So much thy juniors, who their birth received
Half a millenium since the date of thine.
  But since, although well qualified by age
To teach, no spirit dwells in thee, nor voice
May be expected from thee, seated here
On thy distorted root, with hearers none,
Or prompter, save the scene, I will perform
Myself the oracle, and will discourse
In my own ear such matter as I may.

One man alone, the father of us all,
Drew not his life from woman; never gazed
With mute unconsciousness of what he saw,
On all around him; learn'd not by degrees,
Nor owed articulation to his ear;
But, moulded by his Maker into man
At once, upstood intelligent, survey'd
All creatures, with precision understood
Their purport, uses, properties assign'd
To each his name significant, and, fill'd
With love and wisdom, render'd back to Heaven
In praise harmonious the first air he drew.
He was excused the penalties of dull
Minority. No tutor charged his hand
With the thought-tracing quill, or task'd his mind
With problems. History, not wanted yet,
Lean'd on her elbow, watching Time, whose course,
Eventful, should supply her with a theme . . .

WILLIAM COWPER

FAREWELL

Not soon shall I forget — a sheet
Of golden water, cold and sweet,
The young moon with her head in veils
Of silver, and the nightingales.

A wain of hay came up the lane —
O fields I shall not walk again,
And trees I shall not see, so still
Against a sky of daffodil!

Fields where my happy heart had rest,
And where my heart was heaviest,
I shall remember them at peace
Drenched in moon-silver like a fleece.

The golden water sweet and cold,
The moon of silver and of gold,
The dew upon the gray grass-spears,
I shall remember them with tears.

KATHARINE TYNAN

OLTON POOLS

Now June walks on the waters,
And the cuckoo's last enchantment
Passes from Olton pools.

Now dawn comes to my window
Breathing midsummer roses,
And scythes are wet with dew.

Is it not strange for ever
That, bowered in this wonder,
Man keeps a jealous heart?

That June and the June waters
And birds and dawn-lit roses,
Are gospels in the wind,

Fading upon the deserts,
Poor pilgrim revelations? . . .
Hist . . . over Olton pools!

JOHN DRINKWATER

From THE PRELUDE

. . . One summer evening (led by her) I found
A little boat tied to a willow tree
Within a rocky cave, its usual home.
Straight I unloosed her chain, and stepping in
Pushed from the shore. It was an act of stealth
And troubled pleasure, nor without the voice
Of mountain-echoes did my boat move on;
Leaving behind her still, on either side,
Small circles glittering idly in the moon,
Until they melted all into one track
Of sparkling light. But now, like one who rows,
Proud of his skill, to reach a chosen point
With an unswerving line, I fixed my view
Upon the summit of a craggy ridge,
The horizon's utmost boundary; far above
Was nothing but the stars and the grey sky.
She was an elfin pinnace; lustily
I dipped my oars into the silent lake,
And, as I rose upon the stroke, my boat
Went heaving through the water like a swan;
When, from behind that craggy steep till then
The horizon's bound, a huge peak, black and huge,
As if with voluntary power instinct,
Upreared its head. I struck and struck again,
And growing still in stature the grim shape
Towered up between me and the stars, and still,
For so it seemed, with purpose of its own
And measured motion like a living thing,
Strode after me. With trembling oars I turned,
And through the silent water stole my way
Back to the covert of the willow tree;
There in her mooring-place I left my bark, –
And through the meadows homeward went, in grave
And serious mood; but after I had seen
That spectacle, for many days my brain

Worked with a dim and undetermined sense
Of unknown modes of being; o'er my thoughts
There hung a darkness, call it solitude
Or blank desertion. No familiar shapes
Remained, no pleasant images of trees,
Of sea or sky, no colours of green fields;
But huge and mighty forms, that do not live
Like living men, moved slowly through the mind
By day, and were a trouble to my dreams.

Wisdom and Spirit of the universe!
Thou Soul that art the eternity of thought,
That givest to forms and images a breath
And everlasting motion, not in vain
By day or star-light thus from my first dawn
Of childhood didst thou intertwine for me
The passions that build up our human soul,
Not with the mean and vulgar works of man,
But with high objects, with enduring things –
With life and nature – purifying thus
The elements of feeling and of thought,
And sanctifying, by such discipline,
Both pain and fear, until we recognise
A grandeur in the beatings of the heart.
Nor was this fellowship vouchsafed to me
With stinted kindness. In November days,
When vapours rolling down the valley made
A lonely scene more lonesome, among woods,
At noon and mid the calm of summer nights,
When, by the margin of the trembling lake,
Beneath the gloomy hills homeward I went
In solitude, such intercourse was mine;
Mine was it in the fields both day and night,
And by the waters, all the summer long.

And in the frosty season, when the sun
Was set, and visible for many a mile

The cottage windows blazed through twilight gloom,
I heeded not their summons: happy time
It was indeed for all of us – for me
It was a time of rapture! Clear and loud
The village clock tolled six, – I wheeled about,
Proud and exulting like an untired horse
That cares not for his home. All shod with steel,
We hissed along the polished ice in games
Confederate, imitative of the chase
And woodland pleasures, – the resounding horn,
The pack loud chiming, and the hunted hare.
So through the darkness and the cold we flew,
And not a voice was idle; with the din
Smitten, the precipices rang aloud;
The leafless trees and every icy crag
Tinkled like iron; while far distant hills
Into the tumult sent an alien sound
Of melancholy not unnoticed, while the stars
Eastward were sparkling clear, and in the west
The orange sky of evening died away.
Not seldom from the uproar I retired
Into a silent bay, or sportively
Glanced sideway, leaving the tumultuous throng,
To cut across the reflex of a star
That fled, and, flying still before me, gleamed
Upon the grassy plain; and oftentimes,
When we had given our bodies to the wind,
And all the shadowy banks on either side
Came sweeping through the darkness, spinning still
The rapid line of motion, then at once
Have I, reclining back upon my heels,
Stopped short; yet still the solitary cliffs
Wheeled by me – even as if the earth had rolled
With visible motion her diurnal round!
Behind me did they stretch in solemn train,
Feebler and feebler, and I stood and watched
Till all was tranquil as a summer sea.

WILLIAM WORDSWORTH   423

MOUNTAINS

With dignity ye surge into the sky,
O mountain fortresses: pure is the gleam
Of the far worlds caught in your naked slabs:
Well tempered are ye in the season's forge,
Cold progeny of the fire-breathing sun.
Ye heed not the soft mists and wooing clouds
That your locked hollows gently seek to explore.
Proudly above the clinging claim of life
Ye rise to break the elemental storms:
Proudly ye sluice the drooping vines below,
Gaunt monuments of fire that lost its soul.

MICHAEL MCKENNA

IN A DREAR-NIGHTED DECEMBER

In a drear-nighted December,
Too happy, happy tree,
Thy branches ne'er remember
Their green felicity:
The north cannot undo them,
With a sleety whistle through them;
Nor frozen thawings glue them
From budding at the prime.

In a drear-nighted December,
Too happy, happy brook,
Thy bubblings ne'er remember
Apollo's summer look;
But with a sweet forgetting,
They stay their crystal fretting,
Never, never petting
About the frozen time.

Ah would 'twere so with many
A gentle girl and boy!
But were there ever any
Writh'd not at passèd joy?
To know the change and feel it,
When there is none to heal it,
Nor numbèd sense to steal it,
Was never said in rhyme.

JOHN KEATS

O DREAMY, GLOOMY, FRIENDLY TREES

O dreamy, gloomy, friendly Trees,
   I came along your narrow track
To bring my gifts unto your knees
   And gifts did you give back;
For when I brought this heart that burns –
   These thoughts that bitterly repine –
And laid them here among the ferns
   And the hum of boughs divine,
Ye, vastest breathers of the air,
   Shook down with slow and mighty poise
Your coolness on the human care,
   Your wonder on its toys,
Your greenness on the heart's despair,
   Your darkness on its noise.

HERBERT TRENCH

BINSEY POPLARS

FELLED 1879

My aspens dear, whose airy cages quelled,
Quelled or quenched in leaves the leaping sun,
All felled, felled, are all felled;
    Of a fresh and following folded rank
        Not spared, not one
        That dandled a sandalled
     Shadow that swam or sank
On meadow and river and wind-wandering weed-winding bank.

  O if we but knew what we do
     When we delve or hew —
  Hack and rack the growing green!
     Since country is so tender
    To touch, her being so slender,
    That, like this sleek and seeing ball
  But a prick will make no eye at all,
  Where we, even where we mean
        To mend her we end her,
     When we hew or delve:
After-comers cannot guess the beauty been.
  Ten or twelve, only ten or twelve
     Strokes of havoc unselve
     The sweet especial scene,
    Rural scene, a rural scene,
    Sweet especial rural scene.

GERARD MANLEY HOPKINS

From IN MEMORIAM.

Dip down upon the northern shore,
    O sweet new-year delaying long;
    Thou doest expectant nature wrong;
Delaying long, delay no more.

What stays thee from the clouded noons,
    Thy sweetness from its proper place?
    Can trouble live with April days,
Or sadness in the summer moons?

Bring orchis, bring the foxglove spire,
    The little speedwell's darling blue,
    Deep tulips dash'd with fiery dew,
Laburnums, dropping-wells of fire.

O thou new-year, delaying long,
    Delayest the sorrow in my blood,
    That longs to burst a frozen bud
And flood a fresher throat with song.

    .   .   .   .

Old Yew, which graspest at the stones
    That name the under-lying dead,
    Thy fibres net the dreamless head,
Thy roots are wrapt about the bones.

The seasons bring the flower again,
    And bring the firstling to the flock;
    And in the dusk of thee, the clock
Beats out the little lives of men.

O not for thee the glow, the bloom,
    Who changest not in any gale,
    Nor branding summer suns avail
To touch thy thousand years of gloom:

And gazing on thee, sullen tree,
   Sick for thy stubborn hardihood,
   I seem to fail from out my blood
And grow incorporate into thee.

·   ·   ·   ·

Now fades the last long streak of snow,
   Now burgeons every maze of quick
   About the flowering squares, and thick
By ashen roots the violets blow.

Now rings the woodland loud and long,
   The distance takes a lovlier hue,
   And drown'd in yonder living blue
The lark becomes a sightless song.

Now dance the lights on lawn and lea,
   The flocks are whiter down the vale,
   And milkier every milky sail
On winding stream or distant sea;

Where now the seamew pipes, or dives
   In yonder greening gleam, and fly
   The happy birds, that change their sky
To build and brood; that live their lives

From land to land; and in my breast
   Spring wakens too; and my regret
   Becomes an April violet,
And buds and blossoms like the rest.

·   ·   ·   ·

Calm is the morn without a sound,
   Calm as to suit a calmer grief,
   And only thro' the faded leaf
The chestnut pattering to the ground:

Calm and deep peace on this high wold,
    And on these dews that drench the furze,
    And all the silvery gossamers
That twinkle into green and gold:

Calm and still light on yon great plain
    That sweeps with all its autumn bowers,
    And crowded farms and lessening towers,
To mingle with the bounding main:

Calm and deep peace in this wide air,
    These leaves that redden to the fall:
    And in my heart, if calm at all,
If any calm, a calm despair;

Calm on the seas, and silver sleep,
    And waves that sway themselves in rest,
    And dead calm in that noble breast
Which heaves but with the heaving deep.

      .   .   .   .

To-night the winds begin to rise
    And roar from yonder dropping day:
    The last red leaf is whirl'd away,
The rooks are blown about the skies;

The forest crack'd, the waters curl'd,
    The cattle huddled on the lea;
    And wildly dash'd on tower and tree
The sunbeam strikes along the world:

And but for fancies, which aver
    That all thy motions gently pass
    Athwart a plane of molten glass,
I scarce could brook the strain and stir

That makes the barren branches loud;
 And but for fear it is not so,
 The wild unrest that lives in woe
Would dote and pore on yonder cloud

That rises upward always higher,
 And onward drags a labouring breast,
 And topples round the dreary west,
A looming bastion fringed with fire.

LORD TENNYSON

To see a World in a Grain of Sand,
And a Heaven in a Wild Flower,
Hold Infinity in the palm of your hand,
And Eternity in an hour.
A Robin Redbreast in a Cage
Puts all Heaven in a Rage.
A dove-house fill'd with Doves and Pigeons
Shudders Hell thro' all its regions.
A dog starv'd at his Master's Gate
Predicts the ruin of the State.
A Horse misused upon the Road
Calls to Heaven for Human blood.
Each outcry of the hunted Hare
A fibre from the Brain does tear.
A Skylark wounded in the wing;
A Cherubim does cease to sing.
The Game Cock clipt and arm'd for fight
Does the Rising Sun affright.
Every Wolf's and Lion's howl
Raises from Hell a Human Soul.
The wild Deer, wandr'ing here and there,
Keeps the Human Soul from Care.
The Lamb misus'd breeds Public Strife,
And yet forgives the Butcher's knife.
The Bat that flits at close of Eve
Has left the Brain that won't Believe.
The Owl that calls upon the Night
Speaks the Unbeliever's fright.
He who shall hurt the little Wren
Shall never be belov'd by Men.
He who the Ox to wrath has mov'd
Shall never be by Woman lov'd.
The wanton boy that kills the Fly
Shall feel the Spider's enmity.

He who torments the Chafer's Sprite
Weaves a bower in endless Night.
The Catterpiller on the Leaf
Repeats to thee thy Mother's grief.
Kill not the Moth nor Butterfly,
For the Last Judgment draweth nigh.
He who shall train the Horse to war
Shall never pass the Polar Bar.
The Beggar's Dog and Widow's Cat,
Feed them and thou wilt grow fat.
The Gnat that sings his Summer's Song
Poison gets from Slander's tongue.
The poison of the Snake and Newt
Is the sweat of Envy's Foot.
The poison of the Honey Bee
Is the Artist's Jealousy.
The Prince's Robes and Beggar's Rags
Are Toadstools on the Miser's Bags.

WILLIAM BLAKE

From DEJECTION: AN ODE

Late, late yestreen I saw the new Moon
With the old Moon in her arms;
And I fear, I fear, my Master dear!
We shall have a deadly storm.

         Ballad of Sir Patrick Spence

Well! If the Bard was weather-wise, who made
  The grand old ballad of Sir Patrick Spence,
  This night, so tranquil now, will not go hence
Unroused by winds, that ply a busier trade
Than those which mould yon cloud in lazy flakes,
Or the dull sobbing draft, that moans and rakes
    Upon the strings of this Æolian lute,
    Which better far were mute.
  For lo! the New-moon winter-bright!
  And overspread with phantom light,
  (With swimming phantom light o'erspread
  But rimmed and circled by a silver thread)
I see the old Moon in her lap, foretelling
  The coming-on of rain and squally blast.
And oh! that even now the gust were swelling,
  And the slant night-shower driving loud and fast!
Those sounds which oft have raised me, whilst they awed,
    And sent my soul abroad,
Might now perhaps their wonted impulse give,
Might startle this dull pain, and make it move and live!

A grief without a pang, void, dark, and drear,
  A stifled, drowsy, unimpassioned grief,
  Which finds no natural outlet, no relief,
    In word, or sigh, or tear —
O Lady! in this wan and heartless mood,
To other thoughts by yonder throstle woo'd,
  All this long eve, so balmy and serene,
Have I been gazing on the western sky,
  And its peculiar tint of yellow green:
And still I gaze — and with how blank an eye!

And those thin clouds above, in flakes and bars,
That give away their motion to the stars;
Those stars, that glide behind them or between,
Now sparkling, now bedimmed, but always seen:
Yon crescent Moon, as fixed as if it grew
In its own cloudless, starless lake of blue;
I see them all so excellently fair,
I see, not feel, how beautiful they are!

    My genial spirits fail;
    And what can these avail
To lift the smothering weight from off my breast?
    It were a vain endeavour,
    Though I should gaze for ever
On that green light that lingers in the west:
I may not hope from outward forms to win
The passion and the life, whose fountains are within.

O Lady! we receive but what we give,
And in our life alone does Nature live:
Ours is her wedding-garment, ours her shroud!
    And would we aught behold, of higher worth,
Than that inanimate cold world allowed
To the poor loveless, ever-anxious crowd,
    Ah! from the soul itself must issue forth
A light, a glory, a fair luminous cloud
    Enveloping the Earth —
And from the soul itself must there be sent
    A sweet and potent voice, of its own birth,
Of all sweet sounds the life and element!

SAMUEL TAYLOR COLERIDGE

ODE

INTIMATIONS OF IMMORTALITY FROM RECOLLECTIONS OF EARLY CHILDHOOD

There was a time when meadow, grove, and stream
The earth, and every common sight,
   To me did seem
  Apparelled in celestial light,
The glory and the freshness of a dream.
It is not now as it hath been of yore; –
   Turn wheresoe'er I may,
    By night or day,
The things which I have seen I now can see no more.

  The Rainbow comes and goes,
  And lovely is the Rose,
  The moon doth with delight
Look round her when the heavens are bare,
  Waters on a starry night
  Are beautiful and fair;
 The sunshine is a glorious birth;
 But yet I know, where'er I go,
That there hath past away a glory from the earth.

Now, while the birds thus sing a joyous song,
  And while the young lambs bound
  As to the tabor's sound,
To me alone there came a thought of grief:
A timely utterance gave that thought relief,
  And I again am strong:
The cataracts blow their trumpets from the steep;
No more shall grief of mine the season wrong;
I hear the Echoes through the mountains throng,
The Winds come to me from the fields of sleep,
  And all the earth is gay;
   Land and sea

Give themselves up to jollity,
    And with the heart of May
Doth every Beast keep holiday; —
    Thou Child of Joy,
Shout round me, let me hear thy shouts, thou happy
      Shepherd-boy!

Ye blessèd Creatures, I have heard the call
    Ye to each other make; I see
The heavens laugh with you in your jubilee;
    My heart is at your festival,
    My head hath its coronal,
The fulness of your bliss, I feel — I feel it all.
      Oh evil day! if I were sullen
      While Earth herself is adorning,
        This sweet May-morning,
      And the Children are culling
        On every side,
      In a thousand valleys far and wide,
      Fresh flowers; while the sun shines warm,
And the Babe leaps up on his Mother's arm: —
      I hear, I hear, with joy I hear!
      — But there's a Tree, of many, one,
A single Field which I have looked upon,
Both of them speak of something that is gone:
      The pansy at my feet
      Doth the same tale repeat:
Whither is fled the visionary gleam?
Where is it now, the glory and the dream?

Our birth is but a sleep and a forgetting:
The Soul that rises with us, our life's Star,
      Hath had elsewhere its setting,
        And cometh from afar:
      Not in entire forgetfulness,
      And not in utter nakedness,
But trailing clouds of glory do we come
      From God, who is our home:

Heaven lies about us in our infancy!
Shades of the prison-house begin to close
            Upon the growing Boy,
But He beholds the light, and whence it flows,
            He sees it in his joy;
The Youth, who daily farther from the east
            Must travel, still is Nature's Priest,
            And by the vision splendid
            Is on his way attended;
At length the Man perceives it die away,
And fade into the light of common day.

Earth fills her lap with pleasures of her own;
Yearnings she hath in her own natural kind,
And, even with something of a Mother's mind,
            And no unworthy aim,
            The homely Nurse doth all she can
To make her Foster-child, her Inmate Man,
            Forget the glories he hath known,
And that imperial palace whence he came.

Behold the Child among his new-born blisses,
A six years' Darling of our pigmy size!
See, where 'mid work of his own hand he lies,
Fretted by sallies of his mother's kisses,
With light upon him from his father's eyes!
See, at his feet, some little plan or chart,
Some fragment from his dream of human life,
Shaped by himself with newly-learnèd art;
            A wedding or a festival,
            A mourning or a funeral;
                And this hath now his heart,
            And unto this he frames his song:
                Then will he fit his tongue
To dialogues of business, love, or strife;
            But it will not be long

Ere this be thrown aside,
And with new joy and pride
The little actor cons another part;
Filling from time to time his 'humorous stage'
With all the Persons, down to palsied Age,
That Life brings with her in her equipage;
As if his whole vocation
Were endless imitation.

Thou, whose exterior semblance doth belie
Thy Soul's immensity;
Thou best Philosopher, who yet dost keep
Thy heritage, thou Eye among the blind,
That, deaf and silent, read'st the eternal deep,
Haunted for ever by the eternal mind, —
Mighty Prophet! Seer blest!
On whom those truths do rest,
Which we are toiling all our lives to find,
In darkness lost, the darkness of the grave;
Thou, over whom thy Immortality
Broods like the Day, a Master o'er a Slave,
A Presence which is not to be put by;
Thou little Child, yet glorious in the might
Of heaven-born freedom on thy being's height,
Why with such earnest pains dost thou provoke
The years to bring the inevitable yoke,
Thus blindly with thy blessedness at strife?
Full soon thy Soul shall have her earthly freight,
And custom lie upon thee with a weight,
Heavy as frost, and deep almost as life!

O joy! that in our embers
Is something that doth live,
That nature yet remembers
What was so fugitive!
The thought of our past years in me doth breed
Perpetual benediction: not indeed

For that which is most worthy to be blest —
Delight and liberty, the simple creed
Of Childhood, whether busy or at rest,
With new-fledged hope still fluttering in his breast: —
          Not for these I raise
            The song of thanks and praise;
     But for those obstinate questionings
          Of sense and outward things,
          Fallings from us, vanishings;
          Blank misgivings of a Creature
Moving about in worlds not realised,
High instincts before which our mortal Nature
Did tremble like a guilty Thing surprised:
            But for those first affections,
            Those shadowy recollections,
        Which, be they what they may,
Are yet the fountain light of all our day,
Are yet a master light of all our seeing;
        Uphold us, cherish, and have power to make
Our noisy years seem moments in the being
Of the eternal Silence: truths that wake,
            To perish never;
Which neither listlessness, nor mad endeavour,
            Nor Man nor Boy,
Nor all that is at enmity with joy,
Can utterly abolish or destroy!
            Hence in a season of calm weather
            Though inland far we be,
Our Souls have sight of that immortal sea
            Which brought us hither,
            Can in a moment travel thither,
And see the Children sport upon the shore,
And hear the mighty waters rolling evermore.

Then sing, ye Birds, sing, sing a joyous song!
            And let the young Lambs bound
            As to the tabor's sound!

We in thought will join your throng,
        Ye that pipe and ye that play,
        Ye that through your hearts to-day
        Feel the gladness of the May!
What though the radiance which was once so bright
Be now for ever taken from my sight,
        Though nothing can bring back the hour
Of splendour in the grass, of glory in the flower;
        We will grieve not, rather find
        Strength in what remains behind,
        In the primal sympathy
        Which having been must ever be;
        In the soothing thoughts that spring
        Out of human suffering;
        In the faith that looks through death,
In years that bring the philosophic mind.

And O, ye Fountains, Meadows, Hills and Groves,
Forebode not any severing of our loves!
Yet in my heart of hearts I feel your might;
I only have relinquished one delight
To live beneath your more habitual sway.
I love the Brooks which down their channels fret,
Even more than when I tripped lightly as they;
The innocent brightness of a new-born Day
        Is lovely yet;
The Clouds that gather round the setting sun
Do take a sober colouring from an eye
That hath kept watch o'er man's mortality,
Another race hath been, and other palms are won.
Thanks to the human heart by which we live,
Thanks to its tenderness, its joys and fears,
To me the meanest flower that blows can give
Thoughts that do often lie too deep for tears.

WILLIAM WORDSWORTH

THE WATER-FALL

With what deep murmurs, through Time's silent stealth,
Doth thy transparent, cool, and wat'ry wealth
        Here flowing fall,
        And chide, and call,
As if his liquid, loose retinue stay'd
Ling'ring, and were of this steep place afraid;
        The common pass,
        Where, clear as glass,
        All must descend
        Not to an end,
But quick'ned by this deep and rocky grave,
Rise to a longer course more bright and brave.

Dear stream! dear bank! where often I
Have sate, and pleas'd my pensive eye;
Why, since each drop of thy quick store
Runs thither whence it flow'd before,
Should poor souls fear a shade or night,
Who came (sure) from a sea of light?
Or, since those drops are all sent back
So sure to Thee that none doth lack,
Why should frail flesh doubt any more
That what God takes He'll not restore?
O useful element and clear!
My sacred wash and cleanser here;
My first consigner unto those
Fountains of life, where the Lamb goes!
What sublime truths and wholesome themes
Lodge in thy mystical, deep streams!
Such as dull man can never finde,
Unless that Spirit lead his minde,
Which first upon thy face did move
And hatch'd all with His quick'ning love.
As this loud brook's incessant fall
In streaming rings restagnates all,

Which reach by course the bank, and then
Are no more seen: just so pass men.
O my invisible estate,
My glorious liberty, still late!
Thou art the channel my soul seeks,
Not this with cataracts and creeks.

HENRY VAUGHAN

A CONTEMPLATION UPON FLOWERS

Brave flowers, that I could gallant it like you
    And be as little vaine!
You come abroad, and make a harmlesse shew,
    And to your bedds of Earth againe;
You are not proud, you know your birth
For your Embroiderd garments are from Earth.

You doe obey your moneths, and times, but I
    Would have it ever Springe,
My fate would know noe Winter, never dye,
    Nor thinke of such a thing;
Oh that I could my bed of Earth but view
And Smile, and looke as chearefully as you:

Oh teach me to see Death, and not to feare,
    But rather to take truce;
How often have I seene you at a Beere,
    And there looke fresh and spruce;
You fragrant flowers then teach me that my breath
Like yours may sweeten, and perfume my death.

HENRY KING

443

LIFE

I made a posie, while the day ran by:
Here will I smell my remnant out, and tie
   My life within this band.
But time did beckon to the flowers, and they
By noon most cunningly did steal away
   And wither'd in my hand.

My hand was next to them, and then my heart:
I took, without more thinking, in good part
   Time's gentle admonition:
Who did so sweetly death's sad taste convey,
Making my minde to smell my fatall day,
   Yet sug'ring the suspicion.

Farewell, deare flowers, sweetly your time ye spent,
Fit, while ye liv'd, for smell or ornament,
   And after death for cures.
I follow straight without complaints or grief,
Since, if my scent be good, I care not if
   It be as short as yours.

GEORGE HERBERT

INDEX OF AUTHORS

445

447